The Process of Priority Formulation

Westview Replica Editions

This book is a Westview Replica Edition. The concept of Replica Editions is a response to the crisis in academic and informational publishing. Library budgets for books have been severely curtailed; economic pressures on the university presses and the few private publishing companies primarily interested in scholarly manuscripts have severely limited the capacity of the industry to properly serve the academic and research communities. Many manuscripts dealing with important subjects, often representing the highest level of scholarship, are today not economically viable publishing projects. Or, if they are accepted for publication, they are often subject to lead times ranging from one to three years. Scholars are understandably frustrated when they realize that their first-class research cannot be published within a reasonable time frame, if at all.

Westview Replica Editions seem to us one feasible and practical solution to the crisis. The concept is simple. We accept a manuscript in camera-ready form and move it immediately into the production process. The responsibility for textual and copy editing lies with the author or sponsoring organization. If necessary we will advise the author on proper preparation of footnotes and bibliography. The manuscript is acceptable as typed for a thesis or dissertation or prepared in any other clearly organized and readable way, though we prefer it typed according to our specifications. The end result is a book produced by lithography and bound in hard covers. Edition sizes range from 200 to 600 copies. We will include among Westview Replica Editions only works of outstanding scholarly quality or of great informational value and we will exercise our usual editorial standards and quality control.

The Process of Priority Formulation:
U.S. Foreign Policy in the Indo-Pakistani War of 1971
Dan Haendel

How are foreign policy objectives and priorities formulated by decision makers in the U.S. government? Dan Haendel answers this question by examining the decision-making process during the Indo-Pakistani War, focusing on the behavior of government institutions and individuals as they attempted to cope with the events of 1971. After a discussion of post-World War II U.S. foreign policy in South Asia, the area's importance to the United States during the Cold War, and the internal crisis in Pakistan leading up to its war with India, the author considers the U.S. government's response to the Indo-Pakistani clash. He discusses the organizational structure for the conduct of U.S. foreign policy, the relative importance of the various governmental decision-making units, and the impact of an individual such as Kissinger within the organization. Using, as his basic source, information gathered in interviews with the participants, he provides an account of deliberations with the U.S. government.

This work introduces to the field of foreign policy analysis the concept of priority formulation. Examining the argument that a decision maker establishes a *subjective* and *personal* scale, the author points out that beliefs and values are likely to determine the approach used by the decision maker in coping with complex stimuli and in structuring problems.

Dan Haendel, a captain in the U.S. Army, is an assistant staff judge advocate at Fort Belvoir, Virginia. He received J.D. and Ph.D. degrees from the University of Pennsylvania, and was previously a research associate at the Foreign Policy Research Institute and a member of the editorial research staff of *Orbis*.

The opinions reflected in this book are solely those of the author, and do not necessarily reflect the views of the Judge Advocate General or any government agency.

The Process of Priority Formulation

U.S. Foreign Policy in the Indo-Pakistani War of 1971

Dan Haendel

Westview Press
Boulder, Colorado

A Westview Replica Edition

All rights reserved. No part of this publication may be reproduced or transmitted in any form or by any means, electronic or mechanical, including photocopy, recording, or any information storage and retrieval system, without permission in writing from the publisher.

Copyright © 1977 by Dan Haendel

Published in 1977 in the United States of America by

  Westview Press, Inc.
  1898 Flatiron Court
  Boulder, Colorado 80301
  Frederick A. Praeger, Publisher and Editorial Director

Library of Congress Cataloging in Publication Data

Haendel, Dan, 1950-
  The process of priority formulation.

  Bibliography: p.
  Includes index.
  1. India-Pakistan Conflict, 1971--United States.
2. United States--Foreign relations--1969-1974. 3. United States--Foreign relations--Administration. I. Title.
DS388.H28   353.008'92   77-21372
ISBN 0-89158-322-X

Printed and bound in the United States of America

לכבוד אבא, אמא, דורון, וורדה

ולזכר סבא אנשל, סבתא שושנה, וסבתא מרים   ז"ל

TABLE OF CONTENTS

LIST OF ILLUSTRATIONS	p. xiii
ACKNOWLEDGMENTS	p. xv
INTRODUCTION	p. 1
CHAPTER I: THE INDO-PAKISTANI CONFLICT AND THE COLD WAR	p. 26
Background	p. 30
Leadership and Focus of Orientation	p. 36
The Neutral Period	p. 39
The Search for Means of Defense: A Convergence	p. 42
The American Search	p. 42
The Pakistani Search	p. 45
Pakistan's Disillusionment with the United States	p. 50
Divergence of Interests	p. 50
In Search of Other Friends	p. 56
Summary	p. 63
CHAPTER II: THE UNFOLDING OF A CRISIS -- FROM NONCRISIS TO MIDDLE-LEVEL CRISIS	p. 66
The Problem of Integration	p. 66
Yahya Khan's Regime	p. 73
The 1970 Elections	p. 79
The March 25 Crackdown	p. 86

Indian Involvement .... p. 89

American Involvement .... p. 91

Summary .... p. 102

CHAPTER III: THE STRUCTURE OF DECISION-
            MAKING .... p. 105

The President and the NSC .... p. 109

The Bureaucrats and Advisors .... p. 126

Congress and Interest Groups .... p. 129

Public Opinion and the Media .... p. 134

Summary .... p. 136

CHAPTER IV: U.S. DECISION-MAKING:
            ORGANIZATION AND POLICY ..... p. 140

The White House and State Department p. 142

Mrs. Gandhi's Visit .... p. 155

WSAG Meetings .... p. 160

Summary .... p. 181

CHAPTER V: APPLICATION OF DECISION-MAKING
           THEORY TO MIDDLE-LEVEL CRISIS   p. 185

Risk and Uncertainty .... p. 188

Organizational Behavior .... p. 196

Middle-Level Crisis .... p. 207

Systems Theory .... p. 214

Three Models .... p. 222

Summary .... p. 237

CHAPTER VI: THE RATIONAL MAN MODEL: THE RATIONALE OF THE NIXON APPROACH   p. 241

A Triangular Relationship: U.S., Pakistan, and China .... p. 246

A Triangular Affair: U.S., USSR, and China .... p. 249

The Nixon Report's Explanation of the 1971 South Asia Events .... p. 252

The Nixon Administration's Considerations .... p. 256

The Enterprise Episode .... p. 258

The Nixon Report: Taking Action ...... p. 264

U.S.-USSR Relations .... p. 267

The China Factor .... p. 271

The Nixon Report: The Unmentioned Factors .... p. 275

Summary .... p. 278

CHAPTER VII: THE PSYCHOLOGICAL MODEL: THE PIQUE THEORY .... p. 281

Elite Images .... p. 283

Belief Sets .... p. 301

Summary .... p. 307

CHAPTER VIII: THE INCREMENTAL MODEL: CHANGE OR NO CHANGE .... p. 311

    Contrasting the China and Pakistan Policies .... p. 315

    A Bureaucratic Perspective .... p. 323

    Summary .... p. 333

CHAPTER IX: THE GLOBAL-REGIONAL CONTROVERSY: A PROBLEM OF FOCUS .... p. 336

    The Rational Man, Expected Values, Utility Theory, and Bayes' Theorem ... p. 339

    Preference Ranking .... p. 348

    Value Formation .... p. 358

    Looking at the Events in 1971 .... p. 365

    Congressional Concerns .... p. 378

    Summary .... p. 382

CONCLUSION .... p. 386

BIBLIOGRAPHY .... p. 409

INDEX .... p. 418

LIST OF ILLUSTRATIONS

Concentric Circles of Power .... p. 114
Continuum of Leadership Behavior .... p. 205
Situational Cube .... p. 212
Input-Output Model .... p. 218
Probability Analysis .... p. 344
Bayes' Theorem .... p. 347
South Asia and the Major Powers .... p. 372

ACKNOWLEDGMENTS

A dissertation is made up of chapters. Numerous paragraphs strung together make up a chapter. A paragraph is nothing more than a combination of sentences while a sentence is merely a few properly ordered words. Accordingly, a dissertation should be quite easy to put together, but as many who have had the misfortune to be processed through this ritual would attest, the task is substantially more difficult to accomplish. Teachers, colleagues, and friends, however, have made the experience more rewarding and enjoyable than it otherwise would have been.

First, I am indebted to the members of my PhD. defense committee. I would like to express my sincere gratitude to my dissertation supervisor, Professor Norman D. Palmer whose justified reputation as a scholar and gentleman needs no elaboration. Professor Palmer was also my supervisor in my first University of Pennsylvania teaching assignment in U.S. foreign policy and his encouragement was invaluable. Professor Donald Smith stimulated my interest in South Asia and suggested that

I pursue the subject matter of this dissertation. His genuine concern and warmth as a fine human being are appreciated by his students. Dr. William Quandt served as a "secondary supervisor." He took time out from his busy schedule to read over previous drafts of this dissertation and comment extensively on them. His insight and organizational ability have taught me much and his help was far greater than would normally be expected from a member of a PhD defense committee. Dr. Quandt, I thank you. Last, but by no means least, I would like to thank Ambassador William R. Kintner. Ambassador Kintner has been my teacher at the University of Pennsylvania and "Honorable Boss" at the Foreign Policy Research Institute. He has tolerated my idiosyncratic behavior ranging from tennis equipment and general disorderliness in the office to late night working hours.

Second, I am deeply indebted to the numerous U.S. Government officials who granted me interviews. They provided me with invaluable insight and information. Most of the interviews were conducted in March and May 1975. Because of the sensitivity of the subject matter, individuals interviewed were assured anonymity. Accordingly, they are footnoted in a fashion that does not allow for identification. As agreed with these individuals, only members of my defense committee had access to the identification of those officials who were interviewed.

Third, I would like to thank the Foreign Policy Research Institute for use of its facilities. Its previous Director, Dr. Robert L. Pfaltzgraff, deserves my thanks for placing numerous services at my disposal. I appreciate the typing task that was ably performed by Beatrice Polston, Joan Ellen Milkovits, and Marcia Dissinger on the previous drafts of this dissertation.

Fourth, I would like to thank my friends and colleagues. John Johnson deserves my thanks for keeping me in good physical condition by being able to entice me rather easily to abandon my dissertation work in favor of squash and tennis. John has been my close friend during our three years of studies at the University of Pennsylvania Law School, and I will always treasure his friendship. Major Sherwood D. Goldberg has served as a friend and mentor. I have learned more about international relations and other subjects from him than from many of my teachers. One teacher who does not fall in that category is Dr. Alvin Z. Rubinstein. I only regret that I disappointed him by choosing, for purely personal reasons, not to write a dissertation on the Middle East. Mr. Christopher Garrahan is a teacher who has had a profound influence on my development and I remain indebted to him. Robert Meadow has been my office-mate for five years both at the University of Pennsylvania and the Foreign Policy Research Institute. We have both developed professionally and otherwise during that period and were, I trust, of help to one another. Other individuals whom I would like to thank, but must mention by name only are Professor Franklin R. Root, Gerald T. West, Robert Collins, Joseph and Judy Semo, Lieutenant Mark Kennedy, Farid Lavipour, Resa Silver, Professor Henry Wells, Dr. Charles Elder, Dr. Brian Healy, Mimi Maguire, Bill Jones, Andy Krinsky, Steve Kawalick, and Eric Frank.

Fifth, Ellen Goldberg deserves my special thanks. Ellen has been a friend and companion. In addition to her help in editing, she typed the final draft of the first half of this dissertation. I trust that her work as a Finance Analyst at Citibank is more interesting. Her encouragement was exemplified by such needling questions as "When are you going to be finished?", "Aren't you through yet?", and "When are we going on vacation?"

Finally, I wish to thank my family. My parents have always encouraged my educational efforts without ever putting me under pressure to perform. Doron, my brother, is a free spirit, and I trust that he will succeed in his artistic endeavors. Varda will probably always remain in my memory as my little sister despite the fact that she has already developed into a young woman. It is to my family and to my three deceased grandparents, may their memories be blessed, that this dissertation is, with love, dedicated.

INTRODUCTION

This study is undertaken with the primary objective of determining and explaining American foreign policy decision-making in the Indo-Pakistani War of December 1971. The effort has the more general purpose of contributing to the understanding of the formulation of foreign policy objectives and priorities. Accordingly, the focus will be on the institutions and personalities of the American government and their behavior as they attempt to cope and manage what we will characterize as a middle-level crisis.

Decision-making is a broad area of inquiry. In the field of international relations, specialists have become cognizant of the need to examine the management of the foreign policy apparatus by looking not only to the governmental structures involved but also at the decision-making process in its dynamic and human dimensions.[1] Both Steinbruner and the Rudolphs have recently

---

[1] For example, Glenn D. Paige, The Korean Decision (New York: The Free Press, 1968).

emphasized the concept of complexity.[2] Steinbruner points to the mushrooming of bureaucracies that are created in response to the increasing complexity of problems in a modern era. He argues that a increasingly diverse bureaucracy that is created to solve a complex problem strains the managerial capacity of the system to deal with the original complex problem. The Rudolphs expand this thesis by pointing out the difficulties associated with an effort to coordinate the bureaucracy that is mobilized to deal with a complex issue.

The decision-maker will be able to attain limited solace from the observation that foreign policy issues are complex. His interest is in managing, coping, and/or arriving at an output or decision. He must make a decision and implement it. Under this analysis the conscious decision not to decide is also a decision.

We will be examining a decision. In particular, we will be involved with the question of the formulation

---

[2] John D. Steinbruner, The Cybernetic Theory of Decision: New Dimensions of Political Analysis (Princeton, N.J.: Princeton University Press, 1974); Lloyd I. Rudolph and Susanne H. Rudolph, "The Coordination of Complexity in South Asia," A Report Prepared for the Commission on the Organization of the Government for the Conduct of Foreign Policy, Spring 1975.

of high policy decisions, to use Brecher's label, or priority formulation. Brecher classifies foreign policy decisions on the basis of a time continuum, a spectrum of initiation, and a scale of importance as these relate to the implementation of a decision. He defines a foreign policy decision

> as the selection, among perceived alternatives of one option leading to a course of action in the international system. A decision is made by an individual or individuals or a group authorized by the political system to act within a prescribed sphere of external behavior.[3]

An argument advanced in this study suggests that events occur which may be characterized on a continuum from noncrisis to middle-level crisis and to crisis. This continuum is intended to reflect the objective events or the reality, in contradistinction to the concept of priority formulation which seeks to probe the subjective and personal evaluation of decision-makers who confront this objective stimuli. A crisis is defined as an event which entails high threat to high

---

[3] Michael Brecher, The Foreign Policy System of Israel: Setting, Images, Process (New Haven: Yale University Press, 1972), p. 374.

values, occurs as a surprise and must be resolved in a short period of time. A middle-level crisis is characterized either by the absence of <u>at least</u> one of the four elements of a crisis, that is, the absense of high threat, high value, surprise, or short period of time, or any of these factors being at a level other than high on a low-middle-high scale. In other words, the concept of middle-level crisis encompasses the continuum of events between noncrisis and crisis. This study is devoted to an examination of one type of middle-level crisis. The proposition will be advanced that the locus of a decision within the American government shifts to the Executive Office from the field and the bureaucracy as a noncrisis develops into a middle-level crisis.

The primary contribution this study attempts to make in the field of foreign policy analysis is through the introduction of the analytical concept of priority formulation. Priority is defined as the quality or state of being superior in ranking. We will posit that a decision-maker establishes a <u>subjective</u> and <u>personal</u> priority scale that is in essence a preferential rating scale. In order to cope with complex stimuli, a decision-maker will attempt to reduce to or express in a systematized statement a rank order of the issues meriting prior attention. In arriving at his <u>subjective</u> and <u>personal</u> preference ranking, a decision-maker's cognition, belief set, and values are likely to determine the model or approach he utilizes in structuring the problem he faces. In other words, a decision-maker is not a <u>tabula rasa</u> as he proceeds in his effort to process an issue. He will likely have a "world view," previous experiences, cognition, beliefs, values and preferred outcomes which he will apply to stimuli that confront him. Prior to confronting the various problems, a decision-maker's rank order of possible issues will yield his subjective estimation regarding the allocation of attention that each issue-area warrants, depending on his view of their relative importance. In other words, in confronting an issue, decision-makers must decide the importance of the issue itself in comparison to other issues in order to determine the amount of attention the issue warrants.

    We will argue that each decision-maker has a measurable preference among various choices that exist in situations characterized by risk. Utility theory provides a means for determining the alternative that a rational decision-maker will choose by examining his preferences in terms of their utility. By knowing the decision-maker's utility function, the probability he assigns to the occurrence of events, and the consequences of each possible outcome, we should be able to determine a decision-maker's choice by assuming that he will seek to maximize his utility. Therefore, the utility of a preferred decision outcome is postulated to be personal and subjective.[4]

The purpose of utilizing the concept of priority formulation is to describe and predict foreign policy decision-making. We will present the thesis that in attempting to describe and predict a decision-making process, an analyst should seek to uncover the method through which a decision-maker simplifies into workable conceptions the complex phenomena that he faces. The human mind has a limited capacity for information processing. Therefore, a decision-maker will attempt to manage his affairs by conceptually simplifying the problem or imposing a model on it. Accordingly, the key explanatory variable is posited to be the concep-

---

[4] William T. Morris, The Analysis of Management Decisions (Homewood, Illinois: Richard D. Irwin, Inc., 1964), pp. 49-50.

tual simplification or model that a decision-maker possesses in order to process issues. Priority formulation is at the heart of the decision-making process because of the focus it provides an analyst for examining an issue from the <u>subjective</u> and <u>personal</u> perspective of each decision-maker. By utilizing the concept of priority formulation as an analytical tool, an analyst will be able to utilize decision-making theory as an integrated whole. While priority formulation focuses on the preference ranking of an individual decision-maker, other decision-making approaches can then be utilized to explain the process of integration or lack of it that occurs when a number of decision-makers assemble to reach a decision.

Priority formulation has been a neglected concept. Recent works on decision-making theory have utilized a trilogy approach, such as Allison's Rational Man, Organizational, and Bureaucratic Models, to separate three different explanations for a decision without integrating the decision process or attempting to formulate an explanatory variable for the integration of the models. We are advancing the concept of priority formulation as an analytical tool with explanatory power that can be used to integrate the various models that have been developed in the decision-making literature. While various decision-making models have mentioned the concept of priority, these models have dealt with the issue of priority formulation only tangentially and not as the core of the decision-making process. We will utilize three decision-making models, both in order to provide alternative and complementary explanations for U.S. decision-making and policy toward South Asia during 1971 and to underscore the contribution that each of the models makes to the concept of priority formulation.

Foreign policy analysis has recently focused on Allison's[5] three models: the Rational Man, Organizational, and Bureaucratic. Steinbruner labels his three paradigms: Analytic, Cybernetic and Cognitive. In this study we have chosen the labels of Rational Man, Psychological and Incremental Models. While the labels do signify some significant differences in the orientations used, the studies seem to indicate a basic agreement that the models that have developed in response

---

[5] Graham T. Allison, Essence of Decision: Explaining the Cuban Missile Crisis (Boston: Little, Brown and Co., 1971).

to the Rational Man Model have not sought to modify that model's assumptions. They are in fact a challenge to that model and can be viewed as alternative and separate explanatory models of reality. Nevertheless, each model can also add a certain dimension of explanation to the other.

The Indo-Pakistani War of 1971 will be examined according to the different perspectives afforded by the Rational Man, Psychological, and Incremental Models. The assumptions of each of the models provide a degree of explanatory power to the analysis of U.S. foreign policy in South Asia during 1971 that is missing when only one of the models is utilized. To be sure, a model or paradigm is a simplified version of reality. The complexity of the reality is reduced to a few basic working assumptions in a model. The purpose of a model is to explain the reality in **relatively** simple terms and simultaneously maintaining the essence of that reality. The dissection of the real phenomenon allows the analyst to separate the strands or factors of the decision-making process thereby, hopefully, gaining greater insight into the event he strives to explain.

Steinbruner argues that the common denominator of his three paradigms is the human mind. As he rightly points out, in the sense that human beings are involved in processing the information entering the system, it is in fact the human brain that processes the stimuli. Steinbruner's cybernetic paradigm is in many respects similar to the Incremental Model. The paradigm posits a highly structured environment and does not take into account a human mind that can make inductive inferences. The shortcomings of the explanatory power of the cybernetic paradigm led Steinbruner to place particular emphasis on the cognitive theory which examines the process whereby human beings structure their beliefs. By providing a structured environment, the cognitive theory is used to supplement the cybernetic paradigm in order to offer an alternative to the analytic paradigm which by itself cannot explain much of observed reality.

Steinbruner's and Allison's tools of analysis are helpful in explaining the Nixon Administration's effort to formulate and implement policy. Decisions under complexity provide the basis by which to distinguish most readily among Steinbruner's paradigms. He defines a decision as a "choice made by either an individual or a group of individuals (and it matters which) in pursuit of some purpose."[6] The complex decision problem exists when the following conditions are present:

1. (a) Two or more are affected by the decisions.
   (b) There is a trade-off relationship between the values such that a greater return to one can be obtained only at a loss to the other.
2. There is uncertainty (i.e., imperfect correspondence between information and the environment) of a special character...
3. The power to make the decision is dispersed over a number of individual actors and/or organizational units.[7]

The special character of uncertainty is labeled "structural uncertainty" because of the uncertainty associated with the possible outcomes or estimated occurrence probabilities. Furthermore, the decision-makers may not agree on the decision problem itself, that is, "the values at stake, the weight to be given to them, the resolution of major uncertainties."[8] Uncertainty is likely to be suppressed by a decision-

---

[6] Steinbruner, op. cit., p. 16.
[7] Ibid., p. 16.
[8] Ibid., p. 18.

maker. By suppressing uncertainty, a decision-maker is acting to simplify the environment he is facing. He behaves on the assumption that a particular future will unfold and is likely to modify his actions to account for his subjective projections.

In addition to the focus on the institutions and personalities, this study will devote particular attention to the interaction between the actors involved within the American government. By undertaking this analysis, the relative importance of the actors will be determined. We will posit that where a consensus cannot be achieved, the preference of the actor with the most influence will be imposed on the other decision-makers. Where a consensus can be reached, the preferences of the various participants will be reflected in the decision output. Following this assessment, an attempt will be made to ascertain the priorities of these actors and specify the formulation of priority setting in American foreign policy in the Indo-Pakistani War of December 1971.

During the course of the study, the role of various government bodies, especially the Executive Office, the National Security Council and various other groups, the State Department, the Defense Department and Congress, will be examined in order to determine where the various decisions were made and explain the rationale for those decisions. According to the Rational Man Model, the decision-maker weighs the outcomes as he seeks to arrive at a rational decision, while in both the Psychological and Incremental Models a decision is generated without the outcome having been taken into account. With each of these models, or, according to Steinbruner, paradigms, there is a high degree of interaction that occurs among the participants, the governmental bodies, and the preferences of those involved. Such an analysis will call for the examination of the organizational structure and process by which the handling of problems such as the Indo-Pakistani War of December 1971 occurs. More specifically, an examination of the role of the Presidency is particularly crucial for an understanding of American foreign policy in these events. This aspect of the study will focus on the pre-eminence of the Presidency in such decisions and the Nixon Administration's utilization of this pre-eminence.

The importance of the role of personal actors in determining the priorities and policy of the United States will be examined. The difficulties associated with this undertaking cannot be underestimated or glossed over. An effort will be made to determine the assumptions and values toward both the Global System and the South Asia subordinate system held by the key U.S. foreign policy-makers, such as Richard Nixon and Henry Kissinger, who were involved with American policy in the Indo-Pakistani War. Such an undertaking will require an examination of U.S. global interests and policies as well as policies and interests in South Asia in 1971. In terms of the focus of the study on priority formulation, the explanation for the limited priority of South Asia within the overall global framework and the overriding importance of the global factors for the United States need to be established.

Propositions dealing with decision-making in middle-level crisis situations will be offered and applied to the Indo-Pakistani War of 1971. These propositions examine additional factors such as the alliance relationship with Pakistan and the importance of previously held values of U.S. decision-makers involved in the priority setting process.

By-products of this study include clarifications of several points. First, the effort will be made to uncover whether U.S. decision-makers were indeed working "behind the scenes" and were instrumental, through their influence on Yahya Khan, in saving the life of Sheikh Mujib. This question also brings to the forefront the utility of the apparent U.S. preference for quiet diplomacy during this middle-level crisis. Second, the issue arises whether there existed any possibility, or indeed whether there was active consideration, of direct U.S. intervention in the Indo-Pakistani War. Third, concerning the issue of priorities, we will examine the reason for the adoption by the U.S. government of a decision not to remain neutral in the conflict and, in fact, to visibly align itself with the losing side. Finally, an effort will be made to explain the basis for Nixon's and Kissinger's assumptions that the U.S.-China policy would be jeopardized by even a neutral United States policy toward the war.

The basic chronological scope is the period from the Pakistani elections of 1970 through the events that culminated in the Indo-Pakistani War of December 1971. The American involvement in South Asia from the time of the partition of the Indian subcontinent until the events of December 1970 will be set out very briefly in order to establish the setting for the decisions to be analyzed. This American involvement will tend to be reported from the perspective of U.S.-Pakistani relations rather than U.S.-Indian relations primarily because of the focus of this study on the internal developments within Pakistan as the triggering event that led to the Indo-Pakistani War and the importance of the American alliance with Pakistan. In addition, the dependent variable or policy that is being explained is the "tilt toward Pakistan" while the focus on past U.S.-Pakistani relations seems to be an appropriate independent variable for analysis. A brief analysis will be provided of the South Asian events for the one year period and especially for the month of December 1971. However, the primary focus will be devoted to the American government's efforts through its actors, both organizational and personal, to cope with this middle-level crisis.

The substantive scope will extend to the formulation of American foreign policy and priority formulation as it related to the Indo-Pakistani War of 1971. Consequently, certain events such as the Pakistani elections, the Pakistani Army's crackdown of March 1971, the refugee problem, the Gandhi-Nixon meetings, and the beginnings of American contacts for the establishment of improved relations with China are highlighted.

The study is divided into nine chapters in addition to an introduction and conclusion. The first chapter provides the background of post-World War II U.S. foreign policy in South Asia and seeks to explain the importance attached to the region by U.S. decision-makers during the Cold War era. Chapter II contains an analysis of Pakistan's failure in national integration and the unfolding of a middle-level crisis -- that is, an account of events from the election and the March 25, 1971 crackdown to the outbreak of the war.

The next two chapters deal with the attempts of the U.S. Government to cope with the dynamic South Asian events. Entitled "The Structure of Decision-Making," Chapter III examines the organizational structure for the conduct of U.S. foreign policy in general and toward South Asia in particular. We will seek to establish the relative weight or importance of the various governmental decision-making units and discuss the impact that an individual such as Kissinger can have on the influence of an organization. The argument will also be made that an institution within the U.S. Government is likely to have certain goals that may differ significantly from other agencies. Chapter IV presents an account and data gathered primarily from interviews with the American participants. An analysis of the deliberations and actions of the U.S. Government agencies and personalities involved in the Indo-Pakistani War is also undertaken.

Chapter V begins by presenting a theoretical construct of decision-making and organizational management and applies it to the decision-making process of the U.S. Government. This chapter is presented in order to structure the problem from various theoretical perspectives. Chapters VI, VII, and VIII analyze the American foreign policy decision-making process in light of three different perspectives, the Rational

Man, Psychological, and Incremental Models, respectively. Chapter VI examines the assumptions of the Nixon Report and of many U.S. decision-makers in order to assess the probabilities and desireabilities assigned by individual decision-makers to the events in South Asia. We will examine why, despite their awareness of low, if any, probability of success, Nixon and Kissinger chose to pursue low priority goals for other reasons. For example, they may have wanted to place the American position on record and present a signal to the international community regarding the American stand on future crises. Furthermore, the proposition will be advanced that the locus of a decision in the American government shifts to the Executive Office as a non-crisis develops into a middle-level crisis. A second proposition examined in this section is that the previously held values of the key U.S. decision-makers are linked to the establishment of priorities. In addition, as the locus of decision in a middle-level crisis shifts to the Executive Office, the generalists, on a generalist-regionalist continuum, rather than the regional experts become the decision-makers. We will attempt to provide reasons for these observations if they are indeed confirmed.

Chapter VII examines the proposition that Nixon's and Kissinger's bias in favor of Pakistan and their negative image of India and her leaders explain the U.S. "tilt toward Pakistan" policy. In this chapter we make use of elite images and belief sets to derive the desireabilities of individual decision-makers. Through the derivation of the desireabilities and probabilities in the Rational Man Model, we will establish in Chapter IX the methodology for the systematized statement or formula for the calculation of an individual decision-maker's preference ranking.

Entitled "The Incremental Model: Change or No Change," Chapter VIII suggests the process whereby changes in priorities may occur. We will suggest how a problem can be restructured, from a regional to a global problem, so as to provide a different conceptual frame of reference. The process of arriving at a consensus and getting the participants on the same wavelength, through such methods as invoking Presidential authority and logrolling, will be examined. We will also deal with the problems involved in implementing a decision.

Entitled "The Process of Priority Formulation," Chapter IX seeks to establish the priorities and objectives of the actors involved in the decision-making process. The objectives and values of the decision-makers are then linked to the relative power of the various decision-makers to achieve the predominance of their respective priorities. The effort is also made to reduce the process of priority formulation argument into a quantitative explanation or model. This effort is aimed at integrating the contributions and insights provided by the Rational Man and Psychological Models in particular by utilizing the concepts of probabilities and desireabilities to arrive at a preference ranking. Thus, priority formulation attempts to view the decision-making process in terms of an individual decision-maker's subjective and personal evaluation. These individual priorities are then processed in a group decision setting.

The differing perspectives of the decision-makers with respect to the importance of the global versus the regional outlook are examined as these views relate to the formulation of foreign policy priorities. The argument will be made that a Superpower's previous bilateral and regional commitments, if taken seriously, are linked to and place a constraint on its priority formulation. It will be proposed that the events which occur within a regional subsystem will not be examined on the basis solely of their relative merits or in isolation from global concerns if those events within the regional subsystem are not viewed as a high priority by the foreign policy decision-makers of the United States. One can also argue that events in high priority regions such as the Middle East will also not be processed in disregard of global considerations. However, the thrust of the argument being made is that events in low priority regions are more amenable to being formulated for non-regional or global goals than events which occur in a high priority region. Thus, for example, the U.S. could formulate a policy toward South Asia in 1971 for the furtherance of a global policy and China connection while disregarding the consequences of a negative Indian reaction. In a high priority area, such as the Middle East, ignoring consequences that may emanate from alienating a regional power may lead to severe repercussions. Consequently, the Arab oil embargo of 1973 was allegedly implemented in reaction to the U.S. arms supply to Israel during the 1973 Middle East War. Therefore, in high priority areas the regional factors and consequences are likely to be given more weight in policy formulation than in low priority areas.

Nevertheless, the proposition is suggested that the establishment of priorities and the actions undertaken in a regional subsystem by the United States Government are a function of its foreign policy goals on the global level. In other words, both in low and high priority regions and nation-states, the determination of particular actions and policies will be derived from the global role and objectives that U.S. foreign policy decision-makers seek. The difference that seems to exist in policy formulations stems from the weight given to the regional factors.

In the "Conclusion" an attempt is made to assess the consequences for U.S. policy in South Asia as well as the global consequences that emanated from the course of action taken by the Administration during the Indo-

Pakistani War of 1971. In addition, an evaluation will be made of the value of applying theoretical constructs to analyze events. We also summarize the findings that were made throughout the study.

The utilization and development of decision theory is undertaken with the view toward providing a better understanding of a decision, U.S. foreign policy in the Indo-Pakistani War of 1971 in this case. The Rudolphs have shown some of the structural or organizational aspects of complexity associated with the event. They did not, however, discuss the aspects of uncertainty associated with the decision nor did they focus on the non-crisis aspect of the event in order to distinguish it from crisis decision-making. Furthermore, they did not delve into the psychological dimensions of the decision-making process or into the different preference rankings of the various decision-makers. Their focus on the structural or institutional aspect of decision-making seems to be accounted for by the purpose of their task. Their examination was undertaken with the objective of recommending changes in the organizational structure for U.S. foreign policy decision-making in

South Asia. The purpose of this study is to apply Allison's and Steinbruner's three theoretical models to the U.S. decision-making process with a view toward describing and predicting U.S. foreign policy formulation through the introduction and development of the analytical tool and concept of priority formulation as the core of the decision-making process.

I: THE INDO-PAKISTANI CONFLICT AND THE COLD WAR

The purpose of this chapter is to provide a brief historical sketch of the international relations of South Asia. We will seek to demonstrate the varying degrees of importance that South Asia had for U.S. foreign policy during the 1945-1971 period, depending on other global developments in addition to the views held by the American Presidents involved. The onset of the Cold War between the U.S. and the Soviet Union occurred during the same period that the partition of the Indian subcontinent into India and Pakistan took place. Because of the Cold War, South Asia took on increased significance and priority for U.S. policy makers and planners as the policy of containment was implemented. South Asia became important for U.S. foreign policy in order to deny the region to the Soviet Union by assuring that the Soviets not be able to penetrate the area. South Asia was also to be part of the forward American defense perimeter in order to contain the Soviet Union. On the one hand, India's non-aligned status in the Cold War angered many American leaders, especially John Foster Dulles who equated India's neutrality with immorality. Pakistan, on the other hand, took advantage of the American-Soviet struggle by becoming the lynchpin of the American security scheme of SEATO and CENTO, thereby seeking to assure American military supplies for confrontations with India. Thus, a regional conflict was provided with a global dimension at an early stage. To further complicate the situation, Pakistan's geopolitical position was precarious because of its division into East and West Pakistan, which were separated by over one thousand miles of Indian territory.

Robert Strausz-Hupé claims that international politics is "dominated by the quest for power," and that "at any given period of known history, there were several states locked in deadly conflict, all desiring the augmentation or preservation of their power."[1] Hans Morganthau tends to view international politics as a struggle for power in which men attempt to control

---

[1] Robert Strausz-Hupé and Stefan T. Possony, _International Relations_ (New York: McGraw-Hill, 1954), pp. 5-6 as quoted in James E. Dougherty and Robert L. Pfaltzgraff, _Contending Theories of International Relations_ (Philadelphia: Lippincott, 1971), p. 67.

the minds and actions of other men.[2] One can also argue that international politics is dominated by a nation-state's struggle for survival. In short, since without existence no other goals can be attained, existence clearly becomes the main objective of a nation-state's foreign policy with other behavior being the means to the attainment of that end.

Thus far, the underlying assumptions of this explanation for the behavior of a nation-state has been that rationality is a key factor in foreign policy. Yet in an analysis of a nation-state's foreign policy the irrational element must also be taken into account since the decisions are, after all, taken by human beings.[3]

An analysis of Pakistan's foreign policy during the 1947-1965 period reveals that the conduct of Pakistan's foreign policy has been preoccupied with

---

[2] Hans J. Morgenthau, *Politics Among Nations: The Struggle for Power and Peace* (New York: Alfred A. Knopf, 1967), pp. 25-26.

[3] Otto Klineberg, *The Human Dimension in International Relations* (New York: Holt, Rinehart and Winston, 1964), p. 6. Also Dean G. Pruitt and Richard C. Snyder, *Theory and Research on the Causes of War* (Englewood Cliffs, N.J.: Prentice-Hall, 1969).

assuring Pakistan's national survival. During the early 1950's the Pakistanis turned to the U.S. for arms to be used against India at a time when the U.S. was prepared to offer such assistance in order to bolster Pakistan against possible Communist aggression. This was the beginning of an entangling American alliance in South Asia that imposed a constraint on American decision-makers who were most enthusiastic about the U.S.-Pakistani alliance, particularly Richard Nixon, were the key actors in formulating and implementing U.S. policy toward South Asia in 1971.

  U.S. foreign policy during the Cold War period should have been more accurately aware of the fact that Pakistan agreed to join in an alliance with the U.S. primarily in order to arm itself against India. Pakistan's search for a strong and reliable ally seems to be particularly crucial as an explanation for Pakistan's actions in the Indo-Pakistani conflicts. This search seems to explain Pakistan's shifting alliance behavior in the international environment. In this light, Aslam Siddiqui's thesis, which is reflected in the title of his book, <u>Pakistan Seeks Security</u>, seems to be particularly apropos.[4]

The United States is the global power that was most directly affected by the consequences of Pakistan's foreign policy during the 1947-1965 period. The reason for this should be obvious: the United States is the major power that was most involved with Pakistan at both the domestic and international levels during this period. Yet with the American arms supply to India during the Sino-India conflict of 1962 and the American arms embargo to India and Pakistan because of the Indo-Pakistani War of 1965, the Pakistanis became disillusioned with the attitude of the United States and sought other "friends." Therefore, the implications drawn from Pakistan's behavior are equally applicable to other states that come into close association with Pakistan.[5]

Background

The hostility and mutual distrust between India and Pakistan have their roots in the struggle between

---

[4] Aslam Siddiqui, Pakistan Seeks Security (Lahore: Longmans, Green and Co., 1960).

[5] B. L. Sharma, The Pakistan-China Axis (Bombay: Asia Publishing House, 1968), pp. 84-87.

Hindus and Muslims which resulted in the creation of Pakistan.[6] Much of the Pakistani insecurity stems from the struggle for the creation of the state and the Hindu and Indian opposition to partition. The differences between Hindus and Muslims and the fear of many Muslims of being dominated by the Hindus in a united India following Great Britain's withdrawal caused many Muslims to demand a separate state. Communal tensions were manifested in riots which broke out during the late nineteenth century. "The growth of Indian nationalism during the twentieth century brought an accompanying increase in the number of intensity of intercommunal riots and took the clash between Mulims and Hindus out of religion and economics into politics."[7]

While Tariq Ali focuses on class interests and views the creation of Pakistan as the result of the

---

[6] For a general background of Pakistan's history see Keesing's Research Report, Pakistan from 1947 to the Creation of Bangladesh (New York: Charles Scribner's Sons, 1973); Richard S. Wheeler, The Politics of Pakistan: A Constitutional Quest (Ithaca: Cornell University Press, 1970); Herbert Feldman, From Crisis to Crisis: Pakistan 1962-1969 (London: Oxford University Press, 1972); Damodar P. Singhal, Pakistan (Englewood Cliffs, N.J.: Prentice-Hall, 1972).

[7] W. Norman Brown, The United States and India and Pakistan (Cambridge: Harvard University Press, 1963), p. 143.

grip which the feudal landlords had on the Muslim league, an analysis based solely on a materialistic interpretation of history is particularly deficient in this case.[8] Matters of emotion, attitude, and idealogy may be equally, if not more, significant.[9] G.W. Choudhury's thesis is that the creation of Pakistan can only be explained in terms of culture. While this may not necessarily be the only explanation, it is certainly a cogent one. "These communities belonged to two different civilizations, which were based on conflicting ideals and conceptions."[10]

The Muslims were genuinely alarmed at the prospect of Hindu domination. This fear led to the demand, which was made by Jinnah in 1940, for a separate Muslim state. Muslims who sought a separate state propounded the "two nation" theory which asserted that Muslims and

---

[8] Tariq Ali, Pakistan: Military Rule or People's Power (New York: William Morrow and Company, 1970), p. 27.

[9] Keith B. Callard, Pakistan's Foreign Policy: An Interpretation (New York: Institute of Pacific Relations, 1957), p. 1.

[10] G.W. Choudhury and Parvez Hasan, Pakistan's External Relations (Karachi: Pakistan Institute of International Affairs, 1958), p. 3.

Hindus constitute two equal nations. This position was, of course, totally unacceptable to the Congress Party leadership which claimed that India was being established as a secular state. Callard points out that there are problems in attempting to reconcile nationalism with traditional Islam, but that this difficulty has been "partly resolved by Pakistan which caused Islam to make room for nationalism."[11]

Insecurity is a characteristic that has plagued Pakistan from its inception. In 1946 the Cabinet Commission rejected the establishment of Pakistan on administrative, economic, and military grounds. In 1947 the Mountbatten Plan for partition was accepted, but the Pakistanis were fearful that Great Britain would support India. Due to the fact that most of the arms remained within India following partition, the Pakistanis were acutely aware of the vulnerability of the new Muslim state. This fear was significant because most Pakistanis were convinced that the Hindus were striving to rule South Asia. As a result of this fear, the process of

---
[11] Callard, op. cit., p. 5.

selective perception went into effect and statements made by India's leaders reaffirmed the Pakistani belief of India's goal of absorbing the Muslim state. The Indian leadership did not conceal its desire for a united India, and this expectation is manifested in the All-India Congress Committee resolution of June 14, 1947.

> Geography and the mountains and the seas fashioned India as she is, and no human agency can change that shape or come in the way of her final destiny. Economic circumstances and the insistent demands of international affairs make the unity of India still more necessary.... The A.I.C.C. earnestly trusts that when the present passions have subsided, India's problems will be viewed in their proper perspective and the false doctrine of two nations in India will be discredited and discarded by all.[12]

Clearly such an Indian view presented a direct challenge to the sovereignty of Pakistan as well as to its very legitimacy for existence. But Choudhury claims that Jinnah's proclamation "Pakistan has come to stay" is the creed of all Pakistanis.[13]

---

[12] As quoted in William L. Barnds, *India, Pakistan, and the Great Powers* (New York: Praeger, 1972), p. 72.

[13] Choudhury, *op. cit.*, p. 5.

In light of the 1971 South Asian events, whether Choudhury would make the same statement today is open to serious questioning. Yet for the period immediately following partition the statement appears to be an accurate portrayal of the mood in Pakistan. In The Myth of Independence Bhutto puts forth the justice of the Pakistani case against India and claims that the confrontation will continue.[14] Such a perception and the resulting anxiety lead to an increased hostility level and aggression toward India.

Many issues between India and Pakistan remained outstanding after partition and these disputes, which were largely the result of partition, served to maintain the basic conflict. Among the disputes were the refugee problem, the Pakistani assets, the distribution of the Indus Valley canal waters, economic issues, Kashmir, and others.[15] "Pakistan's 'birth defect,' the absense of Kashmir in the national union,

---

[14] Zulfikar Ali Bhutto, The Myth of Independence (London: Oxford University Press, 1969), p. 187.
[15] Brown, op. cit., pp. 165-169.

has left its elite with the mentality of the handicapped who are obsessed with their incompleteness."[16] In addition, Pakistan also had numerous internal problems. Clearly, the "first duty of the Government under such conditions was to organize itself and seek security."[17] Obviously, therefore, from the Pakistani perspective this security was essential in order to protect the weak Muslim state in the face of Hindu threats.

Leadership and Focus of Orientation

Donald Smith has pointed out that before 1947 the Pakistani leadership did not have a cohesive foreign policy orientation because their main concern was the achievement of partition.[18] Yet the outlook for the foreign policy of the Pakistani leadership had been shaped during the period prior to 1947.

---

[16] Wayne Wilcox, The Kashmir Problem and the Indo-Pakistani War of 1965 (unpublished manuscript, Columbia University), pp. 1-2.

[17] Choudhury, op. cit., p. 6.

[18] Professor Donald Smith in International Politics of South Asia, seminar at the University of Pennsylvania, Spring 1972.

While Pakistani leaders tended to share the view of colonial rule as a matter of exploitation, the United States was spared from the inclusion in this category. Moreover, in part due to the negative reaction of Great Britain's support for India during the partition crisis, Pakistanis had a negative attitude toward European powers and, consequently, tended to share the sentiment for Asian solidarity. But the focus of the leadership was on Islam largely because this was the basis for Pakistan's raison d'etre. In international affairs a logical extension of the "two nation" theory and the idea of the political identity of Muslims would suggest that Pakistan align herself with other Muslim states. Such an interpretation is also supported by traditional Islam which tends to view the world as the dichotomy of true believers as opposed to the unbelievers.

Since Islam was viewed as a total way of life, the role of Islam came to be considered equally applicable to foreign affairs. Guy Wint suggests that the Pakistanis had two possible options for their foreign policy orientation. They could utilize Islam, which had been the foundation of Pakistani nationalism, as the guide for their foreign relations. Such an orientation would be aimed at other Islamic states. Alternatively, Islam could be abandoned as an anachronism for the conduct of foreign affairs in the twentieth century. This alternative would allow Pakistan to pursue its national interests in foreign relations on the basis of non-ideological national interests.[19]

The Pakistani outlook and perception of insecurity seem to be a major factor in explaining its foreign policy behavior since partition. While the shifts appear to be sudden and drastic, they may be explained largely in terms of the view "the enemy of my enemy is my friend." Allport emphasizes the we--they dichotomy in human behavior.[20] Not only does this dichotomy solidify the "we" feeling, but it also allows for the attribution of evil to the "they."

---

[19] Guy Wint in Arif Hussain, Pakistan: Its Ideology and Foreign Policy (London: Frank Cass & Co., Ltd., 1966), p. xi.

[20] Gordon Allport, The Nature of Prejudice (Garden City, N.Y.: Doubleday, 1958), p. 40.

This perspective may help to explain the Pakistani search for supporters as a means to assure adequate strength in confrontations with India.

The Neutral Period

Choudhury characterizes the 1947-1953 years as the period of nonalignment and non-commitment.[21] While this may be true in terms of Pakistan's position in the bipolar Cold War world, it does not mean that Pakistan was not actively seeking support for her position vis-à-vis India. The goal became the protection of Pakistan from Indian aggression and the "supreme test of friendship has been the willingness to support the cause of Pakistan against India."[22]

The myth-factor in Islam is discussed by Hussain, but he recognizes its utility as the "only positive factor which leads some kind of cohesion to the Pakistani nation."[23] Liaquat Ali Khan's program stated the main objective to be the search for security. Apparently some expectation existed that the Common-

---

[21] Choudhury, op. cit., p. 7.
[22] Callard, op. cit., p. 14.
[23] Hussain, op. cit., p. 51.

wealth would provide Pakistan with the necessary support to confront India, notwithstanding the fact that the British had often conciliated the Indians.[24] But the Pakistanis were disappointed by the lack of results, since they were unable to utilize the Commonwealth as an instrument against India.

With the failure to mobilize the Commonwealth against India, Pakistan sought to utilize the notion if Pan-Islamism by which to assert her leadership and attain legitimacy from and equality with India. Pan-Islamism could also be used in furtherance of Pakistani security. During the late 1940's and early 1950's Pakistan sought to promote the unity and achieve the leadership of the Muslim world. As revealed by the statements of Arab leaders, a Pakistani foreign policy with the goal of forming a Muslim bloc met with failure.[25]

---

[24] Mohammed Ahsen Chaudri, "Pakistan and the Commonwealth," in Latif Ahmed Sherwani, et al., Foreign Policy of Pakistan: An Analysis (Karachi: The Allies Book Corporation, 1964), pp. 64-65.

[25] Hussain, op. cit., p. 139.

The Arabs were preoccupied with other matters. For example, the Palestine issue was of greater concern to the Arab world than events in the subcontinent. Moreover, the ideal of Pan-Islamism was also running into obstacles in view of the problems faced by one of its strongest advocates, Pakistan. The Pakistanis were involved in a dispute with Afghanistan, another Muslim state. The area of Pakhtunistan is claimed by both sides. Ayub Khan considered Afghanistan's attitude to be an effort at expansionism. He also clearly revealed the view which Hussain had chosen to label a myth, namely that Islam is an important factor in Pakistan's foreign relations. Ayub stressed the importance of Islam as a factor that should have resulted in good relations between Pakistan and Afghanistan, but he lamented the fact that his expectations were not fulfilled.[26]

Pakistan's attempts to mobilize support within the Arab and Muslim world were by and large unsuccessful, notwithstanding the fact that Pakistan served as

---

[26] Mohammad Ayub Khan, Friends Not Masters: Political Autobiography (New York: Oxford University Press, 1967), pp. 175-177.

host to numerous Islamic conferences. India succeeded in securing the leadership of the so-called nonaligned Third World and many Muslim states found this position very appealing. But the Pakistanis were still very much aware of what they perceived to be the Indian danger to Pakistan's existence. Therefore, other sources of support were necessary in order to assure Pakistan's survival.

The Search for Means of Defense: A Convergence

The American Search

Following World War II American foreign policy was geared toward the containment of Communism. While Kennan's thesis of containment was applied by the Truman Administration to Europe and the Far East and plans were drawn up for a worldwide security system, not until the advent of the Eisenhower Administration did the United States fully attempt to establish a global security system. By viewing the world in terms of a good-evil dichotomy, Dulles found it necessary to mobilize all possible nation-states in the struggle against

Communism, thereby not allowing for a policy of neutralism which he considered immoral.[27] Under these circumstances the United States viewed Pakistan primarily in terms of the Cold War.

In the eyes of many U.S. decision-makers, geopolitical and strategic considerations made Pakistan increasingly important in any global defense arrangements against the possibility of Communist attack in Asia. Chester Bowles has ridiculed this rationale as follows: "For the U.S. to spend more than 800 million dollars to build up West Pakistan's military capacity against the USSR is about as rational as if the Soviets were to arm Mexico to counterbalance the United States."[28] However, the USSR did send missiles to Cuba in 1962. Not only could Pakistan provide the United States with air bases adjacent to the Soviet Union, but Pakistan is also strategically located in proximity to the Middle

---

[27] John C. Campbell, Defense of the Middle East: Problems of American Policy (New York: Praeger, 1960), p. 53.

[28] Chester Bowles, "U.S. Arms to Pakistan: A Tragedy of Errors," The Washington Post, August 15, 1971.

East and its oil reserves.

> In 1953, the United States was thinking in terms of a defensive arc in the Middle East. Dulles had outlined the concept of a 'northern tier' defence system which would embrace primarily those countries directly contiguous to the Soviet Union. In this scheme, the United States grasped the significance of Pakistan. Conscious of the fact that the defence of the Middle East could not be based on the Arab States, the United States looked upon Pakistan as a possible alternative to fulfill that important role. America thus became interested in associating Pakistan with the chain of local defensive arrangements, which constituted her first line of defence.[29]

Pakistan came to be viewed as an important link in the American global defense system.[30] With the "Agreement for Friendly Cooperation" with Turkey, Pakistan became indirectly linked to NATO while becoming a member of the Baghdad Pact and SEATO. In May 1954 Pakistan also signed the Mutual Defense Assistance Program with the United States. The United States had apparently succeeded in encircling the Communist states and Pakistan had been a significant link in the chain.

---

[29] Khurshid Hasan, "U.S.-Pakistan Relations," in Sherwani, et al., op. cit., p. 51.

[30] Khalid B. Sayeed, "The Role of the Military in Pakistan," in Jacques Van Doorn, Armed Forces and Society (The Hague: Mouton, 1968), p. 291.

The Pakistani Search

Pakistan's perceived weakness in confronting India seems to be the significant factor which drove Pakistan to become extremely security-conscious and, therefore, seek aid from other sources. The "nonalignment period" was characterized, as has been pointed out, by Pakistan's turning first to the Commonwealth and then to the Muslim world for support. However, this search did not yield results and one is left to wonder what would have been the value of support from the Muslim states, especially since the Pakistanis themselves had serious doubts about its worth.

With the American search for allies against Communism the stage seems to have been set for what Uri Ra'anan had labelled the convergence of interests.[31] "The two factors which have decisively influenced and conditioned the course of her relations with the

---

[31] Uri Ra'anan, "The Role of the Military in Pakistan," in Jacques Van Doorn, Armed Forces and Society (The Hague: Mouton, 1968), p. 291.

[32] Hasan in Sherwani, et al., op. cit., p. 49.

United States have been the desire to strengthen herself against India and to get more economic and military aid."[32]

The United States had approached Pakistan about joining the Middle East Defense Organization in 1952, but due to Arab opposition the United States did not pursue the idea further. "Sensing the keen interest of the United States for some sort of defensive arrangement in the area, Pakistan seized upon the opportunity and made a formal request to the United States for military aid in February 1954 on the plea that the demand was for adequate defence were becoming progressively heavy and imposing an increasingly burdensome strain on the country's economy and that assured of the adequacy of her defence for safeguarding her security and preserving her independence, Pakistan will be able to devote her resources increasingly to the development of her human and material wealth, so as to achieve greater economic stability and prosperity."[33]

---

[32] Hasan in Sherwani, et al., op. cit., p. 49.
[33] Ibid., p. 52.

The convergence of interests existed but each of the parties was seeking distinct goals. While the United States was interested in Pakistan in order to contain Communism, Pakistan entered into the alliance in order to improve her position vis-à-vis India.[34] When no events occurred which would bring to the surface the different motivations for the alliance, no conflicts took place between the objectives of the United States and Pakistan. The advantages which accrued to Pakistan in her relations with India because of the ties with the United States were substantial in terms of aid, although Pakistan became a participant in the Cold War in the process. Moreover, Pakistan was to become disappointed with the American position.

> The United States, as clearly evinced by her reservation to the SEATO Treaty, was exclusively interested in containing possible threats of communist aggression. She was chary of supporting Pakistan against India.[35]

However, the very fact of possible American support for Pakistan brought Indian criticism and

---

[34] Siddiqui, op. cit., p. 104.
[35] Hasan in Sherwani, et al., op. cit., p. 55.

apparently some offers to Pakistan regarding possible normalization of relations.[36] In 1953 Mohammad Ali (Bogra) met with Nehru to discuss the feasibility of a political settlement. At the same time, however, General Ayub Khan was seeking military aid from the United States. Nehru argued that through the supply of American military aid to Pakistan the Cold War would be introduced to South Asia. Nehru offered a possible settlement, but it was rejected by the Pakistani military which viewed the offer as an Indian effort to keep Pakistan in a weak military posture.[37]

While Pakistan derived the above advantages from its alliance with the United States, there were some very serious consequences resulting from the relationship. Alvi and Khusro point out that the Soviet Union had no reason for attacking Pakistan, while other observers explain that the Pakistani

---
[36] Brown, op. cit., p. 371.
[37] Wilcox, op. cit., p. 3.

leadership perceived no danger from the Soviet Union.[38]

> There is one circumstance, however, which can bring about conflict between Pakistan and the Soviet Union-- our involvement in the U.S. alliance.... By our involvement in military pacts we are not safeguarding ourselves against any danger but are bringing a danger into being. We are endangering the safety and the well-being of our people and squandering badly needed resources in pursuit of a policy which offers no benefits to our people, which concerns a quarrel not of our making and in which we have no need to be involved.[39]

Therefore, rather than only obtaining greater security from possible Indian aggression, Pakistan, by joining the Western camp in the bipolar world, acquired the enmity of the Soviet Union. Under the circumstances, the Soviet Union's only interest in the Middle East was to destroy those bases which would be used to attack the Soviet Union. Consequently, in attempting to pursue a policy which would assure the survival of the state, Pakistan's leaders may have brought the nation-state's very existence into question. The U-2 incident seems to have highlighted this possibility. Moreover, Pakistani troops were ap-

---
[38] Hamza Alvi and Amir Khusro, Pakistan and the Burden of U.S. Aid (Karachi: Syed and Syed, 1965), p. 15.
[39] Ibid., p. 15.

parently also to be used to defend Western interests in the Middle East.[40]

Pakistan's Disillusionment with the United States

Divergence of Interests

With the end of the Dulles era the United States began to abandon its insistence that every nation-state choose between the West or the Communist camp. In fact the Kennedy Administration encouraged the nonaligned nations.[41] By the early 1960's changes in military technology had made American bases overseas less essential and the Kennedy Administration had a significant degree of sympathy for India. Furthermore, the U.S. no longer enjoyed its strategic invulnerability vis-a-vis the USSR, and a period of U.S.-USSR reconciliation had begun to emerge following the Cuban Missile Crisis. By the early 1960's Ayub Khan and the Pakistani leadership took serious cognizance of the changes in the American attitude and position. "By this time it was becoming clear to

---

[40] Ibid., p. 16.
[41] Barnds, op. cit., pp. 166-167.

us that, in the event of India attacking us, it was most unlikely that the U.S.A. would honour its commitment and come to our assistance."[42]

The divergence of interests was becoming clear. From the Pakistani perspective Pakistan had the disadvantage of an alliance with the U.S. without obtaining the advantages it had sought. Pakistan was viewed as an enemy by the Soviet Union because of the presence of the U.S. military bases in Pakistan, but the U.S. did not provide Pakistan with security against a possible Indian attack. Moreover, argued the Pakistanis, the Soviet Union extended diplomatic support to India in the conflict between India and Pakistan, and while the U.S. was ready to support Pakistan against Communist states, Pakistan in fact needed diplomatic support against India and this support was not readily available.[43]

Under the Kennedy Administration American policy in South Asia evolved into what Kissinger has labeled "a love affair with India." Kennedy's desire

---
[42] Khan, op. cit., p. 153.
[43] Hasan in Sherwani, et al., op. cit., p. 58.

to make India the show-piece of Western accomplishments in the Third World was a cause for consternation to Pakistan's leaders. Furthermore, the "Camelot" Administration's Realpolitik outlook focused on the containment of China, and India was chosen to play the leading role in this effort in South Asia.

Pakistan's leaders were concerned that the U.S. might provide military aid to India. G.W. Choudhury claims that Ayub Khan received assurances from Kennedy that the U.S. would not provide military aid to India unless South Asia were threatened and that Pakistan would be consulted in advance.[44] With the outbreak of the Sino-Indian War of 1962, the U.S. provided military aid to India under emergency circumstances. Not only did the Pakistanis consider the amount of U.S. military aid to India excessive, thereby constituting a threat to Pakistan, but Ayub Khan also felt that Kennedy had not fulfilled his promise to consult with Pakistan before providing military aid to India.

---

[44] G.W. Choudhury, India, Pakistan, Bangladesh and the Major Powers (New York: The Free Press, 1975).

The Sino-Indian War brought to the forefront the shifting pattern of tacit, if not explicit, alliance interests between the states in South Asia and the major powers. Pakistan sought to improve her relations with China and the USSR while simultaneously maintaining good relations with the U.S. When the Soviet Union extended its support to India rather than China in the dispute, signs of the schism between the major Communist powers emerged. During the 1960's the U.S. Government opposed closer relations between Pakistan and China and continued to view India, despite her relations with the Soviet Union, as the counter to China. Not until the Nixon Administration's awareness of the advantages that could accrue to the U.S. from the Sino-Soviet conflict and the focus on China's role as a check on India's hegemony in South Asia did the pattern of alignments change once again.

Since the United States was no longer willing to provide the type of support that the Pakistani leadership considered necessary, the Pakistanis in turn sought to restructure their foreign policy accordingly. Following the Sino-Indian clashes in 1959,

Ayub Khan had proposed to India a joint defense of the subcontinent, but his suggestion was rejected. The reason for Ayub Khan's proposal remains unclear. Apparently in order to decrease American influence in Pakistan, as well as in reaction to the innovations in American foreign policy in the U-2 incident, Ayub Khan began to retreat from over-identification with the West and move toward a normalization of relations with the Soviet Union and China. As Pakistan limited its ties with the United States, the Cold War tensions in South Asia were reduced to some degree. However, as Ayub Khan pursued Pakistan's relations with Chian, a new element was introduced to South Asian relations.[45]

    The Sino-Indian War of 1962 brought out quite clearly the different interests of Pakistan and the United States in South Asia. India rejected Ayub Khan's proposal for a joint defense, and India sought and received $120 million in emergency military aid from the United States. "...India turned to the West for military supplies and assurances and began a massive

---

[45] Wilcox, op. cit., p. 7.

conventional forces build-up, much of which was purchased and deployed to be useful only against Pakistan."[46]

The Pakistanis were especially resentful of the fact that the United States, their ally, did not consult them, as had been promised, prior to sending military equipment to India. "The Western decision to give military aid to India has produced a strong reaction in Pakistan and seemingly destroyed the raison d'etre of Pakistan's policy of alignment with the United States."[47]

With the awareness that the United States had interests in South Asia that superseded its support of Pakistan, the Pakistanis not only proceeded to attempt to become less dependent on the United States but sought out other friends or "patrons" as well. Since the main reason for Pakistan's seeking such friends is her antipathy to India, the Sino-Indian conflict set the stage for a different convergence of interests.

---

[46] Ibid., p. 8.
[47] Hasan in Sherwani, et al., op. cit., p. 59.

In Search of other Friends

Pakistan's relations with the Soviet Union had been strongly affected by Pakistan's pacts with the United States. The Soviet Union's position was one of support for India and Afghanistan in their disputes with Pakistan. Starting in 1959, when Pakistan and the Soviet Union for the first time signed an agreement for trade and assistance in the exploitation of natural resources, relations between the two states began to improve.[48]

Norman Palmer claims that the Soviet Union's basic interest in India prevents too much Soviet support for Pakistan. Yet Pakistan sought to change the Soviet Union's openly pro-Indian stance to a position closer to neutrality.[49] Palmer views these efforts

---

[48] For details see Norman Palmer, South Asia and United States Policy (Boston: Houghton Mifflin Company, 1966), p. 278.

[49] Norman Palmer, Recent Soviet and Chinese Penetration in India and Pakistan: Guidelines for Political-Military Policy (McLean, Va.: Research Analysis Corporation, 1970), p. 72.

as characteristic of Pakistan's "new realism" in her foreign policy orientation.

Prospects for receiving strong Chinese support against India seemed brighter than attaining such Soviet aid. Despite Pakistan's alliance with the West, China seems to have desired to maintain friendly relations with Pakistan since trade between the two states increased and Pakistan did not become a target of Chinese abuse. Pakistan's disillusionment with its American ally has been pointed out above, and the Chinese were interested in Pakistan as an avenue of access to South Asia. The basis of convergence for the Chinese and Pakistanis was their mutual desire to keep India in check. "The result of the Sino-Indian conflict ... has been a Sino-Pakistan relationship which even in its ... embryonic form, has brought a significant measure of Chinese influence through the mountain frontier of the subcontinent to the shores of the Indian Ocean."[50]

---

[50] Alastair Lamb, Asian Frontiers (New York: Praeger, 1968) as quoted in Norman Palmer, Penetration, op. cit., p. 57.

In order for good Sino-Pakistani relations to be established certain obstacles had to be eliminated. The most important of these was the demarcation of their undefined borders. As early as October 1959 Ayub Khan stated that Pakistan would approach the Chinese for a peaceful settlement of the border problem.[51] Aziz and Palmer agree that Pakistan and China had been negotiating their border agreement prior to the outbreak of the Sino-Indian War. The Pakistanis have sought China's friendship in order to augment their power in their confrontation with India.

> Pakistan realizes that it cannot expect really substantial economic or military aid from China. It seems to regard China as its external shield against possible Indian aggression.[52]

As mentioned earlier, the Pakistanis were particularly upset by the manner in which the West rushed to India's aid during the Sino-Indian War and the fact that the Indians were in fact deploying much of the military equipment on Pakistan's frontiers. While the

---

[51] Qutubuddin Aziz, "Relations between Pakistan and the People's Republic of China," in Sherwani, et al., op. cit., p. 85.

[52] Palmer, Penetration, op. cit., p. 68.

United States asked Pakistan to open the way for reconciliation with India, Pakistan viewed the danger as emanating from India and not China.[53] In fact, Indian leaders feared a Pakistani conspiracy with China in the 1962 war.

Following the Sino-Indian 1962 War, Pakistan's leadership did not fail to take advantage of India's fears. In 1963 Foreign Minister Bhutto is reported to have said:

> A conflict does not involve Pakistan alone. Attack from India on Pakistan today is no longer confined to the security and territorial integrity of Pakistan. An attack by India on Pakistan involves the territorial integrity and security of the largest state in Asia and, therefore, the new element and this new factor that has been brought in the situation is a very important factor.[54]

That survival was still the major perceived foreign policy goal of Pakistan is clearly revealed by this statement. Possibly because of increased Pakistani confidence as a result of the newly found Chinese "patron," Pakistan adopted the policy of

---
[53] Bhutto, op. cit., p. 131.
[54] Sharma, op. cit., p. 103.

"leaning on India." This policy culminated in the 1965 Indo-Pakistani War.

The solidification of Sino-Pakistani relations occurred during and after the 1965 Indo-Pakistani War.[55] In February 1964 Chou En-lai had visited Pakistan and publicly endorsed Pakistan's position on the Kashmir issue. This statement was particularly significant in light of the fact that the Chinese had previously refrained from taking a position on the Kashmir dispute. The Chinese, of course, had their own motivations for their position. The Chinese leaders sought to solidify their relations with Pakistan and reduce India's influence in the Third World. Moreover, the Chinese were interested in weakening American influence in Pakistan and reducing Pakistan's pursuit of Soviet support.[56]

---

[55] For further elaboration on Sino-Pakistani relations see Anwar Hussain Ayed, China and Pakistan: Diplomacy of an Entente Cordiale (Amherst: The University of Massachusetts Press, 1974).

[56] Sheldon W. Simon, "The Kashmir Dispute in Sino-Soviet Perspective," Asian Survey, March 1967, pp. 176-187.

In March 1965 Ayub Khan made an official visit to China and during the Rann of Kutch dispute China sided unequivocally with Pakistan. The possibility of Chinese and Pakistani collusion haunted India during its war with Pakistan when on September 16, 1965, the Chinese presented India with an "ultimatum" demanding that the Indian government

> dismantle all its military works for aggression on the Chinese side of the China-Sikkim boundary or the boundary itself within three days..., and immediately stop all its intrusions along the Sino-Indian boundary and the China-Sikkim boundary, return the kidnapped Chinese border inhabitants and the seized livestock and pledge to refrain from any more harassing raids across the boundary.[57]

Even though the Chinese did not implement their threat, the Indians became understandably apprehensive. Moreover, not only did China provide Pakistan with badly needed credit but with the American arms embargo Pakistan needed a source of military equipment. The Chinese provided Pakistan with 100 T-59

---

[57] As quoted in Palmer, *Penetration*, op. cit., p. 64.

tanks, 50 MIG-19 jet fighters, and 10 IL-28 bombers.[58] Such actions seem to have provided the Chinese with a widespread favorable attitude in Pakistan. Thus, the stage was being set for improved Sino-Pakistani relations which were to play a significant role in the 1971 events in South Asia.

With the emerging internal crisis in East Pakistan, the Chinese were frank with Yahya concerning his poor handling of the situation. The Chinese leaders were particularly concerned with the opportunities that a crisis in East Pakistan could present the Indians and their fear of Indian hegemony in South Asia was a major factor in their urging Yahya to find a reasonable compromise for Pakistan's internal difficulties.

The Johnson Administration seems to have paid little attention to South Asia primarily because of the preoccupation with Vietnam but also because of the American desire to maintain the status quo in the region. Johnson also opposed Pakistan's relations

---

[58] Ibid., p. 6.

with China. In April 1967 the U.S., as part of its low profile policy in South Asia, announced a limit on arms shipments to both India and Pakistan. The Pakistanis felt such a policy had its primary effect on them because the Indians were receiving their military supplies from the Soviet Union and would not be affected by the U.S. arms policy. Accordingly, even though it did not formally withdraw, Pakistan reduced its participation in SEATO and CENTO and proceeded to cement its relationship with China, the new source of its arms supplies. After some initial hesitation the Chinese, for their part, were ready to supply Pakistan with arms and diplomatic support in order to counter India, the state the Chinese viewed as the key in the Soviet Union's containment policy aimed against them.

Summary

This chapter has sought to describe and analyze the politics and conflicts between India and Pakistan within the South Asia regional system. We have observed the differing "White House views" on the relative importance of South Asia that emerged during the Truman, Eisenhower, Kennedy, and Johnson Administrations. In addition, we have attempted to establish the patterns of relationships between these two regional powers and their respective major power supports. The intrusion of the major powers into the South Asian regional system has served to widen the scope of the conflict and in the process a regional conflict is transformed into a global issue. This development is not unique to South Asia, however. The internationalization of a conflict can also be observed in such arenas as Europe, the Arab-Israeli conflict, Vietnam (1964-1972), and Angola (1976). A key contribution that may result from tracing the development of the Pakistani domestic crisis is the distinction between those regional crises which will become matters of global concern and conflict from those that will not.

    We will proceed to attempt to analyze the development of a Pakistani domestic issue into a regional war and international middle-level crisis for U.S.

foreign policy decision-makers. Pakistan's major foreign policy concern at the regional level was its survival in light of the dangers it perceived emanating from India. However, the Pakistani central government's failure to integrate East and West Pakistan into one community and its brutal suppression of the Bengalis were major factors that propelled the South Asia region into a conflict that resulted in the dismemberment of the Pakistani state.

The internationalization of a regional conflict will occupy major attention in this work. We have examined the origins of the American involvement in South Asia and the role that the region occupied within the global framework of American foreign policy. We will then proceed to analyze the conflicts between the subjective evaluations of U.S. foreign policy decision-makers and attempt to explain their different value hierarchies.

II: THE UNFOLDING OF A CRISIS -- FROM NONCRISIS
TO MIDDLE-LEVEL CRISIS

The Problem of Integration

In this chapter we will analyze Pakistan's failure in national integration and the unfolding of a middle-level crisis that confronted U.S. decision-makers. The failure of Pakistan to integrate its East and West wings was climaxed with the massacre following the March 25, 1971 crackdown. Prior to the March 25 holocaust, and the refugee issue that was its by-product, Pakistan's internal difficulties were confined within its boundaries and were a Pakistani domestic issue. The results of the 1970 Pakistani election reinforced political conflicts among its leaders. These conflicts evolved into an internal crisis for the polity. The March 25 crackdown created the refugee issue which was the basis for India's involvement in the conflict and cast the problem at a regional level as Pakistan and India confronted each other regarding the fate of the Bengali refugees. Simultaneously, the U.S. became increasingly involved in negotiations with India and Pakistan during the unfolding of the regional crisis, and the Nixon Administration aligned itself with Ayub Khan's regime. We will proceed to examine the dynamic development of a middle-level crisis for the Nixon Administration. The analysis begins with the domestic and regional crises as the origins of the global middle-level crisis.

In his famous work Politics Among Nations, Hans J. Morgenthau describes a nation as "an abstraction from a number of individuals who have certain characteristics in common, and it is these characteristics that make them members of the same nation."[1] These characteristics are usually said to be such common aspects as culture, religion, history, land, and language. However, recent integration literature has concerned itself with integration beyond the nation-state level. Lindberg and Scheingold's Europe's Would-Be Polity[2] and Haas' Beyond the Nation State[3] are examples of this literature. After com-

---

[1] Morgenthau, op. cit., p. 97.

[2] Leon N. Lindberg and Stuart A. Scheingold, Europe's Would-Be Polity: Patterns of Change in the European Community (Englewood Cliffs, N.J.: Prentice-Hall, 1970).

[3] Ernst B. Haas, Beyond the Nation State (Stanford: Stanford University Press, 1964).

paring the integration literature with the literature that seeks to describe and analyze developments within a nation-state, one is struck by the similar problems that are, in fact, present at both levels. In short, the integration problem is present at the nation-state level especially in the case of a nation that only recently achieved its independence. If numerous different groups comprise the newly-constituted nation-state, the integrative process may be its most crucial problem in seeking to attain political unity. Language is one of the aspects or manifestations of a nation, yet having one language, of itself, seems to be neither a necessary nor sufficient condition for a nation.

In The Integration of Political Communities, Philip Jacob and Henry Teune point out that political integration refers to more than one dimension of behavior.[4] Jacob and Teune employ the term focus of

---

[4] Philip E. Jacob and James V. Toscano (eds.), The Integration of Political Communities (Philadelphia: J.B. Lippincott Company, 1964), p. 10.

cohesion and conclude that "the essence of the integrative relationship is seen as collective action to promote mutual interests."[5] Previous research has pointed to ten factors that may exert integrative influence upon people: 1) geographical proximity; 2) homogeneity; 3) transactions, or interactions, among persons or groups; 4) knowledge of each other; 5) shared functional interests; 6) the "character" or "motive" pattern of a group; 7) the structural frame or system of power and decision-making; 8) the sovereignty-dependency status of the community; 9) governmental effectiveness; and 10) previous integration experiences.

Language is indicative of culture and history and consequently arouses emotional sentiments. The bond created by language and other integrative factors is important in determining the cohesion of the group and the benefits which a group, the nation in this case, may be able to attain.[6] In the Pak-

---

[5] Ibid., p. 5.

[6] Karl W. Deutsch, Nationalism and Social Communication (Cambridge, Massachusetts: MIT Press, 1966).

istani case a major point is whether a nation needs to have a common language or whether various types of distributive functions of a national government are sufficient for integration. If language is viewed as the key element for the integration process of the nation-state, Pakistan did not have a unique language to facilitate internal communication and foster a "we" feeling.[7]

The geographical distance between West and East Pakistan was only one of the many factors that were to become obstacles to the goal of Pakistan's national integration. Separated by one thousand miles by India, East and West Pakistan were divided by numerous other factors that were to outweigh the bond that Islam was able to provide in the short term. Islam served as the basis for the Pakistani effort toward integration during the partition of India with the British withdrawal in 1947.

However, the differences between East and West Pakistan also included such fundamental factors as language, culture, and physical characteristics of the

---

[7] K.R. Minogue, *Nationalism* (New York: Basic Books, 1967), p. 119.

population.[8] During the 1947-1970 period, the Bengalis protested against economic and political discrimination practiced against them by the central government. Discrimination against the Bengalis took the form of greater allocation of economic resources for the development of the West than for the East, as well as the systematic exclusion of Bengalis from government services including the military.

The conflict between East and West Pakistan began with Pakistan's independence. Following partition, the Constituent Assembly met and adopted various provisions, two of which were to alarm the representatives from East Bengal. The Bengali representatives feared that in spite of their numerical majority in the population they would receive a minority of the seats in the legislature. Moreover,

---

[8] For a more detailed analysis see Rounaq Jahan, Pakistan: Failure in National Integration (New York: Columbia University Press, 1972).

Urdu was to be the national language. The conflict was between Bengal and Punjab, and the language issue reflected the mutual suspicion and hostility.[9] The breakdown of the languages spoken in Pakistan was as follows:

Bengali	54.6%
Punjabi	28.4
Urdu	7.2
Sindhi	5.8
Pushto	7.1
English	1.8

The geographic split of Pakistan was thus reinforced by the linguistic cleavage. Those who advocated the exclusive use of Urdu feared that the preservation and promotion of Bengali in East Pakistan would be likely to weaken the bond with West Pakistan while strengthening the ties between Indian and Hindu Bengal. The supporters of Urdu argued that the advancement of Bengali was detrimental to the interests of national unity.[10]

Only after riots in East Bengal was a compromise reached in May 1954. This compromise called for the official recognition of both Urdu and Bengali.

---

[9] Keith Callard, Pakistan: A Political Study (New York: The Macmillan Company, 1957), p. 97.

[10] Ibid., p. 181.

By this constitutional recognition, Bengali received equal status with Urdu. Notwithstanding this achievement, the Bengalis resented the obstacles they confronted in achieving that recognition and still believed that they were being denied full equality in practice.

> The language question has been merely the most flagrant example of a series of issues on which Bengalis feel that they have had to fight desperately to secure satisfaction that should have been theirs without argument, as a matter of simple justice.[11]

In 1957 the resentment of the Bengalis led the East Pakistan Assembly to pass a resolution demanding "full regional autonomy." An analogous demand in 1971 by the Awami League resulted in the military crackdown by Yahya Khan's regime and the eventual rise of the independent state of Bangladesh.

Yahya Khan's Regime

Yahya Khan assumed the Presidency of Pakistan on March 25, 1969. He did so following the military rule of Ayub Khan during the previous decade. Violence, strikes, and economic troubles were character-

---
[11] Ibid., p. 183.

istic of both wings of Pakistan toward the end of Ayub Khan's rule. Ayub's efforts to give greater power to the bureaucracy and, in effect, make it his political party, while simultaneously stripping opposing political parties of their power, did not result in the integration of Pakistan.[12] By 1969 the erosion of Ayub's political and military control had become sufficiently serious to warrant a meeting of a Round Table Conference of political leaders on March 10, 1969. Failure to reach a consensus on the actions to be taken regarding the serious demonstrations that were taking place led to Ayub's resignation and Yahya'a rise to power.

Upon taking office Yahya accepted the following three demands from the leaders of the Round Conference:

---
[12] Anwar Hussain Syed, "Reflections on the Ayubian Decade in Pakistan," *Pakistan Administrative Staff College Journal*, IX, December 1971, p. 28.

1. That free and fair elections should be held throughout the country on the basis of one man-one vote for a constituent assembly which would give Pakistan its first democratic constitution.

2. That, as the country had been without a democratic constitution from the date if its birth in August 1947, the General should agree to push matters on.

3. That he should break up the One Unit and restore the provinces as they were in 1965.[13]

In addition to accepting these demands, Yahya proclaimed Martial Law, a seemingly contradictory action, but one which he felt was necessary. During the March 1969-December 1970 period Yahya Khan repeatedly emphasized the transient nature of his rule whose purpose was to allow the establishment of a constitutional government through elections. He stated that he had

---
[13] Donald Watt, "Pakistan From Within: A Threeway Split," Commonwealth Journal of International Affairs, No. 245, January 1972, p. 15.

...no ambition other than the creation of conditions conducive to the establishment of a constitutional government... It will be the task of those elected representatives to give the country a workable constitution and find solutions to all other political, economic, and social problems that have been agitating the minds of the people.[14]

In short, the decision was made to return the reins of government to the civilian sector and national elections were to be held. Yahya first publicly discussed the question of autonomy as a serious potential problem in his July 28, 1969 speech.[15] The issue of autonomy for the two wings of Pakistan was also the subject of his November 28, 1969 speech[16] in which he stated his position in favor of maximum autonomy for the two wings of Pakistan provided that the national integrity of Pakistan were not put in question.

---

[14] Yahya Khan's March 28, 1969 Radio Broadcast, as quoted in S.G.M. Budruddin, Election Handbook 1970 (Karachi: Publishing and Marketing Associated Ltd., 1970), p. 99.

[15] Yahya Khan's July 28, 1969 Radio Broadcast, as quoted in Ibid., p. 103.

[16] Yahya Khan's November 28, 1969 Radio Broadcast, as quoted in Ibid., p. 109.

On March 30, 1970 a Legal Framework Order was published. This document established the rules for the elections to the National Assembly. The key provisions were that Pakistan should be a federation with maximum autonomy granted to the provinces, but that the territorial integrity of the state must be maintained.

The Legal Framework Order was to provide the interim structure of authority and constitutional boundaries within which the parties could contest the elections.

> This order, promulgated on 30 March 1970, had five major points: (1) the country should be a federation, the unity of which 'is not in any manner impaired'; (2) the constitution must provide for Muslim ideology, civil rights, and the independence of the judiciary; (3) the provinces should have maximum autonomy within the needs of the federal government to 'discharge its responsibilities in relation to external and internal affairs, and to preserve the country'; (4) the people of all parts of the country should be full participants in all national activities; and (5) 'within a specified period, economic and all other disparities between the provinces and between different areas in a Province are to be

removed by the adoption of statutory and other measures.'17

Notwithstanding Yahya's promise to hold the elections, it is difficult, in hindsight, to understand his reasons for allowing them to take place since it seemed clear that the Awami League would emerge triumphant. Because of the abolition of the One-Unit, the West could no longer be considered one bloc. Perhaps the most simple reason the elections were held is also the most convincing: miscalculations and a lack of judgement on the part of Yahya. Perhaps he was indeed

> being misled by the assurances of the pro-West Pakistani elements in East Pakistan. These comprised the Muslim League and the Samaat-i-Islam, both representing the die-hard Muslim core in the Eastern wing. Yahya might also have believed that the National Awami Party headed by the pro-Chinese, 89 year old, Maulana Bhashani would offset Mujibur Rehman's Awami League influence in East Bengal.18

---

17 Wayne Wilcox, *The Emergence of Bangladesh: Problems and Opportunities for a Redefined American Policy in South Asia* (Washington, D.C.: American Enterprise Institute for Public Policy Research, 1973), p. 15.

18 Frank Moraes, "India and Pakistan," *Pacific Community*, October 1971, p. 151.

Yahya apparently assumed that the Awami League would not be able to win a sufficient number of seats in order to control the central government. However, the abolition of the One-Unit principle was to work to the advantage of East Pakistan and to the disadvantage of the Western province of Punjab due to the use of provincial political parties.[19] Thus, numerous political parties surfaced and twenty-five of these had candidates running for seats in the National Assembly.

The 1970 Elections

During the election campaign the forces of nature intervened in the political workings of the Pakistani political system. During the summer of 1970 storms and the serious flooding that followed prompted Yahya Khan's regime to postpone the elections from October 5, 1970 to December 7, 1970. On November 12, 1970, however, a cyclone and tidal wave in East Pakistan caused severe losses in both life and property. Lack of a sufficient or efficient relief

---
[19] Donald Watt, "Pakistan From Within," Commonwealth Journal of International Affairs, January 1972, p. 16.

effort by the Pakistani government was viewed by the East Pakistanis as further evidence of the lack of concern for the fate of the Benagalis on the part of the West-dominated central government. Whether or not it was true that the relief effort was inadequate only because the people to be rescued were Bengalis, Bengalis apparently believed that the lack of adequate relief was due to their ethnic stock and inferior position in the Pakistani political system.[20] The resentment and unity which such a belief aroused within the Bengali community, accompanied by the confirmation of their belief of being subject to a long history of victimization from discrimination at the hands of West Pakistan, may explain the size of the Awami League's overwhelming victory in East Pakistan in the 1970 elections.

East and West Pakistan were allocated 169 and 143 seats respectively in the National Assembly. The Awami League won 167 of East Pakistan's 169 seats while Bhutto's Pakistan People's Party (PPP) won 81 out of the West's 143 seats. Thus, the Awami League

---

[20] Dom Moraes, The Tempest Within (New Delhi: Vikas, 1971).

had succeeded in obtaining a majority in the National Assembly, thereby presenting Yahya with an unacceptable winner.

Yahya Khan's initial reaction to Mujibar Rahman's victory was to meet with him in order to convince him to agree to soften his election demands as embodied in the "Six Points." Following the meeting Yahya publicly expressed his desire for an early convening of the National Assembly and referred to Sheik Mujibar Rahman as "the future Prime Minister."[21] By January 12, 1971 Yahya seems to have had a change of heart and talked about the possibility of having talks between the two major parties, that is, the Awami League and Bhutto's PPP.[22] But, in fact, the Awami League had enough seats to form a government with no need for a coalition with any other political party.

Bhutto, however, was interested in projecting a position of formidable political power. He sought

---

[21] Jamna Das Akhtar, Saga of Bangla Desh (Delhi: Oriental Publishers, 1971), p. 263.

[22] The Dawn, January 12, 1971.

to appear to represent all of West Pakistan but was unsuccessful in doing so because other political actors, such as the President of Baluchistan, refused to agree to have Bhutto speak for West Pakistan.[23] Having failed to build a West Pakistan coalition against the Awami League, Bhutto sought the support of the ruling military regime.[24]

The efforts to reach a compromise involved triangular relations between Yahya, Bhutto, and Mujib. Despite his opposition to Mujib's "Six Points," Bhutto assured Yahya of his sincerity in search for a viable solution at their Larkana meeting. But the Bhutto-Mujib talks in late January indicated the difficulty in reaching a compromise in order to preserve the integrity of Pakistan.[25] During the months of February

---

[23] For an account of the various negotiations see Rehman Sobhan, "Negotiating for Bangla Desh," South Asian Review, July 9, 1971.

[24] For an account, see The Dawn, February 12-17, 1972.

[25] G.W. Choudhury, The Last Days of United Pakistan (Bloomington: Indiana University Press, 1974), pp. 152-153.

and March, Yahya's and Mujib's forces sought to strengthen their respective forces. Yahya sent reinforcements to East Pakistan by way of Ceylon because of India's ban on Pakistani overflights.

Bhutto increased the severity of the political crisis by announcing on February 16, 1971 that the PPP would boycott the National Assembly scheduled to convene on March 3, 1971. The Awami League's alleged refusal to compromise on its "Six Points" and India's alleged threats were his stated reasons for the boycott. Bhutto further escalated his threats by announcing his intentions of calling for a general strike in West Pakistan of the National Assembly were to meet on March 3.

A turning point in the failure of political integration and political succession came when Yahya Khan decided on March 1 to postpone the convening of the Assembly. Apparently Bhutto had succeeded in generating an atmosphere of crisis and raising the spectre of an Indian attack. As a result, he was able to reconfirm the military elite's suspicion that an

Awami League-dominated government would result in the decreased effectiveness of the Pakistan military. Those in Yahya's central government who accepted Bhutto's arguments were able to prevail over those who urged that the implications in East Pakistan be considered.

The escalation which Bhutto had begun was also matched by Yahya Khan as well as Sheik Mujib. Yahya dismissed Admiral S.M. Ahsan as governor of East Pakistan and Mujibar Rahman called for a general strike in East Pakistan for March 2. Yahya made several efforts to defuse the coming crisis despite the confrontations that were already taking place between the Pakistani Army and the Bengali population. He called for a meeting of the parties to the conflict for March 10 in Dacca and stated his agreement to have the National Assembly convene on March 25, provided the national integrity of Pakistan be maintained. By this time, however, East Pakistan had begun to operate like an independent state and Sheik Mujib made several demands on Yahya, including the ending of martial law. Furthermore, Mujibar Rahman asked the people of

East Pakistan not to pay taxes and to keep the government and university establishments closed in order to show both Yahya and Bhutto the extent of his power.[26]

The decision to postpone the convening of the National Assembly served to exacerbate the Pakistani political developments which had already evolved from a noncrisis into an internal political crisis. The postponement showed the Bengalis that the central government was willing to intervene on behalf of a political party that had received only 81 seats in the National Assembly compared to the Awami League's 167 seats. A movement that had sought autonomy for East Pakistan began to be transformed into a demand for secession. Therefore, it seems that the actions on the part of the central government induced the consequence it feared most, a movement for secession by the Bengalis.

As each side prepared for a showdown, Yahya and Mujib began what was to be their final effort to

---

[26] See Wilcox, The Emergence of Bangladesh, op. cit., p. 23.

find a political settlement. The atmosphere in Dacca was not friendly toward Yahya. The flags of Bangladesh rather than Pakistan were flown in Dacca on National Day. Yahya construed Mujib's demands and final plan to be nothing short of the dismemberment of Pakistan. Yahya's goal was to keep Pakistan united, but the methods he used would insure it would break up.[27] On March 25 the military operation against the Bengalis began, and South Asia was plunged into a crisis as a civil war became an international issue.

The March 25 Crackdown

The radicalization of the autonomy movement into a militant secessionist movement instituted a cycle as the central government responded with the use of force. This response made the movement more militantly secessionist, which in turn caused the central government to resort to an even greater military force. This cycle soon led to the March 25 crackdown that included

---

[27] Interview with U.S. Government official, February 1976.

the outlawing of the Awami League as well as the
military occupation of East Pakistan by the central
government's armed forces. The "solution" to a domestic political problem was to propel the issue from a regional noncrisis and eventual crisis to a global middle-level crisis.

Yahya Khan left Dacca on March 25 and in his March 26 radio broadcast, he declared East Pakistan a "rebel" province and ordered the army to restore law and order. The events that followed can in essence be described as a massacre and reign of terror. Students, professionals, and leaders were systematically murdered and Hindus along with supporters of the Awami League were rounded up and executed with exceptional ferocity.[28]

The Pakistani Army's crackdown included the indiscriminate shelling and bombing of civilian areas.

---

[28] For an account of these tragic events see Robert Payne, Massacre (New York: The Macmillan Co., 1973); Bangla Desh Documents (New Delhi: Ministry of External Affairs, 1971); Bangla Desh and Indo-Pak War (New Delhi: Ministry of Information, 1972); White Paper on the Crisis in East Pakistan (Islamabad: Ministry of Information and National Affairs, 1971).

Murder, rape, and looting were commonplace crimes perpretrated on the Bengali population by the Pakistani military for several months following the March 25 crackdown.

On May 5, 1971 the U.S. State Department acknowledged that American tanks and jets delivered to Pakistan for the original purpose of providing defense against possible Chinese attack were being used in the crackdown in East Pakistan.[29] The executions and destruction perpetrated by the Pakistani Army provided the impetus for the refugees to flee to India. Following the March 25 crackdown, the millions of refugees who streamed into India from East Pakistan were a contributing factor in catapulting an internal crisis into a regional crisis between India and Pakistan.

The Pakistani Army's ability to quash its enemies and exercise a degree of control over East Pakistan provided support for those in the U.S. Government who argued that the danger of further increase in tensions had receded. Nonetheless, problems of logistics

---

[29] AP report from Washington published in The Statesman, May 6, 1971.

and the rise of the guerrilla movement within East Pakistan along with an increased effectiveness of Indian aid to the geurrillas combined to make the Pakistani Army's control over the province more costly and tenuous during the summer of 1971. The Indian invasion, however, was to be the decisive factor in the "liberation" of Bangladesh.

Indian Involvement

India's concern in East Pakistan's internal crisis began with its moral and diplomatic support for Sheik Mujib's Awami League prior to the March 25 crackdown. In February 1971 India banned the flights of Pakistani planes between West and East Pakistan. With the crackdown, India served as a sanctuary for the Mukti Bahini and its government in exile. Indian intervention in the crisis began with the training and supplying of the Mukti Bahini forces that used Indian territory as a base from which to launch attacks on East Pakistan. As the number of Bengali refugees reached ten million, the ultimate Indian intervention was the invasion of East Pakistan.

"By July the Pakistani Government had received

reliable reports from a friendly great power to the effect that the Indians had begun to prepare for a military confrontation."[30] In order to assure the support of the Soviet Union as a counter to the U.S. and China, India signed its Treaty of Friendship with the Soviet Union in August 1971. The Soviets were interested in extending and formalizing their influence in India as a means of checking China and viewed the Treaty as such a step. Kissinger's trip to China took place in July and on July 15 the announcement was made that President Nixon would visit China in February 1972. According to one account, Kissinger's veiled threat to Ambassador Jha of India that China would intervene should India attack Pakistan and that the U.S. would not aid India as it had in 1962 propelled India to sign the treaty with the Soviet Union in August.[31] Thus, each of the parties was becoming clearly established.

---

[30] Choudhury, The Last Days, op. cit., p. 199. Choudhury states this information was conveyed to him in September 1971 by Yahya and the chief of military intelligence.

[31] Choudhury, The Major Powers, op. cit., p. 206.

However, the Chinese limited themselves to encouraging Yahya to reach an accommodation with the Bengalis. The Chinese were ready to declare their general support for Pakistan but were not willing to commit themselves to intervene on behalf of the Pakistanis. Once the war between India and Pakistan erupted, the Chinese seemed to focus their attention on counteracting the Soviet Union.

G.W. Choudhury recounts that Yahya showed him the correspondence he had been conducting with Nixon and the Chinese leaders. They counseled Yahya to reach a political settlement based on a "brotherly parting of the ways" if the Bengalis would not agree to a solution that entailed a union with the West Pakistanis.[32]

American Involvement

During the mid-1960's there were reports of alleged CIA encouragement of East Pakistan's secessionist sentiments. Pakistani Ambassador Ghulam Ahmad was "assured" by CIA Director Richard Helms on August 26,

---
[32] Choudhury, The Last Days, op. cit., p. 192.

1966, that the "'CIA is not engaged in any subversion activities in East Pakistan... or against President Ayub and his regime,' but there persisted among Pakistanis a widespread feeling that Americans were not passive witnesses to their internal politics, particularly in East Pakistan."[33]

American visitors were viewed as CIA agents and economists connected with the Pakistan Planning Commission were suspected for their pro-Bengali views. Ambassador Farland was depicted as a pro-India CIA agent bent on subverting Pakistan's interests.

U.S. policy apparently played a peripheral role in the developments prior to the beginning of the election campaign. The Nixon Administration believed that the upcoming elections would constitute a peaceful return to democracy in Pakistan. A new constitution would provide a solid framework for the continuation of a united Pakistan. Moreover, many U.S. officials believed that American efforts to emphasize aid for projects in East Pakistan would rectify the

---

[33] As quoted in Choudhury, *The Major Powers*, op. cit., p. 134.

gap in foreign aid received by West and East Pakistan. "The actions of AID and the words of many advisors in reshaping the Pakistan program, however, convinced some Pakistanis that Americans were actively backing secessionists in Dacca."[34]

The U.S. Consul-General in Dacca, Arch Blood, seems to have been openly sympathetic toward Sheik Mujib and his goals. The Pakistani authorities were apparently aware of the secret meetings held between Blood and Sheik Mujib. Blood's activities were viewed as detrimental to the Pakistani national interest because they were interpreted by the Pakistani authorities as encouraging secession.

The U.S. Ambassador to Pakistan, Joseph Farland, sought to counter Blood's suggestions to Sheik Mujib by advising the Bengali leader that the U.S. did not favor the secession of East Pakistan and would not support his effort. Blood's counsel to Sheik Mujib may have influenced the East Pakistani leader to press for secession but it seems clear that he would

---

[34] Wilcox, The Emergence of Bangladesh, op. cit., p. 18.

have done so regardless of Blood's advice.[35]

In January 1970, according to one account, there was a Senior Review Group meeting to discuss contingencies as a result of the Pakistani election of December 7.[36] For the most part, however, American policy prior to March 25 was limited to observations and reporting. The American embassies were reporting the developing events, but the embassies were advocating the position of their respective host country. At this juncture, no American decisions were made that had any significant impact. The official American position was neutrality, but as Blood's activities indicate, the policy was not being implemented according to the wishes of the Nixon Administration. Within a few weeks following the March 25 crackdown, Blood and several of his staff were recalled. The U.S. policy of nonintervention toward the civil war was thus

---

[35] G.W. Choudhury, The Last Days, op. cit., p. 120.

[36] Interview with U.S. Government official, March 1975.

an indirect method of supporting Pakistan's national unity.[37]

Nixon and Kissinger may have had too many illusions about Yahya Khan's leadership capabilities. While some State Department officials suggest on hindsight that more pressure should have been exerted on Yahya by the U.S. to negotiate with the Bengalis in Calcutta, Yahya seems to have been committed to a course of action in line with the March 25 crackdown. The poor advice he was receiving combined with his serious drinking problem by November only served to cause further erosion of the situation.[38] However, the Nixon Administration did not want to exert pressure in Pakistan because the problem involved a domestic issue, and it was questionable whether the U.S. would be able to exert effective leverage. Early in December President Nixon was reported to have said in

---
[37] Wilcox, The Emergence of Bangladesh, op. cit., p. 24.
[38] Interview with U.S. Government official, March 1975.

Washington:

> We have followed with sympathetic interest the efforts of the Government and people of Pakistan to achieve an amicable settlement in East Pakistan. We have also welcomed the efforts of President Yahya to reduce the tensions in the subcontinent.[39]

The U.S. Congress played a role during the summer months of 1971. One of the leading Congressional critics of the Administration's South Asia policy was Senator Kennedy. Kennedy viewed the South Asia middle-level crisis from a conceptual frame of reference that gave priority to the refugee issue. On August 26, 1971, after his arrival in the United States from his tour of South Asia, Senator Kennedy gave expression to a humanitarian consideration in the conduct of foreign policy[40] when he said:

> We must end immediately all further U.S. arms shipments to West Pakistan ...[and] all other economic support to a regime that continues to violate the most basic principles of

---

[39] The Statesman, December 8, 1971.

[40] For a humanitarian approach to foreign policy see Lincoln P. Bloomfield, In Search of American Foreign: The Humane Use of Power (New York: Oxford University Press, 1974).

humanity. We [must] demonstrate to the generals of West Pakistan and to the people of the world that the United States has a deep and abiding revulsion of (sic) the monumental slaughter that has ravaged East Bengal.[41]

Votes in both the House and Senate were taken with resolutions being passed calling for the termination of all U.S. aid, both military and economic, to the Pakistani government.[42] In August 1971 the U.S. House of Representatives voted to suspend U.S. aid to Pakistan. The House amended the Act authorizing the foreign assistance program by banning the supply of military and economic aid, except food and medicine, to Pakistan until political settlement were reached. On October 14, 1971 the Senate Foreign Relations Committee voted to ban all forms of foreign aid to Pakistan until the President informed Congress that the

---

[41] AP report in Amrita Bazar Patrika, August 27, 1971 as quoted in Subrata Roy Chowdhury, The Genesis of Bangladesh: A Study in International Legal Norms and Permissive Conscience (Bombay: Asia Publishing House, 1972), p. 273.

[42] Marta Nicholas and Philip Oldenburg, Bangladesh: The Birth of a Nation (Madras, India: M. Seshachalam and Company, 1972).

situation in East Pakistan was reasonably stable and the refugees were allowed to return.[43]

These resolutions notwithstanding, U.S. military shipments to Pakistan continued, despite the Administration's claim of an arms embargo being in effect. The Administration argued that arms deliveries to Pakistan provided it with leverage with the Pakistani government, although it was again not demonstrated that the arms supplier does in fact control the recipient. The reign of terror and the refugee problem continued throughout the crisis, that is from March 25 through December 14, 1971, and constituted a significant factor in the crisis.

During the 1971 South Asian events, Associated Press correspondent Arnold Zeitlin was told by a Bengali doctor: "The U.S. Government sends us food to keep us alive and bullets to kill us."[44] Senator Kennedy echoed those sentiments when he said: "It makes no sense to provide the West Pakistan Government

---

[43] The Statesman, October 16, 1971.

[44] The Statesman, August 2, 1971, as quoted in Chowdhury, op. cit., p. 264.

with military supplies which help create refugees while spending millions of dollars to aid those refugees."[45]

Chowdhury cites Fulbright[46] for distinguishing between the two extremes of American national character that range from arrogance to compassion in foreign policy.

> Both the Americas were involved in the East Bengal tragedy -- the arrogant America that sent the bullets which killed the Bengalis and Lincoln's America that called for an immediate suspension of all aid to the military rulers of Pakistan; the arrogant America that helped the perpetuation of the exploitative tyranny of West Pakistan, and Lincoln's America that supported the struggle of the Bengali people for freedom from colonial exploitation. For the world's most resourceful nation, East Bengal might have been a small issue, but it was nonetheless a fundamental one, involving human values, and throwing a big challenge to the American people to decide which of the two sides of its national character was to predominate.[47]

---

[45] The Statesman, August 7, 1971.

[46] William J. Fulbright, The Arrogance of Power (New York: Vintage Books, 1967), p. 245.

[47] Chowdhury, op. cit., p. 265.

The concern and involvement of certain members of Congress was particularly discernible with the refugee issue. Congressional involvement will be dealt with in greater detail in a later section. Suffice it to emphasize at this juncture that one of the key Senators who was concerned with the refugee and arms supplies issues in the South Asian events was Edward M. Kennedy. Senator Kennedy's committee on refugees held hearings on the problem and sought to publicize both issues. The Nixon Administration viewed Kennedy's efforts with a substantial degree of suspicion and perceived them as an attempt to embarass President Nixon and as part of Kennedy's predicted 1972 drive for the White House.

According to numerous accounts, Nixon intervened to save the life of Sheik Mujib and counseled Yahya to exercise restraint and reach a political settlement with the Bengalis. "President Nixon's personal sympathy for Pakistan, his cherished China policy, and the unpleasant image of Pakistan's dismemberment under the guns of Soviet-backed Indian forces motivated him and his government to work diligently toward an honorable settlement to both the Bengalis and the West Pakistanis."[48]

But the American mediation efforts had begun too late and may not have been sufficient to avert a war even if successful, as Kissinger admitted at his December 7, 1971 briefing. During Indira Gandhi's visit to Washington, the Nixon Administration sought to buy time in order to proceed with the attempts to arrange negotiations. Nixon apparently thought he had succeeded in his efforts and this belief and apparent misunderstanding may account for the intensity of the Administration's reaction to the Indian attack.

As an apparent last resort, Yahya made an effort in mid-November to avert war by presenting a secret peace plan to Ambassador Atal of India. This plan was conveyed to Mrs. Gandhi who found it unacceptable.[49] The Indian invasion of East Pakistan

---

[48] Choudhury, The Major Powers, op. cit., p. 208.

[49] For an account of this effort see Choudhury, The Last Days, op. cit., pp. 202-203.

was undertaken within a week following Indira Gandhi's return from her visit to Washington.

Summary

The dynamic nature of the development of a middle-level crisis is the major insight afforded by the description and analysis of the 1971 South Asian events. The political conflicts emanating from the failure of Pakistan's central government to achieve the political integration of its East and West wings was a significant factor in triggering the escalation of the conflict. Pakistan's domestic problems eventually engulfed her in a regional war and international middle-level crisis.

The scope of the conflict grew wider as a result of the Bengali refugee issue. India's involvement in a matter that Pakistan considered an internal affair can be traced to the in-flow of Bengali refugees into India following the March 25 crackdown. With the growing burden of the refugees on India's economy, India became increasingly interventionist in its foreign policy orientation toward East Pakistan. Subsequently, the intensity of the conflict sharpened.

For reasons which will be analyzed in greater detail in later chapters, high level foreign policy U.S. decision-makers have traditionally not attached a high priority to South Asia in comparison to such regions as Europe, the Middle East and Southeast Asia. Nevertheless, U.S. decision-makers did pay some attention to the 1971 South Asian events prior to Indira Gandhi's visit to Washington in November 1971. Some Congressional members were particularly vociferous on two manifestations of 1971 U.S. foreign policy toward South Asia: 1) the arms supplies to Pakistan, and 2) the refugee issue. Those State Department officials who believed that a U.S. foreign policy in support of Yahya's regime and actions was wrong were in agreement with these Congressional critics.

Intervening circumstances, especially the "opening of China," played a significant part in shaping the attitudes and values of several U.S. decision-makers involved in formulating U.S. policy toward South

Asia in 1971. The role of Yahya Khan as interlocutor between the United States and China was an important factor. The Administration sought to maintain the balance of power and status quo in South Asia, thereby preventing the perceived danger of Indian and Soviet hegemony of the subcontinent. A few key U.S. foreign policy decision-makers held the view that the "opening of China" and the maintenance of a regional balance of power in South Asia were intertwined, thus reinforcing the justification for the establishment of the "China connection." Accordingly, the global implications of this regional war cast the conflict as a middle-level crisis for the Nixon Administration.

However, the Nixon Administration was having difficulties coordinating a pro-Pakistan policy. For example, Arch Blood was removed from Dacca for his pro-Bengali sympathies and actions. The conflict between those in the U.S. Government who favored and those who opposed the implementation of a pro-Pakistan policy was also evident in the deliberative and advisory bodies assembled in Washington during 1971 to deal with the South Asia events.

III: THE STRUCTURE OF DECISION-MAKING

In this chapter we will undertake an examination of the organizational decision-making structure for the conduct of foreign policy in general and South Asia in particular. The objective of this analysis is to assess the relative weight or importance of the various governmental decision-making bodies. We will also deal with the impact that an individual such as Kissinger can have concerning the locus of decision-making and the increased authority that accrues to the organization where such an individual is located. In addition, the disagreements and conflicts that emerged between governmental units concerning policy objectives and the means of implementation will be analyzed.

As the chief executive officer of the U.S. Government, the President is responsible for the formulation and implementation of foreign and domestic policies. However, in this chapter we will be examining the conflicts among members of the bureaucracy regarding the proper course of action to be implemented by the U.S. in South Asia. We take this approach in order to explain U.S. foreign policy behavior. This policy is not the output of a unitary actor. Rather, the policy that emerges is likely to be a synthesis of conflicts among the involved decision-makers and organizational units within the inner circle of the American government's foreign policy institutions. The decision-makers may arrive at a policy through consensus, or, in failing to reach such a consensus, the decision-maker or organizational unit with the greatest power is likely to be able to impose its preferences or priorities on the other participants involved. Therefore, a major issue is to assess the relative power of the participating decision-makers in order to establish whose preferences are likely to predominate.

This chapter develops an argument that the characteristics of foreign policy decision-making behavior will vary with the personality of the President, his interest in foreign affairs, and the people he chooses as his chief foreign policy advisors. The National Security Council (NSC) and its arm the Washington Special Action Group (WSAG), are accorded primary attention in this chapter. The importance of these bodies for the South Asia middle-level crisis is due to the purposes they served for the Nixon Administration and his Special Assistant Henry Kissinger. The NSC and WSAG usurped several of the State Department's roles in the foreign policy sphere in order to provide Nixon and Kissinger with a greater degree of control over foreign policy decisions.

However, other governmental units were also involved in formulating U.S. policy toward South Asia. We will examine the input of the State Department, as well as Congress and its committees. Furthermore, primarily by serving as a constraint for the Nixon Administration's foreign policy decision and actions, the media also contributed to the formulation of policy. The interaction between these and other governmental agencies is also analyzed in order to determine the relative importance of the participating institutions.

In his analysis of the Israeli Government's inner circle for foreign policy issues, Brecher acknowledges that to dissect an inner decision-making group is a "hazardous enterprise."[1] He points out

---
[1] Brecher, op. cit., p. 453.

that there exist no precise criteria for measuring an individual's influence regarding a particular decision. Influence will also vary with changing situational factors such as time, issue-area, the individual roles of the office holders, the governmental structure, pressure groups, and perceptions. Furthermore, the numerous factors involved are likely to interact in different ways and thus produce varied results.

Domestic decision-making involves many of the same actors who participate in the foreign policy decision-making process. However, the role of the actors and their degree of influence is different in domestic as opposed to foreign policy decision-making. While domestic decision-making is deliberate and does not usually involve a crisis situation, much of the foreign policy decision-making that has been carefully analyzed has been of the crisis type. One of the major distinguishing features of crisis foreign policy decision-making is the formulation of the decision by a small group of leaders in the Executive Branch. The factors of surprise, high threat, high value, and short time to respond seem to explain the need for Presidential power to react decisively and swiftly.

The President and the NSC

Despite the allocation of several foreign relations duties to the Senate, the President of the United States is the person who under the American constitutional scheme is entrusted with the primary responsibility for the conduct of American foreign policy. The power of Commander-in-Chief and chief diplomat, as well as the initiative of the Executive Office in foreign affairs explains the dominance that the President can exercise over the conduct of foreign relations. Other factors, such as the need for quick and decisive action in a "shrinking" world, also seems to suggest that the power of the President in foreign affairs consists of more than simply the power to persuade.[2]

---
[2] Richard E. Neustadt, Presidential Power: The Politics of Leadership (New York: Wiley, 1960).

The Executive Branch plays the dominant role in the formulation and execution of American foreign policy with the Congress playing the check and balance role. The Judiciary is extremely reluctant to interfere with the Executive's choices in the conduct of foreign relations. Within the Executive Branch the President's role is more than <u>primus inter pares</u> (first among equals). His dominance over the Executive Branch is greater than that branch's dominance over the other branches.

The organizational structures within the Executive Office seemed to have been designed in order to assure the participation of the generalists and the regional experts in the management of crises. If, however, an Administration has a global foreign policy orientation, the regional issues will be viewed as a function of that global policy. Moreover, if the procedural style of operation is imperative coordination, the likelihood is that the Administrator will utilize the organizational structure in order to implement the Administration's previously-made decision rather than to discuss possible alternatives.

The President's power and control over the Executive Branch is extensive. Through political appointments, he is able to place "his men," men who are likely to hold his values and possess a personal loyalty that will lead them to execute his wishes, in the key positions of power within the Executive Branch. Should any of these men seek to counter the President's values or orders, the President has the ultimate power to dismiss his appointees.

A President's values may also direct the focus of his Administration. Thus, a President who perceives himself to be particularly adept in matters of foreign policy, will have a significant impact on the conduct and execution of these relations. President Nixon, for example, considered his major contribution to be in the area of foreign policy and, accordingly, extensively involved himself in the conduct of U.S. foreign relations.

Nixon wanted to dominate foreign policy. His preference, however, was to deal with a few people.

This provided Kissinger with greater power because of the access he had to the President. Kissinger was also able to organize a formidable NSC staff which he used for support. Under these circumstances, the power of the bureaucracy to determine the conduct of U.S. foreign policy will be severely limited. If, in addition, the President takes a direct interest in the particular foreign policy problem under consideration and has a goal that he seeks accomplished, the extent of meaningful deliberation by the bureaucracy regarding policy alternatives will be even more restricted.

American foreign policy in South Asia was characterized by a high degree of Presidential involvement. Imperative coordination in this case necessitated the President's effort to assert his chosen alternative and exercise his power. The utilization of the imperative coordination accounts for the absence of cooperation and consultation between the generalists and the regional experts, as well as the lack of balancing between global, regional, and bilateral factors.[3]

---

[3] Rudolph & Rudolph, op. cit., p. 42.

The President's power in the foreign policy sphere is derived in large part from his control of information. Foreign policy information is gathered by such bodies as the CIA, the Department of State and the Department of Defense. Each of these organizations, along with the National Security Council and its staff, is a component of the Executive Branch. However, the counter-argument could also be made that the President's power to determine foreign policy is constrained by the information that other bodies of the government provide him. Thus, the thesis can be made that the President is a captive of the information supplied him.

The use and abuse of the Presidential power has become one of the major areas of concern of the American polity during the post-Watergate era. Presidential conduct in the foreign policy sphere is especially susceptible to abuse because of the possibility that constitutional, Congressional or other restraints will not be effective. Thus, even with the power to conduct hearings and the power of the purse, the Congressional role is usually viewed as limited to reacting to the Executive Branch. Therefore, there exists the tension in the foreign policy area between the constraints to be imposed on the Executive Branch as opposed to the leeway to be allowed for Presidential initiative and conduct of effective foreign policy. The pre-eminence of the presidency in foreign policy-making is the presumption that does not seem to be questioned by the critics. Rather, the issue is the degree to which other actors will have a role and how that role is to be enhanced.

The foreign policy decision-making structure has been depicted as concentric circles of power.[4]

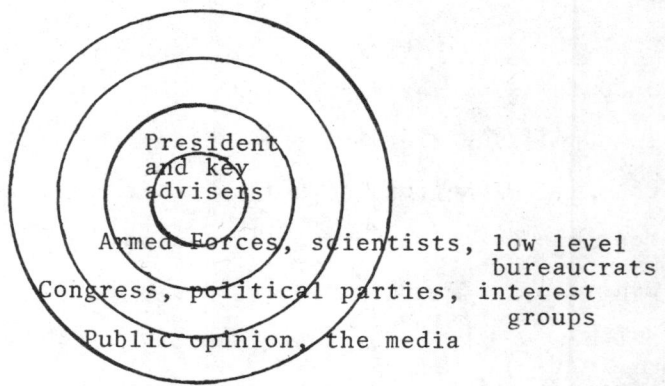

---

[4]John Spanier and Eric M. Uslaner, How American Foreign Policy is Made (New York: Praeger, 1974), p. 55. See also Roger Hilsman, The Politics of Policy Making in Defense and Foreign Affairs (New York: Harper & Row, 1971); Roger Hilsman, To Move A Nation (New York: Dell, 1967).

The structure of the concentric circles intends to reveal in a pictorial fashion the thesis that the President and his key advisors constitute the body that makes the foreign policy decisions. The distance of the respective concentric circles from the core indicates the degree of input and constraint observed and expected from the institutions within each of the concentric circles.

The core, consististing of the President and his key foreign policy advisors, dominates the formulation of foreign policy decision-making. The National Security Council is the institutionalized umbrella organization for the heads of the various U.S. Government organizations involved in foreign policy and national security affairs. The National Security Act of 1947 as supplemented by a number of Executive orders and memoranda is the statutory basis of the NSC. The NSC's function is: "To advise the President with respect to the integration of domestic, foreign, and military policies relating to the national security so as to enable the military services and the other departments and agencies of the government to cooperate more effectively in matters involving the national security." In addition, the NSC has the responsibility "to assess and appraise the objectives, commitments and risks of the United States in relation to our actual and potential military power, in the interest of national security, for the purpose of making recommendations to the President in connection therewith..."[5] The purpose of the NSC system is to insure the participation of certain political and military leaders regardless of the President's whim and to attempt to synthesize their recommendations. However, the NSC system has often been circumvented by past Presidents in favor of an informal circle of advisors many of whom are also members of the NSC. Thus, the NSC structure, because of the President's discretion, may be broadened to include men whom the Chief Executive wishes to be included.

---

[5] National Security Act of 1947, as amended, Public Law 253, 80th Congress, July 26, 1947, 61 Stat. 495, secs. 101(a) and (b).

The personalities of Presidents play a significant role in shaping the structure of their advisory bodies as well as the characteristics of the groups. The NSC is particularly susceptible to being organized or neglected according to the President's preference. The Nixon-Kissinger foreign policy system tended to ignore or give little weight to advice generated by other governmental agencies. They tended to make decisions based on their analyses, many having been generated by the NSC staff. Consequently, the other governmental agencies were not kept informed of major long-term U.S. objectives and priorities.

The President's decision-making style plays a large, and perhaps decisive, role in the method utilized for dealing with issues. Thus, the inner circle can be large or small and one group can be charged with the responsibility for all foreign policy decisions. Alternatively, the participants in the group can be replaced, depending on the issue area involved.

> The informal circle is especially prominent in crisis decision-making. This is where the alternatives are discussed and either accepted or rejected.[6]

---

[6] Spanier and Uslander, op. cit., p. 58.

The NSC system, while seeking to impose an inner circle on the President, does tend to accentuate the importance of certain officials in the Executive Branch. Accordingly, the Secretary of State, the Director of the CIA, the Secretary of Defense, the Chairman of the Joint Chiefs of Staff, and especially the President's National Security advisor can be expected to be the "fixed" participants in the inner circle dealing with foreign policy decision-making. In addition, there will be "variable" participants, those who are asked to take part in the deliberation because of the President's confidence in them. Which of these NSC members or participants becomes the first among equals is likely to depend on the relationship which each of them has with the President. Thus, Nixon's reliance on Kissinger is explicable in terms of the confidence that Nixon had in his National Security advisor, the convergence of their ideas, and their mutual preference for secrecy and quick and decisive action, despite Nixon's reputed hesitation when decisions had to be made.[7]

The NSC was originally intended to be an advisory body. However, under the Nixon Administration the Council had come to be largely utilized to implement and legitimize decisions made by the President, rather than as a body vested with an advisory mandate for authoritative decision-making. Under Kissinger the NSC's staff was used to generate studies that were of an advisory nature. Of course, the NSC could also request that specific studies be undertaken by member agencies of the NSC. According to Kissinger, Nixon would then make the decisions after "further private deliberations."[8] These "private deliberations" were, of course, held primarily with Kissinger. As a result, it is very difficult to separate the respective impact of these two men on U.S. foreign policy decisions.

---

[7] Richard Tanner Johnson, Managing the White House: An Intimate Study of the Presidency (New York: Harper & Row, 1974), p. 214.

[8] Henry Kissinger, letter to Senator Henry M. Jackson, March 3, 1970, "The National Security Council: Comment by Henry A. Kissinger," U.S. Senate, Committee on Government Operations, March 4, 1970.

Nixon's leadership style has been studied by observers who argue that his style influenced the organizational structure for decision-making. Nixon's sense of privacy seems to be at the source of much of the Nixon Administration's limited access to the President and the small size of the inner circle, which in the eyes of many was limited to Kissinger in the foreign-policy issue-area.

> Presidential preferences for closely held decisions and/or personal control of plans and operations blocked non-presidential, line officials from knowledge of operative assumptions relevant for related policy arenas and, in turn, cut off presidential level actors from information, arguments and options relevant to the closely held decisions or operations.[9]

Nixon's character and personal traits were largely responsible for the formalistic decision-making style that he established. This presidential leadership style was in contradistinction to FDR's competitive system. Nixon's "immense sense of privacy and tendency to mask feelings were ill-suited

---

[9] Rudolph & Rudolph, op. cit., p. 42.

to the collegial teamwork that chracterized Kennedy's years."[10]

Nixon's desire for privacy and his proclivity for working alone explain his establishment of a staff whose function was to provide him with options and time to consider those alternatives. Nixon's large staff system was similar to Eisenhower's, and both Presidents used their staffs to research issues and present analyses and alternatives in writing. Eisenhower had a committee structure to consider the alternatives and present a course of action.

> Nixon, on the other hand, sought to avoid the cumbersome committees who did not fit his decision-making style. Nixon wanted his aides to present *him* with the options; he would do the choosing.[11]

Viewing foreign policy as the area of his expertise, Nixon believed that the NSC system could be utilized to exercise an even greater degree of Presidential pre-eminence in foreign policy than had been

---

[10] Johnson, op. cit., p. 210.
[11] Ibid., p. 210.

achieved in the past. In keeping with Nixon's desire for privacy and secrecy, his National Security Advisor, Henry Kissinger, was given the gatekeeper's function in foreign policy analogous to Ehrlichman's position on the domestic side. Through his position as chairman of the NSC, the NSC's Senior Review Group, and WSAG, Kissinger became the major, if not sole, actor in the inner circle for the foreign decision-making.

WSAG was established during Nixon's Presidency and, under Kissinger's chairmanship and domination, was given the mandate to deal with crisis situations. Nixon and Kissinger apparently were seeking to utilize WSAG as a conduit to inform the participating agencies which policies they were to implement. Implementation, however, is an area of particular concern. The Nixon Administration's implementation of the China policy placed severe constraints on the bureaucracy's consideration of the China issue. This limitation was in effect between the July 15 announcement of Nixon's trip to China and the February visit. According to numerous U.S. Government officials, this restriction explains how the bureaucracy was kept in the dark concerning the China factor when the South Asia middle-level crisis of 1971 was unfolding. This issue will be examined in greater detail in the next chapter. Through the use of his NSC staff, Kissinger was able to analyze issues and present the options to the President. The screening of the options and particularly the selection of the issue to be considered for analysis were the major sources of Kissinger's gatekeeper function. By his ability to formulate the issues and decide what areas warranted the attention of the President, Kissinger was utilizing the maxim that knowledge is power.

Many of the policy options provided to President Nixon were formulated by the NSC through National Security Study Memoranda (NSSMs). NSSMs were utilized by the NSC to formulate the priorities of the Administration and focus the President's attention toward certain issue-areas. In short, NSSMs framed the issue after having determined the problem area and formulated the alternatives to be considered by the Chief Executive.

Nixon and Kissinger insisted that NSSMs utilize an options approach. Consequently, these two men emphasized the importance of long-range goals and a conceptual framework as the basis for a decision. This approach served to provide direction and priority for the Nixon-Kissinger foreign policy.

      The NSC's professional staff was in fact in large part duplicating the State Department's work. The NSC's structure for dealing with regional areas duplicated the organizational framework of both State and Defense Departments. In his capacity as Assistant to the President for National Security Affairs, Kissinger's role pre-empted, in part at least, the functions of the Secretary of State and the Secretary of Defense. Within the National Security Council system the Middle East and South Asia were organized under the supervision of Kissinger deputy Harold Saunders who had one assistant for the monitoring of South Asia and another for the Middle East. By concentrating on the planning and policy formulation functions, the NSC system did in fact provide the President with the control he sought over priority formulation and the search and evaluation of alternatives.

Even though the Nixon-Kissinger NSC system provided the desired control over the formulation of priorities and policies in the foreign policy sphere, the limited participation that the system allowed presented several disadvantages. A very serious problem was the degree to which the bureaucracy which had been effectively excluded from the decision-making process could be relied on to implement the decision reached. In addition, Kissinger's role as gate-keeper of the information generated by the NSC system allowed him the opportunity of not reporting conflicts and policy differences that emerged between the government agencies involved in NSC meetings. For example, in discussing the Bangladesh crisis, Johnson suggests that the Anderson papers reveal State Department officials fighting Kissinger

> tooth and nail. They argued for the support of India despite the President's desire to favor Pakistan... the President did what he planned to do, but more for reasons of his own convictions than for the want of other alternatives.[12]

---

[12] Ibid., p. 226.

The Bureaucrats and Advisors

Henry Kissinger has described the weakness of the bureaucracy and the problem this present to the management of foreign policy in the following terms:

> Because management of the bureaucracy takes so much energy and precisely because changing course is so difficult, many of the most important decisions are taken by extra-bureaucratic means. Some of the most important decisions are kept to a very small circle while the bureaucracy happily continues working away in ignorance of the fact that decisions are being made, or the fact that a decision is being made in a particular area. One reason for keeping the decisions to small groups is that when bureaucracies are so unwieldy and when their internal morale becomes a serious problem, an unpopular decision may be fought by brutal means, such as leaks to the press or to congressional committees.[13]

The tendency to include the Middle East and South Asia within the same bureau is also manifested

---

[13] Henry A. Kissinger, "Bureaucracy and Policy-Making: The Effects of Insiders and Outsiders on the Policy Process," in Morton H. Halperin and Arnold Kanter (eds.), Readings in American Foreign Policy: A Bureaucratic Perspective (Boston: Little Brown & Co., 1973), p. 89.

in the State Department and Defense Department. Within the State Department Joseph Sisco served as Assistant Secretary for Near Eastern and South Asian Affairs in 1971. The division between Near East and South Asia emerges at the levels of Deputy Assistant Secretary and Country Directors. The Department of Defense is structured along similar lines within the office of International Security Affairs where James Noyes was in charge of Middle East and South Asia. Interestingly enough, both Sisco and Noyes possess an expertise on the Middle East rather than South Asia.

The major functions of these bureaucracies and advisors is to conduct the daily and routine implementation of U.S. foreign policy and provide information and policy alternatives that are to be discussed by the inner circle. A department such as the Department of State may have severe difficulties in presenting its Secretary with a clear policy statement and concrete, detailed recommendations because of the lack of consensus within the Department. As a result, the ambiguous recommendations generated by the State Department tend to be discounted by an active President who may be in fact playing the role of his own Secretary of State as Nixon did.

The information flow within the Executive Branch provided possible alternative courses of action for U.S. policy in South Asia. The Rudolphs argue that just as "The President is under the 'illusion' that he is giving instruction...," the U.S. officials dealing with South Asia were equally under the illusion that they were providing the President with information and policy alternatives.[14] In fact, however, the decision to "tilt toward Pakistan" had been made previously by Nixon and Kissinger, which pitted them against those whom they needed to implement the policy. That one State Department South Asia officer refused to do any work on the South Asia issue as the events were unfolding because of his disagreement with the Nixon Administration policy is indicative of the intensity of the conflict.[15]

The circles of advisors may be penetrated and shifts of personnel may occur depanding on how the President perceives a particular issue-area, how close he

---

[14] Rudolph & Rudolph. op. cit., p. 48.
[15] Interview with U.S. Government official, March 1975.

is with the individual advisor, and how centralized the decision-making process has become. With Kissinger's control over the NSC's "options" that each department formulated and his chairmanship of the major interagency committees, including the Senior Review Group and WSAG, the second circle was unlikely to be consulted. The Kalbs characterize the foreign-policy management system as follows:

> The upshot was that since Kissinger controlled the system, he controlled the decision-making process. Everyone reports to Kissinger, and only Kissinger reports to the President, was the succinct summing-up of the way the NSC operation worked from the very beginning.[16]

Congress and Interest Groups

Congressional power in foreign policy formulation and implementation has traditionally been weak, notwithstanding the formal powers granted to Congress by the Constitution. Congressional weakness in foreign policy is especially apparent in crisis situations and the Indo-Pakistani War of 1971 is no exception to this general rule.

---
[16] Kalb & Kalb, op. cit., p. 87.

Congress has seldom initiated policies in the foreign policy sphere. Post-Watergate efforts by Congress in this area, including the War Powers Act, the CIA hearings, and opposition to certain operations by a review of the budget, indicate that Congress seems to be playing a checking role. These actions are apparently limited to correcting the abuses of the Executive and placing constraints on the future exercise of seemingly unlimited White House discretion in foreign policy formulation and implementation.

Congress is a deliberative body which depends largely on hearings, testimony, and informal transmission of information by members of the Executive Branch for the acquisition of information. This also applies to foreign policy issues. Moreover, the committee structure divides a problem in a way that seems to allow a committee to examine only a particular facet of the problem. By the time the Committee begins to consider a problem, the Executive Branch may have already acted, thus leaving little else for Congress to do. This may be especially true in crisis situations.

As an initial impression, it would seem reasonable to suggest that the Congressional committees that are traditionally most concerned with foreign policy issues are the Senate's Committee on Foreign Relations and the Committee on Foreign Affairs of the House of Representatives. Each of these committees has subcommittees for specific areas such as the Near East and South Asia, analogous to the State and Defense Department divisions. These subcommittees were not actively involved in dealing with the South Asian events of 1971, although individual Congressmen from these committees did take a particular interest in the issue. Thus, for example, Congressman Peter H.B. Frelinghuysen of New Jersey conducted an investigation in South Asia during the Fall of 1971 and wrote a report to the members of the Foreign Affairs Committee and Congress. In this November 3, 1971 report, entitled <u>Drifting Toward Crisis</u>, Frelinghuysen warns of the imminent danger of war in the subcontinent.[17]

---

[17] <u>Drifting Toward Crisis</u>, A Report by Congressman Peter H.B. Frelinghuysen, Report of a Special Study Mission to Pakistan and India, Committee on Foreign Affairs, November 3, 1971.

Congressional committees that are involved in functional areas may also become concerned with the overseas implications of their expertise. The United States Senate Committee on the Judiciary, for example, has a Subcommittee to Investigate Problems Connected with Refugees and Escapees. As Chairman of this Subcommittee, Senator Kennedy published a report entitled <u>Crisis in South Asia</u> in which he criticized the Administration's handling of the events. Senator Kennedy cast the refugee issue in terms of U.S. foreign policy in the subcontinent.

> If South Asia today is on the brink of war and even greater tragedy, our government's policy bears a special responsibility. For our continued military and economic support of the military regime in Islamabad has encouraged Pakistan intransigency and fed frustrations in India and East Bengal. It is long overdue for us to rescue our foreign policy from a course that has been disastrous both to our best traditions and interests in South Asia.[18]

---

[18] <u>Crisis in South Asia</u>, A Report by Senator Edward M. Kennedy to the Subcommittee to Investigate Problems Connected with Refugees and Escapees of the Committee on the Judiciary United States Senate, Washington, D.C.: USGPO, 92nd Congress, First Session, November 1, 1971, p. IX.

Senator Kennedy did not limit the scope of his investigation of U.S. foreign policy in South Asia to the refugee issue. During the questioning of Christopher Van Hollen, Deputy Assistant Secretary of State for Near Eastern and South Asian Affairs, Senator Kennedy repeatedly raised the issue of U.S. arms supplies to Pakistan and linked the matter to the refugee problem.[19] The publicity generated by the hearings and the disclosure concerning the U.S. arms shipments eventually resulted in the shutting off of U.S. arms supplies to Pakistan. The members of Congress do not seem to have been consulted by the Executive Branch on the issue of U.S. foreign policy in South Asia during 1971. Some members of Congress were active in their opposition to certain South Asian policies of the Nixon Administration but were limited in their effectiveness to the issues of the refugees and U.S. arms shipments to Pakistan. Senator Kennedy's

---

[19] United States Senate, Hearings before the Subcommittee to Investigate Problems Connected with Refugees and Escapees of the Committee on the Judiciary, Relief Problems in East Pakistan and India, Part III, 92nd Congress, First Session, October 4, 1971, Washington, D.C.: USGPO, 1971, pp. 374, 467-475.

motives to be linked to his suspected drive for the White House in the upcoming 1972 elections.[20]

Public Opinion and the Media

Public opinion on the events in South Asia seems seems to have been relatively weak, primarily because of the lack of interest in the area on the part of the American public. Gabriel Almond has emphasized the extent to which the President shapes the public's opinion on foreign affairs, rather than vice versa.[21] Nevertheless, a Harris poll following the Indo-Pakistani War of 1971 reveals that a ratio of two Americans to one disapproved of the way Nixon handled the crisis.

The editorial reaction of several U.S. newspapers to the actions of the Pakistani military in East Pakistan was to analogize the massacre to Hitler's

---

[20] Interview with U.S. Government official, March 1975.
[21] Gabriel A. Almond, The American People and Foreign Policy (New York: Harcourt, Brace, 1950). Also see James N. Rosenau (ed.), Domestic Sources of Foreign Policy (New York: Free Press, 1967); Bernard C. Cohen, The Public's Impact on Foreign Policy (Boston: Little, Brown and Company, 1973).

deeds.[22] For example, The New York Times called for the cessation of aid to Pakistan because the United States seemed to be in a "position of subsidizing, and thus seeming to condone, crimes against humanity unequalled since Hitler's time..."[23]

However, the massacre in South Asia apparently was not considered a matter deserving of consistent, front page coverage in the Western press. Anthony Lewis has touched on a sensitive point that may, in part at least, explain the relatively small coverage and low priority accorded the pre-war events in South Asia and the massacre in particular.

> The West Pakistanis have killed several hundred thousand civilians in the East, and an estimated ten million have fled to India. The oppression has been specifically on lines of race or religion. The victims are Bengalis or Hindus, not Czechs or Poles or Jews, and perhaps therefore less meaningful to us in the West. But to the victims the crime is the same.[24]

---

[22] See, for example, The Washington Post, July 31, 1971 and The New York Times, December 7, 1971.

[23] The New York Times, August 6, 1971.

[24] The New York Times, December 7, 1971.

Summary

The South Asia middle-level crisis of 1971 does indicate the extent to which the initiative in foreign policy matters rests in the White House. The organizational structure of the U.S. foreign policy system largely accounts for this phenomenon. The Nixon Administration utilized the NSC system to centralize the coordinating function within the Executive Office. WSAG was the locus of decision-making during the November-December 1971 period. Kissinger dominated the WSAG deliberations during the 1971 South Asia middle-level crisis, in large part by invoking Presidential authority.

We have demonstrated that the leadership style of the key White House decision-makers was reflected in the foreign policy management system they established. Both Nixon and Kissinger preferred to deal under a cloak of secrecy and make decisions after consulting with one another. Initiative and long-term goals were largely generated by the President and his Special Assistant for National Security Affairs.

Therefore, the establishment of their respective preferences and priorities constitutes the key to an understanding of U.S. policy toward South Asia in 1971.

The suggestion has been made that a check and balance system should also be the modus operandi in the foreign policy area. This suggestion has been made in order to balance the primacy of the NSC and WSAG in foreign affairs. The structural system does exist for Congress to assert its position if it so decides. However, the wisdom of conducting foreign policy crisis management by committee presents a difficult problem. A possible compromise position may be not to have a "super" Special Assistant, while placing the primary responsibility for foreign affairs with the State Department with Congress maintaining a checking role. The NSC's role under this system would be as a balance to the State Department which is a member of the NSC, even though the NSC was established to integrate domestic, foreign, and military policies relating to national security issues.

South Asia has been traditionally perceived by U.S. governmental agencies as an area of low priority.

These governmental organizations were responsible for processing the South Asian policy of 1971 in order to formulate and implement an appropriate American response. However, the Middle East and South Asia have been subsumed within the same bureau in each of these governmental organizations. Consequently, the Middle East, because of its greater implications and significance for U.S. national security and other interests, has received a vastly greater proportion of these decision-makers' attention.

The Rudolphs argue that South Asia as a region of U.S. concern requires a structural prescription. The likelihood seems strong that South Asia would indeed receive more attention from U.S. governmental bodies that deal with foreign policy if South Asia were divorced from the Middle East as an area of focus. Nevertheless, the issue concerning the proper priority that should be accorded to South Asia presents a normative question.

However, it is precisely the values that decision-makers attach to South Asia based on their respective evaluations of the area's importance for the

United States that determines the priority to be given to events that occur within the region. To the degree that crucial U.S. relationships such as those with China and the USSR became involved in South Asia, the attention paid to and importance of South Asia will also increase as a function of these global relations. This is the process of priority formulation that concerns us. The subjective evaluations of the participating decision-makers differ depending on their organizational affiliation and personal views. The process whereby a policy emerges is likely to be characterized by conflict if the subjective preferences and priorities of the decision-makers differ. The personal preference ranking of an individual decision-maker and the interaction among the members of a decision-making group regarding their respective preferences will ultimately be resolved according to the relative power of these individuals.

IV: U.S. DECISION-MAKING: ORGANIZATION AND POLICY

In the preceding chapters we examined, from its regional origins, the unfolding of a middle-level crisis for U.S. decision-makers. We have also dealt with the Nixon Administration's organizational framework for coping with foreign policy issues in order to determine the locus of the decision-making process. In this chapter the conflicts among the preferences of individual U.S. decision-makers regarding the appropriate U.S. policy toward the 1971 South Asia events are examined. Particular emphasis will be given to an analysis of the differing perspectives and South Asia regional expertise of the participating decision-makers. We will delineate their respective institutional affiliations. Furthermore, we will observe what the conflicting decision-makers viewed to be desirable outcomes of the South Asia middle-level crisis and the likelihood of attaining such an outcome.

From March through October 1971, American efforts in Pakistan and India were conducted primarily in the field by the respective U.S. embassies. Although there was a steady flow of information between the field and Washington, particularly the State Department, throughout 1971, no high level official of the Nixon Administration visited Pakistan in order to assess the situation or coordinate the efforts in the field. Kissinger did journey to Pakistan in July 1971, but the purpose of the trip was to disguise his China visit. As the conflict between India and Pakistan intensified over the issue of East Pakistan, the Nixon Administration sought to keep the channels of communication open in the hope that successful negotiations could be initiated.

As early as the spring of 1971, the U.S. embassy in Pakistan predicted that India would attack East Pakistan. However, the South Asian events of 1971 were not viewed with a sense of urgency or importance by the Nixon Administration until the fall of 1971. The shared perception of the relative urgency and importance of the South Asia regional crisis on the part of the Nixon Administration's decision-makers is the crucial factor that made these events a middle-level crisis for the United States.

As the South Asia events of 1971 evolved, the

locus of decision-making shifted from the field and the State Department to the White House and the NSC staff. In this chapter the effort will be made to demonstrate the differences in the type of qualifications possessed by these decision-makers and the differences in the values they attached to South Asia. The conflicts that emerged during the decision-making process and the explanations for them are of particular importance in terms of analyzing U.S. foreign policy toward South Asia during this period.

The White House and State Department

The American government's effort to cope with the middle-level South Asia regional crisis centered in the White House. The National Security Council (NSC) and its arm the Washington Special Action Group (WSAG) served as the forum and instruments to implement the policy that some argue was decided upon solely by Nixon and Kissinger, apparently without meaningful discussion of alternative courses of action. Although Nixon and Kissinger may have in fact considered alternative courses of action, one observer has suggested that the explanation for U.S. policy in South Asia was simply a matter of President Nixon giving the order "tilt" and the United States "tilted."[1] However, interviews with participants in the American government's decision-making process suggest that a considerable degree of disagreement and resistance existed within the Executive Branch as well as between Congress and the Executive. Nevertheless, public sources and interviews with participants in the decision-making process do seem to reveal a decision made by Nixon and Kissinger that was to be "imposed" on others if necessary.

By 1971 Kissinger had managed to acquire control of the conduct of U.S. foreign relations. One former senior Defense Department official argues that because of Kissinger's command and control over the foreign policy machinery, if the President and his national security advisor did not have the time or were not interested in the subject, nothing of any

---
[1] Dr. Alvin Rubinstein, University of Pennsylvania, May 1973.

consequence was done. He and a number of other Defense and State Department officials claim that Kissinger's refusal to share with them essential information presented a severe managerial problem. As a result, events would unfold without being givin attention until they had reached a point of crisis. Only at that point would Nixon and Kissinger begin to deal with the problem. Thus, initiative was left to other nation-states and the U.S. could only react. Perhaps, wryly adds the former senior Defense Department official, this may have been helpful for the U.S. in South Asia during 1971 because the U.S. was unable to commit any major harm.[2]

Kissinger had jockeyed himself in the strategic "bottleneck" position of obtaining and screening important information on foreign policy before it reached Nixon. Even when Secretary of State Rogers sent a foreign policy memorandum to Nixon, Kissinger would be able to see it first. Consequently, Kissinger formulated policy out of the NSC system and normally only

---

[2] Interview with U.S. Government official, March 1975.

had an obstacle if Rogers sought to challenge him directly. One such challenge during the South Asian events involved Rogers' advocacy that the April 1971 arms embargo against Pakistan be fully implemented because of the bad press and Congressional resentment that had been generated. Rogers felt that the price being paid in bad press and bad Congressional feelings was not worth the cost in light of the small amount of arms shipments being sent. Even so, the full implementation of the embargo was not achieved until November 1971.

The special working relationship between Nixon and Kissinger in foreign policy formulation and decision-making explains, in part, the concentration of power within the NSC. An antipathy toward the State Department's pace and ideas was also shared by Nixon and his national security advisor.[3] One observer describes President Nixon's view of the State Department as an "incorrigibly lethargic snail protected by a thick shell of tradition, incapable of creative ideas

---

[3] Interview with U.S. Government official, March 1975.

or firm action."[4]

Nixon's low opinion of the bureaucracy was shared by Kissinger. The two men also shared a distrust of the State Department. The major criticism of the bureaucracy is its alleged inability to think and act in global terms. However, in this case, the White House intentionally kept the State Department in the dark concerning the China connection. Even though the announcement of Nixon's upcoming visit to China was made on July 15, the implications of the visit were not made clear to the South Asia desk in the State Department. The details and general connections between the two areas were kept a secret from the country desk personnel by the White House. For example, possibly because of the fear of leaks, the country desk officer who had made the arrangements for Kissinger's trip to Islamabad, which served as Kissinger's connection to Peking, did not know about the Peking trip.

While the State Department was a major long-

---

[4] Henry Brandon, The Retreat of American Power (Garden City, N.Y.: Doubleday & Company, 1973, p. 24.

term actor involved in the South Asia crisis, the White House (that is, the President and NSC staff) were the primary short-term actors. The State Department, viewing India as the world's largest democracy, tended to be pro-India, while the Defense Department, viewing Pakistan as a good ally, tended to be pro-Pakistan. The U.S. embassies in India and Pakistan tended to recommend and advocate courses of action favorable to the respective countries in which they were located. Although this is not necessarily the proper function of an embassy, the U.S. embassies emerged with the role of pleading the case for each of their respective countries.[5]

The State Department's country desk level felt that it was being kept isolated from the decision-making process and that the important decisions regarding foreign policy were being made by Kissinger and Nixon. As an organization, the State Department had no knowledge of the forthcoming China policy nor of the Administration's view of the role and relation-

---

[5] Interview with U.S. Government official, March 1975.

ship that South Asia had within the global context of U.S.-Soviet-Chinese relations.[6]

Several State Department officials feel that if they had known about the Administrations China policy, they would have adopted a position different from their pro-Indian stance toward the Indo-Pakistani War. During 1971 these officials had proposed that the Administration take a "hard line" toward the Pakistani actions in East Pakistan and that public criticism be made by the U.S. Government. Yet these officials also concede that such measures would have had little or no impact on the actions taken by Pakistan.

As a result of this lack of information, State Department officials were being asked to make recommendations concerning U.S. policy in South Asia without having the benefit of knowledge on the Administration's China policy. The State Department country desk people also failed to realize the Administration's perception of the importance of the South Asian crisis in terms of U.S.-Soviet relations and the prevailing notion that an Indian victory would constitute a Russion victory.

---

[6] Interview with U.S. Government official, March 1975.

Some State Department officials, especially the desk officers, were judging the South Asian events from a regional, if not a country, perspective. The importance of the Soviet factor was either not seen or not taken seriously by the desk officers. The Administration, however, with an eye toward Nixon's upcoming June 1972 visit to Moscow and his China visit, was concerned with a possible outcome that could be construed by other nations as a Soviet victory over a U.S. ally.

Problems of offective communication constituted another major obstacle for the cooperative formulation of U.S. foreign policy by the White House (NSC) and State Department.[7] While the working-level State Department people felt as early as the summer of 1971 that an Indo-Pak War was imminent, they were not encouraged to propound their ideas and beliefs to the White House and were unable to convince the non-area experts of the imminence of war. The White House discounted the State Department's views as dictated by the pro-India bias prevalent within the bureaucracy.

---

[7] Interview with U.S. Government official, March 1975.

An additional strain on communications was the atmosphere of leaks that prevailed in Washington. The State Department was blamed for these leaks which were viewed by the White House as an effort to maneuver the Administration into adopting a pro-India policy. Even if the White House's suspicions were not fully justified, the suspicion served to isolate the State Department's utility in contributing to the decision-making process. Moreover, very poor personal relations between Henry Kissinger and Secretary of State Rogers contributed to the lack of cooperation and coordination between the NSC and the Department of State.[8]

The difference between the State Department desk officers and the White House was not limited to the nation-state each felt the United States should support. The area experts felt that the refugee situation was unacceptable for India and that war would therefore result. At a January 9, 1971 Senior Review Group (a group with a membership which largely overlaps that of WSAG) meeting, the issue of the Pakistani elections was raised and fears of the breakup of Pak-

---

[8] Interview with U.S. Government official, March 1975.

iatan were expressed.[9] By March 1971 the State Department view was that war was likely to erupt and that U.S. policy should be non-involvement in the Indo-Pakistani conflict. During the summer of 1971 the South Asia desk viewed an Indo-Pakistani War to be imminent and had been viewing the situation as an ongoing crisis since March 1971. Efforts to convince the White House of these positions proved unsuccessful. A few WSAG meetings took place in late March and early April in order to assess whether the use of force by Yahya in East Pakistan would prove effective.[10] The problems, in the eyes of the Senior Review Group, constituted a crisis for Pakistan but not for the United States.[11] The White House, unlike the State Department, believed that the March 25 crackdown had been successful in eliminating the secessionist threat. Not until October, but definitely by the time of Indira Gandhi's visit to Washington in November, had the White House begun to view events in South Asia as constituting a crisis.

---

[9] Interview with U.S. Government official, March 1975.

[10] Interview with U.S. Government official, March 1975.

[11] Interview with U.S. Government official, March 1975.

On the one hand, the South Asia area experts in the State Department felt that the United States should accomodate itself to the inevitable process of East Pakistan seceeding from West Pakistan. The non-area experts of the NSC staff, on the other hand, did not share in the assessment that the breakup of Pakistan was inevitable. However, the regional experts who were members of the NSC staff restructured the South Asia issue in terms of a different conceptual frame of reference. This frame of reference had U.S. global relations as its focus. The disagreement between the two schools of thought intensified following the March 25 breakdown. The non-experts and area experts on the NSC staff, had the upper hand through the summer of 1971, felt that the crackdown would be successful, and thought their position that the breakup of Pakistan was not inevitable had been reinforced. The State Department's area experts, however, felt that the suppression of the crackdown would only result in the postponement of the breakup that they viewed as inevitable.[12]

During the summer of 1971 the South Asia desk of

---

[12] Interview with U.S. Government official, March 1975.

the Department of State had begun to formulate contingency plans for imminent war in South Asia. A task force was established and had begun to function. Prior to October many of the decisions involving the South Asia events were made at the State Department.

The decisions were being made at the State Department primarily because of the lack of attention devoted by the NSC to South Asia between the March 25 crackdown and Indira Gandhi's visit. The State Department became primarily involved in the refugee issue and the humanitarian relief efforts of AID. Efforts were also directed at seeking a compromise solution to the problem of East Pakistan, but many State Department officials involved in the attempt were convinced of the futility of the exercise within the framework of a united Pakistan.

By the summer of 1971 the participants at the WSAG meetings had begun to recognize the unfolding 1971 events in Pakistan and the Indian reaction to them as a regional South Asian crisis. Very few of the key WSAG participants knew anything about South Asia, however. Joseph Sisco had contact with the area, although his primary area of concern during this time was the Middle East. Christopher Van Hollen had been more familiar with South Asia and was the "area expert" involved in the deliberations. Serious contingency planning in a subgroup of WSAG chaired by Van Hollen began on November 1. As a result, there was ample time to generate studies and formulate policy options. However, as indicated, for the most part the other members of the group had not been to the area and had not been concerned with the region in their work.

By December 1971 the Indo-Pakistani conflict and the subsequent war had become a high priority item on the agenda of the Administration. Crisis has traditionally been defined as an event constituting a high threat to high values on which a decision must be made in a short time frame. The Indo-Pakistani War was not a crisis in terms of high threat to high values, according to one official, if the China factor is not viewed as the key factor determining U.S. policy.[13] This was a crisis in the "sense of atmosphere;" it

---

[13] Interview with U.S. Government official, March 1975.

"generated adrenaline" but was more a matter of a "show in town and not much in the way of substance."[14] If, however, China is conceded to be the primary factor for the Administration's actions, then the Indo-Pakistani War may be considered to be a crisis in the more traditional sense.

Mrs Gandhi's Visit

As Indira Gandhi's visit approached, decisions began to be made at the White House level with "some State Department people included but their role was really peripheral."[15] Once the Administration had begun to view the situation as a crisis, the people involved in the decision-making process were no longer the area experts who had previously been engaged most prominently with the issue. Within the Nixon-Kissinger global framework, the decision involving a regional crisis was to be made increasingly in light of global affairs. The regional expert does not generally con-

---

[14] Interview with U.S. Government official, March 1975.
[15] Interview with U.S. Government official, March 1975.

sider the global perspective and that is the key consideration of a U.S. decision-maker.[16] If, however, a regional expert is consistently exposed to global concerns, he may restructure the problem through global terms, thereby forming a different conceptual frame of reference from regional experts who do not operate in such a context. Therefore, once the decision begins to be viewed as a crisis by the Administration, the actors involved in making the decisions are not experts and decisions are increasingly made in light of global considerations, especially because of the global factors in the Nixon-Kissinger framework.

By the time of Indira Gandhi's arrival in Washington in November 1971, the White House had begun to view South Asia as a region engulfed by a crisis. The U.S. Government had sought to avert a crisis by providing aid to the refugees, thus hoping to buy time. Simultaneously, the United States proposed mutual troop withdrawals by India and Pakistan, as well as negotiations between Yahya Khan and Indira Gandhi. While the Pakistanis were willing to cooperate to avoid war, the

---

[16] Interview with U.S. Government official, May 1975.

Indians were not, according to U.S. officials. By the fall of 1971 the Indians, burdened by as many as ten million refugees, saw themselves as having very little time and had become impatient. Some Indians also viewed the situation as an opportunity.[17] For example, at the Indian Council of World Affairs meeting of March 31, 1971, the Director of the Indian Institute of Defense Studies, Mr. Subrahmaniyan, stated:

> What India must realize is the fact that the break-up of Pakistan is in our interest, an opportunity the like of which will never come again.[18]

Even though U.S. officials negotiated with an Indian delegation headed by T.N. Kaul, the U.S. negotiators felt that there really was nothing to negotiate since the Indians had already made their decision to attack.[19] The American officials had intelligence

---

[17] Interview with U.S. Government official, March 1975.

[18] *Hindustan Times*, April 1, 1971.

[19] Interview with U.S. Government official, May 1975.

reports indicating that the decision to take military action against East Pakistan had been made before Mrs. Gandhi left India for her negotiations in Washington.

    The negotiations between Nixon and Mrs. Gandhi were paralleled by the meetings between the American and Indian delegations, headed by Joseph Sisco and T.N. Kaul respectively. According to an American negotiator, these meetings "went nowhere."[20] When the meetings were followed by Indian escalation of the border conflict and eventual invasion of East Pakistan, the U.S. negotiators became suspicious of the Indians' motives for having come to Washington. These suspicions served to reinforce the negative attitudes that these American decision-makers had of the Indians, whose views were described as "cantankerous."[21] The feeling on the part of many of the American participants in the decision-making process began to move toward a fatalistic view that war was imminent and inevitable. This led to an increased effort to get negotiations underway between Yahya and Mrs. Gandhi. Even though the United States sought

---

[20] Interview with U.S. Government official, March 1975.

[21] Interview with U.S. Government official, March 1975.

to sponsor these negotiations between India and Pakistan, many State Department officials felt these efforts by Nixon and Kissinger were too little, too late. By the time of Indira Gandhi's visit to Washington many members of the Administration felt that the Indians had already made the decision to attack, that "it was too late," and that "the visit was for windowdressing."[22] According to the Nixon report:

> ...it is clear that a political process was in train, which could have been supported and facilitated by all the parties involved if they had wished. This is the basis for the profound disappointment we felt and expressed when war erupted.[23]

There are U.S. officials who attribute the anger of the White House circle to the President's feeling that he had been mislead by Indira Gandhi.[24] The negative Indian reaction reinforced and highlighted even more

---

[22] Interview with U.S. Government official, March 1975.

[23] Richard Nixon, U.S. Foreign Policy for the 1970's The Emerging Structure of Peace: A Report to the Congress (Washington, D.C.: USGPO, February 9, 1972), pp. 145-146.

[24] Interview with U.S. Government official, March 1975. See also William J. Barnds, "India, Pakistan and American Realpolitik," Christianity and Crisis, June 12, 1972, pp. 146-147.

clearly the Administration's image of the Indians as aggressors. The Indian position, on the other hand, was that they had to act. During her Washington visit, Mrs. Gandhi reportedly said: "the refugee situation in Bengal is about to blow... We just can't wait much longer."[25] Not only did the Administration see its view confirmed by the Indian attack in East Pakistan, but many pro-India officials within the U.S. Government also began to see India as the aggressor.

WSAG Meetings

Following the visit by Indira Gandhi, the number of WSAG meetings accelerated. Between twenty and twenty-five meetings were held between the date of the visit and the end of the war. Many of the participants in the WSAG meetings suggest that the meetings were held merely in order to rubber-stamp a decision previously made by Nixon and Kissinger. Several participants claim that there was some dissent to the Nixon-Kissinger policy at WSAG meetings not reported in the Anderson Papers.

---

[25] Wilcox, The Emergence of Bangladesh, op. cit., p. 45, ft. 34.

Joseph Sisco, Chris Van Hollen and Maurice Williams are said to have openly disagreed with the Nixon-Kissinger policy. Chris Van Hollen was the area expert at the meetings and managed to make his dissenting views, in opposition to a tilt toward Pakistan policy, known to both Kissinger and Rogers. These views were not adopted as the Administration's policy, however. Several participants suggest that by the time of the WSAG meetings, whose contents are now partially available in the Anderson Papers, those involved had developed a consensus and the meetings were held in order to reach a decision on action. Other participants describe an extremely tense atmosphere at the WSAG meetings and suggest that the "consensus" was, in fact, Kissinger's imposing his will and/or Nixon's on the group.

Kissinger explained U.S. policy in South Asia in the following terms at the December 8, 1971 WSAG meeting.

> Dr. Kissinger said that we were not trying to be even-handed. There can be no doubt what the President wants. The President does not want to be even-handed. The President believes that

India is the attacker. We are trying to get across the idea that India has jeopardized relations with the United States. Dr. Kissinger said that we cannot afford to ease India's state of mind. "The Lady" is cold blooded and tough and will not turn into a Soviet satellite merely because of pique. We should not ease her mind. He invited anyone who objected to this approach to take his case to the President.[26]

As mentioned, coinciding with the crisis, between twenty and twenty-five WSAG meetings were held between November 25 and December 14, 1971. WSAG had been meeting for an extended period of time on this subject and there was a degree of familiarity among the participants. The accounts of the participants verify that, in part, Kissinger's dominant personality explains Kissinger's domination of the meetings. Kissinger's chairmanship of WSAG by virtue of his NSC position and the control he had over that organization, combined with the knowledge by the WSAG participants that he had Nixon's full confidence, made Kissinger a formidable force at these meetings. While one participant claims that no participant was really

---

[26] Anderson Papers, see Marta R. Nicholas and Philip Oldenburg, Bangladesh: The Birth of a Nation (Madras: M. Seshachalam and Co., 1972), p. 132.

against the policy, several participants claim that they were opposed to the policy but were intimidated and remained silent.

Kissinger may have in fact been playing the role of Nixon's "messenger boy" during the WSAG meetings. At the December 3, 1971 meeting Kissinger stated:

> I am getting hell every half-hour from the President that we are not being tough enough on India. He has just called me again. He does not believe we are carrying out his wishes. He wants to tilt in favor of Pakistan. He feels everything we do comes out otherwise.[27]

When asked about a Presidential order concerning the cessation of irrevocable letters of credit to India, Kissinger responded, "That is his order, but I will check with the President again."[28] On a possible U.N. strategy, Kissinger said, "The President is in favor of this."[29] In stating that a draft of a speech prepared for UN Ambassador Bush is too even-handed, Kissinger observed: "We have to take action. The President is blaming me, but you people are in the

---

[27] Ibid., p. 115.
[28] Ibid., p. 115.
[29] Ibid., p. 115.

clear." To this Sisco replied contently and sarcastically, "That's ideal!"[30] Concerning the economic steps to be taken regarding Pakistan, Kissinger's answer was:

> Wait until I talk with the President. He hasn't addressed this problem in connection with Pakistan yet...It's hard to tilt toward Pakistan if we have to match every Indian step with a Pakistan step. If you wait until Monday, I can get a Presidential decision.[31]

At the December 4, 1971 WSAG meeting in discussing the preparation of a U.S. statement in the U.N., "Dr. Kissinger replied that he was under specific instruction from the President, and either someone in the bureaucracy would have to prepare this statement along the lines indicated or that it would be done in the White House."[32] At the same meeting he indicated that the leaks were "provoking Presidential wrath. The President is under the 'illusion' that he is giving instructions; not that he is merely being kept, appraised of affairs as they progress."[33]

---

[30] Ibid., p. 116.
[31] Ibid., p. 116.
[32] Ibid., p. 118.
[33] Ibid., p. 119.

The tone for coping with the South Asia crisis differed considerably from the Cuban Missile crisis because of the lack of urgency and high priority involved. By the time of Indira Gandhi's visit to Washington, the Indo-Pakistani confrontation was being viewed as a crisis by the U.S. Administration. However, the non-area decision-makers were "wishing that the crisis would go away because there were more important things to do."[34] These more important things were the Administration's efforts to establish global and improved relations with the Soviet Union and China. The Indo-Pakistani War was, according to this point of view, regarded as a nuisance. While the U.S. policy-makers wished the crisis would go away, the United States, as a global power, was "pulled in."[35] Because the Administration viewed the Soviet role as a mischievous one of doing little to restrain India, the White House viewed the proper American role as "filling a vacuum" in response to the August 1971 Sino-Indian Treaty of

---

[34] Interview with U.S. Government official, March 1975.
[35] Interview with U.S. Government official, March 1975.

Peace, Friendship and Cooperation. From the Administration's perspective the Treaty paved the way for India to check China by way of the USSR and thus provided the Indian leadership with the leeway necessary to attack East Pakistan.

Once the Indo-Pakistani War erupted, U.S. policy-makers conducted background briefings with the purpose of "selling" and justifying U.S. policy to the public. Nixon felt that the criticism leveled against him and the "tilt" policy was unduly harsh and unwarranted. At these briefings, Kissinger's historical role may account for several of his repeated arguments. He emphasized the need for standing with an ally and honoring commitments. He stressed that the United States must maintain its global capability and world power status. In addition, he argued that the United States must take a moral stance against war. However, it should be pointed out that these arguments were not necessarily only for public consumption, since he also emphasized several of these factors during the WSAG meetings.

At the December 4, 1971 WSAG meeting Kissinger emphasized the need for the U.S. to submit the anti-India cease-fire resolution in the United Nations "as quickly as possible" and "alone if necessary."[36] According to Kissinger, "the only move left for us at the present time is to make clear our position relative to our greater strategy."[37] Kissinger was fully aware of the futility of the American efforts in the U.N. in terms of relying on or expecting any U.N. action. Nevertheless, this "exercise in futility" was to be undertaken in order to register the American position.

> Everyone knows how all this will come out and everyone knows that India will ultimately occupy East Pakistan. We must, therefore, make clear our position, table our resolution. We want a resolution which will be introduced with a speech by Ambassador Bush... Dr. Kissinger continued that it was important we register our position.[38]

While China was not prominently mentioned during the WSAG meetings, there were those participants who felt at the time that the only possible explanation

---

[36] Ibid., p. 119.
[37] Ibid., p. 119.
[38] Ibid., p. 119.

that made sense in terms of what Kissinger was attempting to accomplish was the China factor.[39] China, according to these officials, constituted the missing link. One official recalls that Kissinger, visibly upset, made the following statement at one WSAG meeting:

> The Indians are trying to wreck what we're doing with the USSR and what we want to do with China.[40]

At one WSAG meeting, as a result of some dissent regarding the "tilt" policy, Kissinger took the principals of WSAG to see Nixon in order that the President explain the U.S. policy supporting Pakistan to them. When at a later meeting some dissent persisted on the part of the non-principals of WSAG, Kissinger stated that if anybody did not understand the policy, he would personally take them to see Nixon who would explain it to them step by step. The account of this incident is reported in the Anderson Papers in a more cryptic note. "He [Kissinger] invited anyone who

---

[39] Interview with U.S. Government official, March 1975.
[40] Interview with U.S. Government official, March 1975.

objected to this approach to take his case to the President."[41] Nobody volunteered to do it, largely because of fear. As one participant recounts, he wanted to volunteer to do it but was certain that if he did, he would not only not get to see Nixon but would either be shown to the door, that is, fired, or be re-assigned to a village in Zaire.[42]

This episode demonstrates Kissinger's domination of the NSC meetings and their ritualistic nature. Not only was there too much formality at these meetings for a free give-and-take, but there was also an unspoken tension at these meetings that precluded a free exchange. Kissinger would occasionally ask whether anyone wanted to disagree, but those who might have dissented feared at the time, and still believe, that by doing so they be summarily fired.

A close associate of Kissinger describes him as a "hard person to get along with and a bastard to work for."[43]

---

[41] Anderson Papers, Nicholas and Oldenburg, op. cit., p. 132.

[42] Interview with U.S. Government official, March 1975.

[43] Interview with U.S. Government official, May 1975.

With the resistance exhibited at several of the WSAG meetings, Kissinger became very disturbed by what he viewed as subterfuge by various participants of his and Nixon's policy regarding the Indo-Pakistani events. He was angered by what he considered to be the disloyalty to the President by those who did not carry out his plans and orders.[44]

Much of the tension of the WSAG meetings was unspoken. As a consequence of the lack of a free give-and-take, many of the participants felt that neither the arguments for possible courses of action nor the search for alternatives were fully made. Nevertheless, these participants feel that Kissinger did know the views of the State Department, even if he dismissed the Department as having a pro-India bias. Kissinger was keenly aware that large segments of the bureaucracy, press, and Congress were opposed to the Nixon-Kissinger policy on the Indo-Pakistani crisis. However, he was also aware of the global goals he sought to achieve, and he together with Nixon apparently

---

[44]Interview with U.S. Government official, May 1975.

decided that the global goals have a higher priority.[45] The feeling on the part of the participants is that Kissinger probably presented Nixon with the alternatives raised at the WSAG meetings but then probably interjected his evaluation that these suggestions are erroneous and proceeded to present the case for him and Nixon to embark on a virtuoso performance in foreign policy. The rationale for the establishment of the NSC system is to provide the President with options. However, there was a serious concern and suspicion on the part of many participants that the President was not getting all the options. Many departments doubted that their position was being presented to the President by Kissinger, and animosity toward the NSC system was harbored by the State and Defense Departments. There was considerable infighting at the NSC to get a department's position heard. The system, in other words, had a bottleneck such that the presentation of options was being viewed as a myth.[46]

Alternative explanations have been offered for the

---

[45] Interview with U.S. Government official, May 1975.

[46] Interview with U.S. Government official, March 1975.

Administration's policy. The driving factors behind the Nixon-Kissinger policy may be viewed as flowing from the calculated global view shared by the two men. They were beginning to lay the groundwork for better relations with China and did not want India to be an obstacle in this process. In addition, the principle of backing allies at a time of need and the implications this would have for the United States as a global power was emphasized by Kissinger at one time in terms of what Jordan, Israel and other U.S. allies and friends would think if the United States did not support Pakistan. Kissinger framed the Indian attack on Pakistan in terms of a direct challenge to U.S. support for its ally as well as whether the U.S. would allow "India to scare us off"[47] from providing Pakistan with needed supplies. The alliance issue was couched in terms of its precedent in global relations.

> Dr. Kissinger states that what we may be witnessing is a situation wherein a country /India/ equipped and supported by the Soviets may be turning half of Pakistan into an impotent state and the other half into a vassal. We must consider what other countries may be thinking of our action.[48]

---

[47]Anderson Papers, see Nicholas and Oldenburg, op. cit., p. 129.

[48]Ibid., pp. 130-131.

Kissinger agreed that the U.S. did not have any legal obligations toward Pakistan because of CENTO "but added that neither did we have legal obligations toward India in 1962 when we formulated the air defense agreement."[49]

Kissinger sought to underline the importance of the problem in terms of security and guarantee issues.

> We must consider what would be the impact
> of the current situation in the larger
> complex of world affairs... we must look
> at the problem in terms of Security
> Council guarantees in the Mid-East and
> the impact on other areas.[50]

Nevertheless, Kissinger also stated that the reason for the U.S. policy was a matter of Nixon's personal loyalty to Yahya and that this could not be reversed by WSAG.[51]

Many of the WSAG participants were puzzled by the meetings and the way in which they were being directed to cope with the crisis. There was a great deal of puzzlement on the part of the bureaucracy at what Nixon and Kissinger were trying to accomplish with a pro-Pakistan policy. One participant notes that Kissinger may have been utilizing

---

[49]Ibid., p. 131.

[50]Ibid., p. 131.

[51]Interview with U.S. Government official, March 1975.

Nixon's alleged concern with the crisis for dramatic effect in order to silence dissent at WSAG meetings by invoking the President's wish.[52] However, with Kissinger funneling the foreign policy information to Nixon and thereby maintaining total control, it is difficult to assess to what degree Nixon was frustrated and angered by the fact that his policy was not being implemented or to what extent Kissinger was exaggerating Nixon's wrath in order to implement the "tilt" policy within WSAG.

While there apparently was disagreement within the bureaucracy on U.S. Government policy as events in South Asia were unfolding in 1971, even today there are serious disagreements regarding the major determinants of U.S. policy in the region. Three years after the events, several senior State Department officials who were involved in the decision-making process maintain that China was only a factor in the background and not the critical factor affecting U.S. policy in South Asia. The officials who place little reliance on the China factor tend to be those who opposed the Administration's policy in the crisis and

---

[52]Interview with U.S. Government official, March 1975.

who portray Kissinger as a manager who bungled the entire affair. The key, according to these officials, was the past commitments to and special relationship with Pakistan. Thus, the Administration was biased in Pakistan's favor as a result of the alliance system. The American political leadership was not ready to view the breakup of a country, especially a U.S. ally, with indifference.[53] The ease of communicating and dealing with the Pakistanis and the historical ties in comparison with the difficulties and problems of dealing with the Indians are also viewed as contributing factors for the "tilt." Therefore, according to this explanation, due to the past association with Pakistan and the strong personal relationship between the United States and Pakistani leadership, the Administration adopted a tilt to Pakistan policy in an effort to avoid war if at all possible.[54] These officials argue that even without the China factor, the United States would have adopted the same policy in

---

[53] Interview with U.S. Government official, March 1975.

[54] Interview with U.S. Government official, March 1975.

the war of 1971.

South Asia is viewed by many U.S. foreign policy-makers as a low-cost area for the United States, thereby providing the U.S. with a considerable degree of latitude in its decisions. The argument which emerges among U.S. foreign policy decision-makers is whether South Asia is to be viewed qua South Asia, that is, in isolation, or whether South Asia is to be viewed in relation to other regions and other U.S. global relations. The Nixon Administration's position was that South Asia in isolation is not of any particular consequence and that it must be viewed within a global context. If South Asia were viewed simply in terms of its regional politics, some argue that the crisis would likely have been handled differently, and the payoff for a policy favoring India would have been easier to perceive.

Participants who view the emerging relations with China as the critical factor in explaining American foreign policy in the Indo-Pakistani War of 1971 argue that on hindsight the importance of the China connection is even greater than they had realized as the events were unfolding. These participants suggest that the emerging relations with China were extremely important to Nixon and Kissinger and that this fact colored U.S. policy in South Asia to a considerable degree.[55] The negative U.S. view of the events in South Asia coincided with the Chinese attitude toward the developments in the area. The Administration's desire to demonstrate to the Chinese the convergence of U.S. and Chinese interests in a region of strategic importance to China and the effort by the United States to show the American resoluteness in supporting a friend and ally prior to Nixon's Peking visit in February 1971 were reinforced by the Nixon White House's negative view of India and bias in favor of Pakistan on a personal and alliance level. The Enterprise episode, which is considered more fully in a later section, may be viewed as a signal through which the Nixon Administration made its position clear concerning the South Asia events to the major powers, regional actors, and the international community.

Participants who emphasize Kissinger's and Nixon's China policy as the key to U.S. policy in South Asia are also those who were and are most closely associated with Kissinger and who aided in shaping that China policy. They

---

[55] Interview with U.S. Government official, March 1975.

strongly believe in the validity of the measures adopted by the Administration during the South Asian events of 1971. His aides explain that Kissinger is a global and not a regional thinker. Thus, Kissinger took account of many variables simultaneously and, therefore, considered the Indo-Pakistani War within the context of the upcoming China visit, the Indo-Soviet Treaty of Peace, Friendship and Cooperation, the U.S. commitment to an ally, and the importance to China of checking a Soviet effort to encircle China by way of India. Kissinger's notion of relations with partners within the emerging global environment called for the United States to honor its commitments. The idea of the United States standing by her friends and allies was intended to project a strong image overseas and demonstrate the continued American involvement in global politics despite the Vietnam debacle. Therefore, it was imperative that at the time of retrenchment in the post-Vietnam era the United States be viewed as a reliable friend and ally by other states.

David Packard's pragmatic approach to the South Asian events focused on the American capability to exercise any leverage and may have been a challenge to Kissinger's argument that the U.S. had to do something and at the minimum register its position.

> After discussing various possible commitments to both Pakistan and India, Mr. Packard stated that the overriding consideration is the practical problem of either doing something effective or doing nothing. If you don't win, don't get involved. If we were to attempt something it would have to be with a certainty that it would affect the outcome. Let's not get in if we know we are going to lose. Find some way to stay out.[56]

Kissinger's ego and his self-image of constituting the U.S. foreign policy apparently also contributed to the importance of the notion of honoring commitments as well as the duty to help establish a stable world order.[57] Since the alliance with Pakistan may have been dead, an issue may exist whether Kissinger was realistic about the extent to which Pakistan was still a U.S. ally. Regardless of that fact, the view persisted that the United States was obligated to pursue its pro-Pakistani policy in order to establish the mutuality of interests that it had with China for the Chinese and perhaps Soviet leadership to

---

[56]Anderson Papers, see Nicholas and Oldenburg, op. cit., p. 131.

[57]Interview with U.S. Government official, March 1975. See Henry A. Kissinger, A World Restored: Metternich, Castlereagh and the Problems of Peace, 1812-1822 (Boston: Houghton Mifflin, 1973).

appreciate.

If the key to understanding the Nixon Administration's policy in the Indo-Pakistani crisis is in the Nixon-Kissinger global view of U.S. relations with the USSR and China, then U.S. policy in the subcontinent in 1971 may be viewed as a function of the American relationship with these two major powers. U.S. policy can then be explained in terms of Kissinger's and Nixon's efforts to establish the rules of the game for the conduct of international relations among the three major powers.[58]

Thus, according to this explanation, U.S. support for Pakistan, while in part due to the residue of the U.S. alliance with Pakistan, Nixon's and Kissinger's bias for Pakistan, and an effort to repay Yahya Khan the debt for aiding in the establishment of the "China connection," is primarily due to the Administration's effort to demonstrate to China that the U.S. will stand by its allies and support them even in hard times. Such a demonstration was particularly crucial for China at this juncture because

---

[58]Interview with U.S. Government official, May 1975.

of the Chinese interest in using the U.S. as a counter to the USSR. According to a close associate, Kissinger thought that the Chinese were very interested in observing how the U.S. would react to its commitment in hard times.[59]

Summary

From the above analysis of the factors involved in the U.S. decision-making process, the 1971 events in South Asia may be considered to constitute a middle-level crisis. The high threat emanated primarily from the danger that the Indian actions, supported by the Soviet Union, were seen by the White House to present to the territorial integrity of Pakistan and to the establishment of future U.S.-Chinese relations. The high values were the priority which the Nixon White House attached to the opening of China, the need to demonstrate to other states that America stood by her ally, Pakistan, and had not retreated from the global theatre, and the desire to check the Soviet Union

---

[59] Interview with U.S. Government official, May 1975.

by not allowing her client state to dismember a sovereign state. The element of surprise, however, does not seem present in this case because of the protracted nature of the conflict. Numerous State Department and CIA officials indicated in their assessments that war in South Asia was imminent and inevitable. While Nixon and Kissinger may have thought they had received Mrs. Gandhi's assurance in November 1971 that India would not initiate an attack, it is difficult to believe that they were surprised when the war began.

In analyzing the development of a crisis, however, it is important to bear in mind its dynamic nature. Each of the elements, that is, high threats, high values, and surprise, may change during the course of the unfolding events, as in fact happened to U.S. policy in South Asia. Thus, for a major power, global relations are primary and regional matters are secondary but may become of particular importance mainly in terms of their global implications. Therefore, the other global powers are to be watched and their behavior judged according to the "trouble they cause" in a global or regional crisis.[60]

---

[60] Interview with U.S. Government official, May 1975.

The Nixon-Kissinger global concern manifested itself in terms of the international relations rules of the game and the degree to which China and the USSR adhered to these rules. Both Nixon and Kissinger became angered by the Soviet actions in relation to India. They viewed Soviet actions as aimed at seeking to restrain India prior to the Indo-Soviet Friendship Treaty of 1971. Nixon and Kissinger viewed this treaty as a signal that the Soviet Union had ceased in its attempt to restrain India and was providing India with the necessary "cover" to attack Pakistan.[61]

Thus, according to this thesis, it is the global world view that was developed and shared by Nixon and Kissinger that explains the U.S. action in South Asia during 1971. Accordingly, China is the key to this explanation, although the role of the USSR is also important. The USSR-China-U.S. triangle involves the dealings of the major powers with each other, and South Asia became one of the first regional arenas where this major power relationship was tested.[62] The argument will be made that Nixon and

---

[61] Interview with U.S. Government official, May 1975.

[62] Interview with U.S. Government official, May 1975.

Kissinger had "shared images" regarding the importance of the events in South Asia. Furthermore, we will present an explanation that Nixon and Kissinger had a preferred outcome in mind and were cognizant of the low probability of its achievement.

We will now seek to provide alternative and complementary explanations for U.S. foreign policy during the 1971 South Asia crisis. The next chapter will introduce various theoretical and analytical tools for viewing this decision-making process. This theoretical chapter will provide the basis for different approaches for analyzing the process of foreign policy formation and implementation. After dealing with the explanations provided by three alternative models, we will proceed to focus and elaborate on the concept of priority formulation.

V: APPLICATION OF DECISION-MAKING THEORY TO MIDDLE-LEVEL CRISIS

This chapter examines several models and concepts that will be applied in the following chapters in order to explain U.S. foreign policy in South Asia during 1971. The concept of priority formulation was introduced in the "Introduction." There we emphasized that an individual decision-maker's personal and subjective evaluations characterize the process of priority formulation. In this chapter, we begin by examining the concepts of risk and uncertainty in order to delineate the significant process whereby an individual decision-maker monitors information flows. This will be followed by a discussion of a decision-maker's belief system and its significance in terms of his subjective resolution of uncertainty.

U.S. Government foreign policy decision-making situations are likely to involve a group of individuals, each with his own preferences and priorities. These individuals have the task of advising the President, the ultimate decision-maker concerning U.S. foreign policy matters. Within a group context, an individual's preferences may change depending on the consensus that develops. Interaction within the group is the level of analysis to be applied following the determination of each decision-maker's preferences and priorities. The group will seek to cope with the complex issue which it confronts. Stress situations are likely to exacerbate the uncertainty aspect of the complex problem, and procedural differences of arriving at a decision are likely to have a significant impact on the substantive aspect of that decision.

We will also elaborate on the concept of a middle-level crisis. The argument will be presented that a middle-level crisis, the 1971 South Asia events, is the stimulus or input that the U.S. foreign policy decision-makers were confronting. The importance of this concept is in the attention it brings to those events that lie on a continuum between the extremes of noncrisis and crisis. A middle-level crisis is placed within the decision-making framework in order to explain how the inputs are processed to arrive at a decision. We will argue that individuals and organizational units process a middle-level crisis differently from a pure crisis. The major distinction is in terms of the priority accorded to a crisis in comparison to a middle-level crisis. Thus, considerably greater attention will be paid to a crisis. Furthermore, in a crisis the locus of decision is less likely to shift from the lower levels of the bureaucracy to the inner circle of the Executive Branch.

A "pure" crisis, because of the priority given the issue, is more likely to be processed from its inception by the inner circle. Being cognizant of the different elements constituting a middle-level crisis, an analyst and decision-maker should be able to assess more accurately the issue they are confronting and be more likely to respond effectively.

Following this elaboration of a middle-level crisis, the assumptions of three decision-making models are examined. These three models, the Rational Man, Psychological, and Incremental, will be utilized in the next three chapters as a means to organize and present alternative approaches for an explanation of U.S. foreign policy in South Asia during 1971.

We will then proceed in Chapter IX to present a more systematic and detailed analysis of the concept of priority formulation. The contributions of each of the three traditional decision-making models are integrated into the priority formulation concept. Thus, the Rational Man Model analyzes the presumptions of a decision-maker who calculates the probabilities and desirabilities of his alternatives in order to determine his rank ordering of preferences. The Psychological Model yields the desirabilities or value that a decision-maker attaches to an event or belief. Finally, the Incremental Model provides us with insight into the group interaction of the respective individual preferences during the deliberations and consensus-building that yield a group decision.

Risk and Uncertainty

Risk and reward are major determinants of the behavior of rational men. While Steinbruner in essence dismisses the distinction between risk and uncertainty,[2] several writers in the field of insurance have dealt with the issue of defining "risk" and "uncertainty" and how they should be assessed. Several distinctions have been made in this area that can be of value for the purpose of decision-making analysis. The most important of these distinctions is that drawn between the "subjective" and "objective" aspects of risk and uncertainty.

Chester Williams and Richard Heins define risk as

---

[1]Parts of this discussion are adapted from Dan Haendel and Gerald T. West with Robert G. Meadow, *Overseas Investment and Political Risk* (Philadelphia, Pa.: Foreign Policy Research Institute, Monograph Series, No. 21, 1975).

[2]See Steinbruner, *op. cit.*, p. 17.

"objective doubt concerning the outcome in a given situation." Uncertainty, however, is defined as "subjective doubt concerning the outcomes during a given period."[3] These authors suggest that if they had defined risk as uncertainty concerning the possible outcome, the distinction between risk and uncertainty would have become a distinction between objective and subjective risk. In <u>Insurance and Economic Theory</u>, Irving Pfeffer also seems to use the objective-subjective distinction to differentiate between risk and uncertainty:

> Risk is a combination of hazards and is measured by probability; uncertainty is measured by a degree of belief. Risk is a state of the world; uncertainty is a state of the mind.[4]

A pioneer in risk analysis, Allan Willett undertook a systematic examination of the various issues associated with the concept of risk. He argued that it is possible to think of risk either in relation to probability or in relation to uncertainty. In normal usage, the degree of risk

---

[3]Chester Williams, Jr. and Richard Heins, <u>Risk Management and Insurance</u> (New York: McGraw-Hill, 1964), pp. 4-7.

[4]Irving Pfeffer, <u>Insurance and Economic Theory</u> (Homewood, Illinois: R.D. Irwin, 1956) p. 42.

is usually associated with the degree of probability of loss. However, Willett argued for the necessity

> to define risk with reference to the degree of uncertainty about the occurrence of a loss, and not with reference to the degree of probability that it will occur. Risk in this sense is the objective correlative of the subjective uncertainty. It is the uncertainty considered as embodied in the course of events in the external world of which the subjective uncertainty is a more or less faithful interpretation.[5]

The implication of such a definition is that "the method by which the degree of risk may be ascertained depends upon the relative perfection of the knowledge of preceding conditions."[6]

The uncertainty Willett refers to imposes costs on society, and its removal constitutes a potential source of gain. Thus, Willett points out that

> the effect of the occurrence of disaster is in itself the same, whether it was foreseen or not. It is the destruction of a certain amount of capital. But the net result of the occurrence of a certain

---

[5] Allan Willett, *The Economic Theory of Risk and Insurance* (Philadelphia: University of Pennsylvania Press, 1951), p. 6.

[6] *Ibid.*, p. 7.

> amount of loss which was definitely foreseen, is different from the net result of the occurrence of the same amount of loss, plus previous uncertainty whether it would be greater or smaller.... The greater the probable variation of the actual loss from the average, the greater the degree of uncertainty.[7]

Willett's conception of risk and uncertainty renders it axiomatic that uncertainty is an unwelcome factor in the decision-making process. The ideal decision-maker seeks to eliminate uncertainty if possible and to reduce or transfer it if not. The psychological weight of uncertainty can logically be displaced by the acquisition of all available information affecting the circumstances he is facing. The net effect of reducing uncertainty is to reduce the effect of risk as well.

Information bridges the concepts of uncertainty and risk. The same information that is useful in accurately calculating risk also serves to reduce uncertainty. It is axiomatic, therefore, that the ideal decision-maker always be in search of the most complete information available.

The distinction drawn by two utility theorists concerning ideal risk and uncertainty conditions may also

---

[7] Ibid., p. 8.

prove useful. In Games and Decisions, Luce and Raiffa note that the decision-maker is in the realm of risk if each course of action leads to one of a set of possible specific outcomes, with each outcome occurring with a known probability.[8] A decision-maker is in the realm of uncertainty if each course of action has as its consequence a set of possible specific outcomes but where the probabilities of these outcomes are completely unknown or are not even meaningful. In other words, if there is enough objective information available to calculate probabilities, one is in the realm of risk; in the absence of such information, one is in the realm of uncertainty.

The subjective resolution of uncertainty can be achieved by 1) reinforcement, 2) the management of inconsistency, or 3) small group interactions. The reinforcement principle argues that a belief will be more strongly held if, on the basis of previous experience, it has been shown to work. The notion of inconsistency management seems to be more helpful in explaining subjective resolution of uncertainty. This explanation suggests that

---

[8]R. Duncan Luce and Howard Raiffa, Games and Decisions (New York: John Wiley and Sons, 1957).

the application of the decision-maker's belief set will be determined by the context within which the event is structured. "That is, the strength of some beliefs depends not upon any direct evidence but rather upon inferential logic connecting them to other established beliefs."[9] This process occurs, for example, when certain fundamental images or analogies are triggered in the decision-maker's mind as he confronts a complex issue. The uncertainty and complexity is reduced, for instance, by labeling one side the "good guys" and the other side the "bad guys." The analogy notion can be seen in decisions that rely on simple historical precedents such as Munich or Vietnam. Thus, for example, Munich is equated with appeasement and evokes a mental value set that rejects appeasement. The word Vietnam is today associated by many Americans with an agony that relates to unnecessary and improper intervention.

The theoretical thinker's characteristics are most pronounced under situations of uncertainty, since his belief system is somewhat independent of the reality principle. Because the thought process of the theoretical thinker is

---

[9] Steinbruner, op. cit., p. 114.

strongly deductive, he is

> less dependent upon incoming information in order to <u>establish</u> coherent beliefs... The <u>theoretical thinker</u> thus can act quickly and with great confidence in those fluid, chaotic situations of short duration which cause a great deal of distress to others operating in different modes of thought.[10]

The theoretical thinker is likely to have a strongly held, highly generalized belief system. These theoretical beliefs are not developed during brief time spans. Steinbruner suggests that theoretical thinking is <u>less</u> likely to occur at the level of the Presidency and Cabinet officers and <u>more</u> likely to be found in small closely knit groups. "Unless some issue seizes high-level policymakers over a considerable period of time, theoretical thinking is likely to be removed from these positions at the intersection of channels and to be located within a particular information channel in an organizational unit, formal or informal, which has a restricted scope of concern."[11] However, Nixon and Kissinger were theoretical thinkers who did have a "world view" and they processed events according to their belief system.

---

[10]<u>Ibid.</u>, p. 132.

[11]<u>Ibid.</u>, p. 135.

The Nixon-Kissinger world view is reflected in the series of Nixon Reports which we will examine during the course of analyzing the Rational Man Model. During the course of the WSAG meetings, Kissinger was invoking Presidential authority and relaying Nixon's "tilt toward Pakistan" to the group. Kissinger admitted that there was no probability of success associated with the "tilt toward Pakistan" policy as far as safeguarding East Pakistan from an Indian attack. Nevertheless, because of their "world view," Nixon and Kissinger argued that the U.S. position, despite its lack of tangible results, had to be made clear to the international community. If Nixon and Kissinger had been in possession of an objective estimate of their policy's probability of success, we would analyze their behavior as risk-taking. However, they were operating in the realm of uncertainty because they were acting on the basis of their subjective estimates. We will utilize the risk-uncertainty distinction in dealing with the Rational Man Model in order to explain the Nixon Administration's concern for the possibility that American inaction in the face of an Indian attack on Pakistan could jeopardize the opening of relations with China. Because of the resistance expressed by various

WSAG members, Nixon and Kissinger found it necessary to convince them or impose on them the "tilt toward Pakistan" policy.

Organizational Behavior

Numerous decision-makers may be organized in a group in order to attempt to cope with a complex problem. These individual decision-makers may have different and, perhaps, conflicting goals. For one outcome to be the result, these decision-makers must be coordinated. The group will process the inputs it receives by employing Standard Operating Procedures (SOPs) and will attempt to reach a result that provides the minimum level of acceptability for the group. Alternatively, the head of the group will arrive at a decision and impose it on the other participants. In the event that the group has failed to adapt to the inputs to which it is subjected, it may seek out more information until it succeeds in its effort to cope or adapt. The organizational routine or SOP utilized will bear on the outcome that will result.

The cybernetic paradigm posits an organization which, having avoided uncertainty and divided a problem into sequential parts, will change its behavior and not its outcome calculation. In other words, a different "response set" will be adopted if the first one does not show itself to be adaptive.

The outcome of the cybernetic paradigm has been identified with incrementalism. "The evolutionary process whereby output in each successive time period represents only a small change from the previous time period is thought to be a primary consequence of the cybernetic process."[12] Steinbruner objects to this identification and argues that a cybernetic mechanism can change its basic behavior pattern and that the analytic paradigm can also yield an incremental decision. Nevertheless, Steinbruner characterizes the cybernetic process as "dominated by established procedure."[13] Consequently, the cybernetic paradigm does not "yield a coherent preference ordering for alternative states of the world under trade-off conditions."[14]

Stress situations are another type of uncertainty, and interesting findings have been uncovered in gaming and

---

[12] Ibid., p. 80.

[13] Ibid., p. 87.

[14] Ibid., p. 86.

simulation experiments. Crisis in these experiments has been explained according to whether the situation is anticipated or unanticipated, the degree of threat presented, and the time available for responding.[15] "The most crisis-loaded situation is an unanticipated, major threat to objectives that compels decision-makers to respond almost immediately."[16]

Robinson, Hermann, and Hermann were interested in the decision-making process in a crisis situation. Among the hypotheses examined, two are of particular interest here. One hypothesis deals with the search for alternatives, that is, "the attempt to seek different possible solutions or methods of handling the situation confronting the nation's decision-makers." [17] The other hypothesis involves the attainment of additional information as a basis for decision-making and choosing among alternatives. The investigators

---

[15] James A. Robinson, Charles F. Hermann, and Margaret G. Hermann, "Search Under Crisis in Political Gaming and Simulation," in Dean G. Pruitt and Richard C. Snyder, Theory and Research on the Causes of War (Englewood Cliffs, New Jersey: Prentice-Hall, Inc., 1969), p. 81.

[16] Ibid., p. 81.

[17] Ibid., p. 85.

expected that in a crisis situation there would be less search for alternatives and a greater search for information. While the former hypothesis was confirmed, the latter was not.

The above findings seem to support very strongly the notion that there exists a positive correlation between the rise of authoritarian leadership and a stress situation. One may hypothesize that in a crisis situation where the group does not seek to expand its options, the group will tend to adopt the alternative proposed by the "authoritarian leader" within the group. It is suggested that this may explain U.S. policy in the Indo-Pakistani conflict as Nixon and Kissinger imposed the "tilt" policy on WSAG. That this process is adaptive can be argued from the perspective that the group needs to achieve its goal, and the time factor does not seem to allow for a full discussion of the virtues of various alternatives. Under these circumstances, the group's most adaptive behavior is either to arrive at a consensus or have the leader impose a decision.

The flow of authority in decision-making processes for groups under stress presents the question of the degree of consultation which takes place on the part of the "authoritarian leader" with his technical advisers. This also raises the question of the proper role for the area experts as decisions are made by the political leadership. Furthermore, one might seriously consider adopting different and possibly non-value laden terms in order to describe the phenomena usually referred to as "authoritarian" and "democratic" leadership. This change of terms may even be necessary were it to be found that "authoritarian" means are more effective than a "democratic" style in coping with crisis situations.

Under conditions of stress, the authoritarian style will have a high degree of appeal because of its capacity to mobilize resources in order to confront the stimuli causing the stress and to provide certainty in ambiguity.[18] If nothing else, Nixon and Kissinger were providing certainty in terms of what they wanted to see accomplished, even though some members of WSAG and the bureaucracy either disagreed with the policy or didn't understand the reasons for it. The Nixon Administration's approach was for Nixon and Kissinger to make the decisions and announce them to WSAG and impose their will on those WSAG members who dissented.

---

[18]See David C. Korten, "Situational Determinants of Leadership Structure," in Dorwin Cartwright and Alvin Zander, Goup Dynamics: Research and Theory (New York: Harper & Row, 1968); A. Paul Hare, Handbook of Small Group Research (New York: The Free Press, 1962); Roger Brown, Social Psychology (New York: The Free Press, 1965), Chapter 10 and 1?

In times of stress it seems that the group strives to liquidate uncertainty and attain a clear-cut goal. In the WSAG meetings at least Kissinger and Nixon were attempting to achieve a direct goal.

The handling by the U.S. Government of the Indo-Pakistani War of 1971 has been used as a case study by the Commission on the Organization of the Government for the Conduct of Foreign Policy (henceforth, the Murphy Commission).[19] The Indo-Pakistani War of 1971 raises serious questions concerning Presidential predominance over foreign policy compared to the participation and influence exercised by the area experts, for example, State Department line officials. There is also the complementary issue of employing strategic and global considerations in the conduct of foreign policy compared with the possible benefits of dealing with the events in a regional subsystem on their own merits, that is, in isolation of or independently from global factors. This discussion seems to be of particular importance in light of the continuing debate concerning Presidential power in foreign policy formulation in addition to the circumstances

---

[19]Lloyd I. Rudolph and Susanne H. Rudolph, "The Coordination of Complexity in South Asia," a Report Prepared for the Commission on the Organization of the Government for the Conduct of Foreign Policy, Spring 1975.

of the particular decision that is analyzed. The U.S. response to the Indo-Pakistani War of 1971 and the policy formulated provide an appropriate occasion for the study of this issue because of the resistance that the policy faced within the U.S. bureaucracy and in various quarters of Congress.

The Rudolphs argue that the complexity in foreign policy formulation requires coordination. They make the distinction between imperative coordination and deliberate coordination.

> Imperative coordination relies upon the mystique of high office, hierarchy in organizational and personal relationships, and will as the source of policy compliance. Deliberative coordination involves the knowledge and judgment of officials, collegiality in formal and informal relationships and reasoned argument and bargaining as the source of policy and compliance.[20]

Imperative coordination is said to be conducted by the President and President's men and is analogous to our discussion of authoritarian leadership. The Rudolph's discussion of deliberative coordination is analogous to the White and Lippitt characterization of democratic leadership.

---

[20] Ibid., p. 11.

White and Lippitt generated characteristics of authoritarian and democratic leadership from the experiments which they conducted. On the one hand, in authoritarian leadership 1) all determination of policy is made by the leader, and 2) the techniques, task and activity are determined by the leader. In cases of democratic leadership, on the other hand, 1) policies are made on the basis of group discussion and decision, and 2) alternatives are determined during group discussions with technical expertise consulted when needed.[21]

The Rudolphs quote Kissinger's statement to the WSAG meeting of December 3, 1971 as a basis for a discussion of imperative coordination: "The President if under the illusion that he is giving instructions..." By invoking the orders of the President, Kissinger was reminding the WSAG participants of the legitimacy and powers of the Office of the President in foreign affairs. Kissinger's reference to Nixon's "illusion" served to emphasize the fact that the President's wishes and orders were not being implemented.

---

[21] Ralph White and Ronald Lippitt, "Leader Behavior and Member Reaction in Three Social Climates," in Cartwright and Zander, op. cit., p. 319.

Furthermore, the possibility existed that some officials were attempting to sabotage the President's will.

Many of the members of the White House staff were the President's men who were appointed to carry out his policies. These men were bing reminded of their proper function. The members of the bureaucracy were being told that they were to implement the President's orders and not their personal preferences. In short, the decision had been made and they were to implement it.[22]

The Rudolphs prefer deliberative coordination in comparison to imperative coordination. The argument in favor of deliberative coordination is premised on the dangers inherent in executive power and attempts to build a framework to mitigate the dangers and simultaneously allow decisions to be reached. "Deliberative coordination is the product of informal argument, rational persuasion and bargaining among professionals representing diverse interests in a context mandated to consider common problems and recommend

---

[22] Rudolph and Rudolph, op. cit., pp. 12.

CONTINUUM OF LEADERSHIP BEHAVIOR

Boss-centered
Leadership ←──────────────────────────→ Subordinate-centered
                                          Leadership

use of authority by the manager						area of freedom for subordinates
Manager makes decision and announces it	Manager sells decision	Manager presents idea & invites questions to change subject	Manager presents decision subject to change	Manager presents problems gets suggestions makes decision	Manager defines limits; asks group to make decision	Manager subordinates to function within limits defined by superior

SOURCE: Robert Tannenbaum and Warren H. Schmidt, "How to Choose a Leadership Pattern," in David R. Hampton, Charles E. Summer, and Ross A. Webber, Organizational Behavior and the Practice of Management, Glenview, Illinois: Scott, Foresman and Company, 1968, p. 502.

joint solutions."[23]

Organizational structures are emphasized and the procedures resemble those associated with the Rational Man Model that is examined in a later section. The procedures call for an analysis of the issue being confronted, consideration of the alternatives and their respective consequences, and the advantages and disadvantages of the possible course of action. The Rudolphs argue that for this type of deliberation to occur, the group meetings must be characterized by an atmosphere of collegiality and a feeling of equality among the participants. They recognize the fact that the President is the only elected official in the Executive Branch and that appointed and bureaucratic officials should be subordinate to the elected officials. Without the equality, collegiality, and free give-and-take that are essential for deliberative

---

[23]Ibid., p. 14. But see Irving Janis, Victims of Groupthink: A Psychological Study of Foreign-Policy Decisions and Fiascoes (Boston: Houghton-Mifflin, 1967). Janis points to the dangers of having an esprit de corps among members of a policy-making group. He argues that in this environment independent critical thinking will be replaced by group-think or shared illusions. The self-imposed constraints on a cohesive group may result in various alternatives not being considered, majority preferences not being questioned, and selective bias for certain information.

coordination, Presidents will exercise imperative coordination. Although Nixon and Kissinger may have understood the arguments presented by those opposing the Administration's policy, they felt that the President's will should, nevertheless be followed. They were not viewing WSAG as an advisory, decision-making body under these circumstances. The alternative to "tilt toward Pakistan" had been chosen. However, in order to implement the policy effectively, a consensus was sought. Each of the WSAG participants represented an organizational unit whose function was to advise and/or implement Presidential decisions. Accordingly, the WSAG meetings dealt with what steps could be taken to implement the "tilt" policy.

Middle-Level Crisis

As we mentioned earlier, the goal of this study is to describe, analyze, and perhaps predict the process of making a decision. It is with this goal in mind that we present these alternative methods for understanding a decision-making process. Decision-making theory focuses on well-defined decisional units and rejects the personification of the nation-state as the basic actor in the international system. Thus, decision-making theory looks to the behavior of human decision-makers who influence and provide the substance of governmental policy.

> It is one of our basic methodological choices to define the state as its official decision-makers -- those whose authoritative acts are, to all intents and purposes, the acts of the state. State action is the action taken by those acting in the name of the state.[24]

While the element of perception is central to much of decision-making theory as will be seen in the Psychological Model, an emphasis solely on perceptions without an examination of the objective situation would be misguided. Accordingly, the objective conditions may be looked upon as the constraints on the decision-maker.[25]

A major goal of foreign policy decision-making theory is to explain the way policy decisions are made. The major decision-making models in the literature of international relations can be classified as: 1) Rational Man Models, 2) Psychological Models, and 3) Incremental Models. Each of these models attempts to explain the structure and process of foreign policy formulation by isolating and analyzing those

---

[24]"Decision-Making as an Approach to the Study of International Politics," in Richard C. Snyder, H.W. Bruck, and Burton Sapin (eds.), Foreign Policy Decision-Making (New York: Free Press of Glencoe, 1963), p. 65.

[25]See Joseph Frankel, The Making of Foreign Policy: An Analysis of Decision-Making (New York: Oxford University Press, 1963).

factors that the model either assumes or finds to be of primary importance.

The decision-making models of foreign policy deal with the policy process at the Presidential level[26] and tend to focus on crisis decision-making. While there has been a call for a systematic analysis of the policy process for both crisis and noncrisis situations,[27] such a suggestion seems to imply that an event is either a crisis or a noncrisis rather than viewing crisis and noncrisis as poles of a continuum.

Charles Hermann defines a crisis and provides a means of viewing this phenomenon as a continuum.[28] We advance the argument in this study that events occur which may be characterized on a continuum from noncrisis to middle-level crisis and to crisis. Hermann specifies threat, time, and surprise as the elements of crisis, although he does characterize it as situation that "(1) threatens high-priority goals of the decision-making unit, (2) restricts

---

[26]See Lincoln P. Bloomfield, The Foreign Policy Process: Making Theory Relevant (Beverly Hills: Sage Publications, 1974), pp. 16-26.

[27]Ibid., pp. 41-42.

[28]Charles F. Hermann, "Some Issues in the Study of International Crisis," in Charles F. Hermann (ed.), International Crisis: Insights From Behavioral Research (New York: The Free Press, 1972), p. 13.

the amount of time available for response before the decision is transformed, and (3) surprises the members of the decision-making unit by its occurrence."[29]

The suggestion we make here is that analogous to the split made for the element of time into time and surprise, the "threatens high-priority goal" should also be divided into threat and priority. The reason for this modification is that all foreign policy decisions that are a crisis may not involve high-priority goals. The presence of three of the factors, threat, time, and suprise is normally viewed as a crisis. A crisis is considered to possess different characteristics from any other possible combination of the factors. The argument here, however, is that even where the goal is mid-priority rather than a high-priority, the situation may be characterized as a middle-level crisis rather than as a noncrisis.

A middle-level crisis is characterized either by the absence of <u>at least</u> one of the <u>four</u> elements of a crisis, that is, the absence of high threat, high value, surprise, or short period of time, or any of these factors being at

---

[29] Ibid., p. 13

a level other than high on a low-middle-high scale. In
short, the concept of middle-level crisis encompasses the
continuum of events between noncrisis and crisis. This
study is devoted to an examination of one type of middle-
level crisis, although a different characteristic will
attach to each middle-level crisis depending on which
element is absent and/or its level of intensity on a low-
middle-high scale. Hermann labels three situations that we
labeled middle-level crisis as "Innovative Situation"
(High Threat/Extended Time/Surprise), "Circumstantial
Situation" (Low Threat/Short Time/Surprise), and "Reflexive
Situation" (High Threat/Short Time/Anticipated).

Of greater significance to the analysis of the
unfolding South Asian events of 1971 is the notion of
viewing the degree of threat, the degree of priority,
the time duration of the threat, and the amount of surprise
as a continuum with "scale positions for every possible
quantity of each property."[30] Here we reproduce Hermann's
model which forms a three-dimensional space from the three
scales of threat, time, and surprise, thereby not accounting

---

[30]Ibid., p. 14.

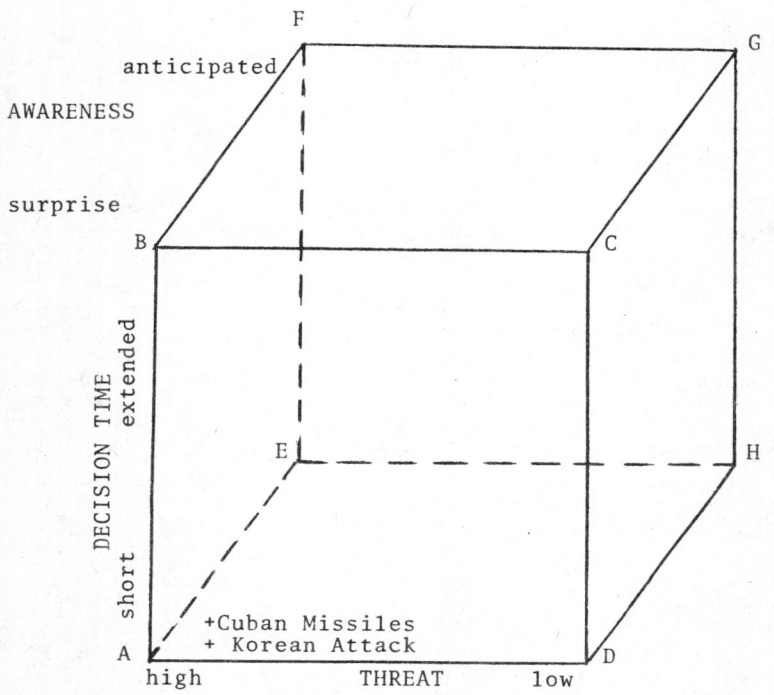

A situational cube representing the three dimensions of threat, decision time, and awareness with illustrative situations from the perspective of American decision-makers.

A. Crisis Situation
   High Threat/Short Time/Surprise
B. Innovative Situation
   High Threat/Extended Time/ Surprise
C. Inertial Situation
   Low Threat/Extended Time/ Surprise
D. Circumstantial Situation
   Low Threat/Short Time/Surprise

E. Reflexive Situation
   High Threat/Short Time/ Anticipated
F. Deliberative Situation
   High Threat/Extended Time/ Anticipated
G. Routinized Situation
   Low Threat/Extended Time/ Anticipated
H. Administrative Situation
   Low Threat/Short Time/ Anticipated

SOURCE: Charles R. Hermann, "Some Issues in the Study of International Crisis," in Charles F. Hermann (ed.), *International Crises: Insights from Behavioral Research* (New York: The Free Press, 1972), pp. 13-15.

for the priority scale that we explained above. In the three dimensional model, the corners of the cube represent the extreme values which constitute the eight ideal types. With the addition of the priority scale, the continuum would consist of sixteen rather than eight possible ideal types. If we were then to construct a model with discrete measures of high, low, and middle for each trait, we would have eighty-one possible ideal types. With the continuum concept, we are, of course, including an infinite number of noncrisis to crisis phenomena within the model. We are suggesting that these middle-level crises are the _objective_ events that confront a decision-maker. However, a desion-maker is not likely to take account of all the nuances that differentiate one type of middle-level crisis from another. Rather, he is likely to possess in his mind a small repertoire of models that he can utilize to process the stimuli he faces. Furthermore, there is a linkage between the objective event and the concept of crisis, because factors such as threat and priority are derived from a decision-maker's subjective evaluation of the events.

  U.S. policy in the Indo-Pakistani War of 1971 is herein described as a middle-level crisis because of the time factor and, in addition, the uncertainty associated with the issue, that is, whether the event did in fact constitute a threat to high-priority goals of U.S. decision-makers. By analyzing the South Asia 1971 events as a middle-level crisis from the vantage of U.S. interests, we are led to a search for the reasons that the Nixon Administration attached such importance to an event in a region that seemingly did not involve the national security of the United States. Moreover, the thesis of this work is that if there was indeed a threat, or more explicitly, a perceived threat, to high priority U.S. goals, these goals were a function of U.S. global interests and were not goals of U.S. foreign policy formulated for South Asia <u>qua</u> South Asia. Once the war erupted the time available for an American response was limited. However, the Administration had sufficient notice that a war was likely to occur as reflected by the fact that a unit of WSAG began considering scenarios and options as early as November 1.

Systems Theory

The linkage between decision-making theory and systems theory is provided by the context or environment within which decision-making occurs. The link is provided by the decision-maker's perceptions because of the presumption that the decision-maker is aware of the existence of his role at various concentric systemic levels. Therefore, this linkage also provides the opportunity for analysis within the total perceived environment as the decision-maker takes into account both the national and international political systems as the setting for his decisions.

Political scientists such as Deutsch, Almond, Easton, and Spiro have utilized the systems theory framework in focusing on the means by which the system converts inputs into outputs.[31] Thus, a political community creates a network of structures or institutions by which to process issues and generate decisions.[32] Accordingly, at the level of foreign policy formulation and implementation, those institutions dealing with the foreign policy stimulus are mobilized into action in order to cope with the particular input. Foreign policy studies have sought to examine the

---

[31] Karl W. Deutsch, The Nerves of Government (New York: Free Press, 1964); Gabriel A. Almond, "Comparative Political Systems," Journal of Politics, August 1956, pp. 391-409; David Easton, A Framework for Political Analysis (Englewood Cliffs, N.J.: Prentice-Hall, 1965); Herbert J. Spiro, World Politics: The Global System (Homewood, Ill.: Dorsey Press, 1966).

[32] See James E. Dougherty and Robert L. Pfaltzgraff, Jr., Contending Theories of Politics and International Relations (Philadelphia: J.B. Lippincott Company, 1971), pp. 102-137.

processes by which decision-makers respond to an input and deal with the numerous issues, both domestic and foreign, that confront them in the formulation of foreign policy.

Charles McClelland has used the systems approach in his article entitled "The Acute International Crisis."[33] McClelland raises the issue of whether there exists a discernible change in the state of the system in the transition from noncrisis to crisis. McClelland offers three propositions for examination: (1) that acute international crises are "short burst" affairs and are marked by an unusual volume and intensity of events; (2) that the general trend in acute international crises will be toward "routinizing" crisis behavior, that is, dealing with problems by means of increasingly "standard" techniques: and (3) that participants will be reluctant to allow the level of violence to increase beyond that present at the onset of the crisis.[34]

The importance of McClelland's thesis is the emphasis

---

[33]Charles A. McClelland, "The Acute International Crisis," in Klaus Knorr and Sidney Verba (eds.), The International System: Theoretical Essays (Princeton: Princeton University Press, 1961).

[34]Dougherty and Pfaltzgraff, op. cit., p. 120.

it places on the changes in the flow of action and
communication. He also emphasizes the feedback feature
of the system such that the output becomes an input in the
next phase of the decision process. The feedback becomes
a continuous flow of demands on the decision process.[35] As
international crises intensify, the sequences of action
become rapid as the time factor for response becomes or is
perceived to be limited and the alternatives are narrowed.
Accordingly, the patterns of interaction within the political
system can be investigated and discerned in order to
distinguish among the different types of crises.

Brecher has brought forward the concept of
"operational environment" which establishes the setting
and parameters for the making of foreign policy. The
objective events will have a direct bearing on the outcome.
However, a decision-maker's policy choices will be influenced
by those inputs that he processes.[36]

A simple systems analysis view of the decision-
making process consists of Inputs, Decisions, Outputs, and
Feedback. The Decision may also be considered the

---

[35]Brecher, op. cit., pp. 3-4.
[36]Ibid., p. 4.

mysterious Black Box that processes and transforms Inputs into Outputs.

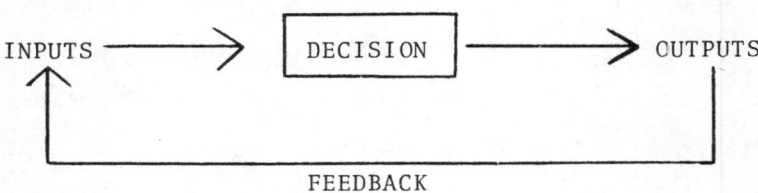

The Inputs are the events that trigger the Decision process. The events itself and the information-gathering phase constitute the Inputs which are then processed at the Decision level in order to arrive at a policy or policies, that is, Outputs. The implementation of a policy may result in a feedback loop which in turn affects the Inputs and initiates a second phase of the process. The Decisions or Black Box has been the focus of the Rational Man, Psychological, and Incremental Models because of their purpose of explaining the way policy decisions are made. While Inputs and Outputs may be observed, Decisions, that is, the process of transforming the Inputs into Outputs, have not been as readily accessible to an investigation. Perhaps the very difficulty of explaining this transformation process is the reason for the interest it has generated among researchers.

International relations specialists have in recent years focused on crisis decision-making in order to explain the Decisions phase. The works that have been generated in this area are among the more well known writings in the discipline of international relations. As will be pointed out below, even though their works have different perspectives toward the Decisions phase, Glenn Paige's The Korean War and Graham Allison's Essence of Decision exemplify the type of work that has been done in the area of crisis decision-making.[37] Works have recently been focusing on the noncrisis decision-making aspects of foreign policy as well, and Newhouse's Cold Dawn is an example of this literature.[38]

Dougherty and Pfaltzgraff criticize decision-making-making theory if undertaken through the static assumptions of "decision-makers making clear-cut choices

---

[37] Paige, op. cit.; Allison, op. cit.

[38] John Newhouse, Cold Dawn: The Story of SALT (New York: Holt, Rinehart and Winston, 1973).

at given points in time and then sitting back to await the results."³⁹ In addition, they emphasize that decisions do not in reality take place in a vacuum, even if for the sake of convenience numerous studies are undertaken as though the decision were made in isolation from other factors. In fact, however, "decisions occur in a fluid context"⁴⁰ and the output of a previous decision will affect the current input. In addition, the national political system and the international system are likely to constitute a constraint or factor in the formulation of a decision. Accordingly, action and events should be viewed as a continuum rather than as discrete phenomena. This work will seek to take account of these criticisms by adopting a dynamic perspective. For example, we have already observed that participants from the State Department and NSC began their involvement in this decision-making process at different times. Furthermore, we have seen that the unfolding South Asia events can be divided into relatively distinct phases. The stages of U.S. foreign policy in the Indo-

---

³⁹Dougherty and Pfaltzgraff, op. cit., p. 319.
⁴⁰Ibid., p. 319.

Pakistani War of 1971 may be divided as follows: 1) the
election period, November 1969- February 1970, 2) the
crackdown period, March 1971, 3) the refugee period,
April- June 1971, 4) the period of Indian intervention in
guerrilla action, July- November 1971, 5) the "crisis"
period, November- December 7, 1971, and 6) the war period,
December 1971.

In terms of the different types of events that can
occur, however, there seems to be a need for an examination
of an event that is in the middle of the crisis-noncrisis
continuum and to consider the possibility and likelihood of
the "movement" of an event to different stages. In other
words, the middle-level crisis event may be viewed as a
<u>dynamic process</u> that moves through various stages as an
Input and demands different Decisions, possibly yielding
various and differing Outputs. Thus, for example, the events
in South Asia in 1971 may have begun as a "Circumstancial
Situation" (Low Threat/Short Time/Surprise) for the U.S.
with the March 25, 1971 crackdown. However, as the dynamic
events unfolded and the Inputs changed, the events in
South Asia may have evolved into a "Routinized Situation"
(Low Threat/Extended Time/Anticipated) between April and
November 1971. With the Nixon Administration's emphasis

on a multipolar world and the U.S. efforts to initiate relations with China, the Indo-Pakistani War may have evolved into a "Reflexive Situation" (High Threat/Short Time/ Anticipated) which has been previously characterized as a middle-level crisis.

Three Models

Within the above crisis-noncrisis continuum framework, we may proceed to examine the contributions that the Rational Man, Psychological, and Incremental Models have made to the understanding of the Decisions phase of the process. To the degree that these Models explain the Decisions phase of the decision, they also explain which Inputs are likely to stimulate the Decisions phase and what are likely to be the Outputs.

The Rational Man Model is an adaptation of the notion of the Economic Man Model that explains the behavior of the actor who seeks to maximize his profits. Thus, the Rational Man Model is characterized by total information which serves as the Input. The Decision is based on the fact that every participant is rational, which results in the Output that will maximize the welfare of the decision-unit. The Rational Man Model is a normative and idealized notion of reality whose major function may in fact be to serve as a benchmark for comparison or standard for the behavior that an investigator observes. The assumptions made by such a model flow from its ideal nature. The model assumes that 1) the actor is able to receive complete and perfect information, 2) all the alternatives can be identified, 3) the advantages and disadvantages of each alternative can be identified and compared, 4) all the actors can agree on the goals and objectives to be achieved, 5) the actors can agree on the best choice of alternatives, and 6) the actors are rational, that is, seek to maximize their welfare, and will not become irrational.

Steinbruner suggests that the two critical assumptions made by the Rational Man Model are that the decision-maker will 1) calculate the various outcomes of a given course of action, and 2) revise the outcome calculations to reflect the acquisition of new information and experience. Some actual decisions will fit this "blueprint," but many will not be explainable by the utilization of these two assumptions. These two assumptions are examined in greater detail in the chapter dealing with priority formulation.

The Rational Man Model has suffered from the confusion of whether its purpose is to serve as a normative model or an accurate description of reality.[41] But the model does serve to point out the importance of a problem-solving strategy that takes into account the goal to be achieved, the possible alternatives, the choosing of an alternative, the implementation of the choice, and a consideration of its consequences.

The criticism of the unrealistic reflection provided by the Rational Man Model led to the formation of the Incremental or Bureaucratic Model. Much of the criticism emerged as a result of comparing the Rational Man Model with case-study writings by participants in actual decision-making situations. These writings reflect the bargaining among participants, pulling and hauling, and bureaucratic "muddling through" that have become the jargon and acknowledged characteristics of the Bureaucratic Model. Herbert Simon's writings on administrative decision-making criticize the Rational Man Model as unrealistic on the grounds that decision-makers are subject to the limitations of knowledge, time, and other pressures.

The Incremental Model was developed by Charles Lindblom and David Braybrooke in their work,

---

[41]Bloomfield, <u>The Foreign Policy Process</u>, <u>op. cit</u>.

A Strategy of Decision.[42] While rejecting the Rational Man
Model as synoptic decision-making, the Incremental Model
also modifies the Psychological Model. However, the major
goal of the Incremental Model is to construct a realistic
model that can be applied to both noncrisis and crisis
decision-making. The model assumes that decision-makers
must develop ways to handle their affairs because they are
pressed for time and harassed. Flowing from this observation
the model proceeds to make a crucial distinction between
"maximizing" and "satisficing." On the one hand, the Rational
Man Model, as discussed above, holds that "maximizing," that
is, seeking the maximum from a given situation, is the
explanation for decision-makers' behavior. The Incremental
Model, on the other hand, emphasizes the importance of
"satisficing" as the explanation for decision-making behavior.
"Satisficing" is the process by which the minimum that will
satisfy the decision-maker, rather than the "true" maximum,
is the decision that will be adopted and pursued. A series
of such ad hoc decisions made in order to "satisfice" each

---

[42]David Braybrooke and Charles E. Lindblom,
A Strategy of Decision: Policy Evaluation as a Social
Process (New York: Free Press, 1963).

particular input results in "disjointed incrementalism."
This, then, is the "science of muddling through," or doing
just enough to get by.

Herbert Simon distinguishes between servomechanisms
and analytic calculations as decision-making models.[43] He
distinguishes between "state" and "process" descriptions of
reality. The former is a "blueprint" model of the environment
as the locus of decision. The "process" description is like
a recipe which works by the completion of a sequence of steps
without a prior conceptualized overall picture of the final
product. The cybernetic paradigm depicts a decision-maker
who has a "repertory of operations which he performs in
sequence while monitoring a few feedback variables."[44]

By eliminating the many aspects of variety, the
decision-making process of servomechanisms results in adaptive
behavior. Thus, the mechanism itself is quite simple and
deals effectively with complexity without going through the
elaborate calculations involved in the Rational Man Model.
But since the cybernetic mechanism operates in response to

---

[43] Herbert A. Simon, "The Architecture of Complexity," in Herbert A. Simon, The Sciences of the Artificial (Cambridge, Mass.: MIT Press, 1968), pp. 84-118.

[44] Steinbruner, op. cit., p. 55.

the environment, the degree of its adaptability will also depend on the environment.

The cybernetic paradigm operates in situations that involve routine decision sequences. The issue of the decision process is extremely well defined and structured, and

> ... the cybernetic paradigm, in positing a decision mechanism based on selective feedback and programmed operations (the recipe), is building upon the notion of hierarchically organized environments. The adaptive capacity of cybernetic decision mechanisms occurs when the decision maker is operating within a stable environmental subsystem.[45]

The cybernetic paradigm proceeds by "satisficing," whereby the first alternative that provides an outcome that meets the decision-makers' values will be adopted. Steinbruner also points to the challenge confronting the analytic paradigm posed by Ashby, who depicts a decision-maker who does not calculate outcomes or payoff values but who is posited to possess a "repertory of behaviors"[46] and processes critical inputs on the basis of past experience. The repertories of behavior are rank ordered in terms of their success by past positive reinforcement and survival is the basic value.

---

[45] Ibid., p. 61.

[46] Ibid., p. 63.

The cybernetic paradigm's decision-maker seeks not to deal with value calculations and handles uncertainty by applying to the critical input a behavior pattern that had worked in the past. The cybernetic paradigm criticizes the analytic paradigm's demands in terms of the absolute amount of information that the rational decision-maker must process in addition to the various calculations that he is presumed to make. The cybernetic paradigm argues that the decision-maker avoids these complex outcome calculations by not taking into account uncertainty or the complex variety inherent in reality. This decision-maker is viewed as possessing procedures or a small number of "responses" and "decision rules" for dealing with inputs. Past experience is the key determinant in the establishment of the utility of the "response set." The "response set" will also act as a screening device for information and inputs. Information not in tune with the preconceived notions of the "response set" will not be taken into account as the decision is made, even though it may have a bearing on what occurs.

The cybernetic paradigm is thus able to control uncertainty largely by avoiding it and eliminating numerous dimensions of variety by the establishment of a few "response sets."

> Complex problems under such a scheme become fragmented into a large number of very specific problems, each addressed by a separate decision maker.
> ... This is the natural cybernetic explanation for the rise of mass bureaucracy.[47]

Graham Allison attempts to formulate a distinction between the Organizational Model and the Bureaucratic Model. The Organizational Model examines the organizational actors, their narrow perceptions, constraints, and their Standard Operating Procedures. Thus, actors behave as spokesmen for the particular organization that they represent, or the actors may be viewed as the organization itself. The policy alternative preferred by each organization may differ from the objective, rational choice as outlined in the Rational Man Model.

However, the Bureaucratic Model also deals with organizational behavior, although focusing on individuals constrained by the organizational context. The Organizational Model, it can be argued, is not readily distinguished from

---

[47]Ibid., p. 69.

the Bureaucratic Model.

> In a sense this Model III /⁻The Bureaucratic Politics Model_7 can be regarded as a refinement or extension of the Organizational Model (II). In essence, it sees foreign policy products as outcomes of a bureaucratic-political process in which bargaining takes place among players positioned hierarchically in the government.[48]

The focus of the Bureaucratic Model is on actions. These actions are processed through action channels. Policy becomes the "authoritative aspirations" that the government seeks to realize as outcomes.

> "Decision games" are played in converting various activities into decisions; "policy games" are played in the process of converting activities into policy; "action games" describe the interactive process of activities that follow decisions. The "unitary actor" is replaced by the pluralistic player whose stands are derived from parochial priorities and perceptions, goals, interests, stakes, deadlines, and perspectives.[49]

Consequently, Allison's Organizational and Bureaucratic Models may be subsumed within the more general Incremental Model. On the one hand, the Organizational Model raises the serious problem of the management and coordination of governmental organizations dealing with the

---

[48]Bloomfield, The Foreign Policy Process, op. cit., p. 25.

[49]Ibid., p. 25.

same problem and emphasizes the organization as the actor. On the other hand, the Bureaucratic Model focuses on the bargaining process, the step-by-step handling of issues, and the different values and objectives of the actors. Both models, however, are characterized by "satisficing." In short, the process characterizing the Organizational and Bureaucratic Models is similar. The Incremental Model's "disjointed incrementalism" posits that the policies that will be considered are those that vary only slightly from previous decisions or the status quo, thereby making innovation rare.

The process of decision-making is also a function of organizational structure. Nevertheless, it is important to note at this stage that while the Executive Branch of the U.S. Federal Government is in primary control of U.S. foreign policy, the Legislative Branch may exercise differing degrees of control depending on the specific foreign policy issues involved. Of even greater significance is the fact that the process of decision-making may be dependent on organizational structure within the Executive Branch for its locus of power, and the "leadership style" of the executive.

The Psychological Model or cognitive paradigm, according to Steinbruner, provides a third perspective from which to explain and seek to predict decision-making behavior. The model emphasizes the importance of attitudes of the individual decision-maker as well as the social context in which he is operating. The writings by North, Snyder, and Paige exemplify this approach.

This model examines 1) the characteristic of the organization, 2) the communication patterns, and 3) the motivational elements of the decision-makers. In analyzing the organizational framework, the Psychological Model considers the formal organizational structure and the formation of new or *ad hoc* decision groups that are created in order to confront a particular problem. Within the formal and the informal organizational framework, the flow of information and the personal interactions that occur are posited as factors that may explain the decision or decisions reached.

The Psychological Model places particularly strong emphasis on the motivation of a decision-maker. The difficulty of grappling with motivations, however, lies in the fact that they cannot be directly observed and can only be inferred. While Snyder distinguishes between "in order to" motives as conscious and verbalizable in contradistinction to "because of" motives as unconscious, both types still cannot be directly observed.[50]

The Psychological Model focuses on the individual decision-makers *qua* individuals in an organizational context. Thus, particular emphasis is placed on factors concerning the individual decision-maker. The model looks to the individual's values that are at stake as he confronts the event and analyzes this in terms of the decision-makers' 1) background characteristics, 2) individual beliefs, and 3) personality characteristics. Boulding states that a

> decision involves the selection of the most preferred position in a contemplated field of choice. Both the field of choice and the ordering of this field... lie in the image of the decision-maker.[51]

Brecher divides the decision-makers' psychological environment into the "attitudinal prism" and "elite image." The "attitudinal prism" corresponds closely to the factors enumerated under what we have labeled the Psychological Model. The personality and societal factors account for the decision-makers' psychological predispositions. The

---

[50]See Richard C. Snyder, et. al., op. cit., p. 144. See also Dougherty and Pfaltzgraff, op. cit., p. 327.

[51]Kenneth Boulding, "National Images and International Relations," The Journal of Conflict Resolution, June 1959, pp. 120-121.

"elite image" consists of the elites' world view which is derived from their perceptions of the external and internal environments.[52]

The "occasion for decision" is the context within which the decision is made. The Psychological Model examines 1) the extent of prior consideration given to the problem being confronted, 2) the time that leaders see themselves as having in order to respond, 3) the value or beliefs held by the decision-makers, and 4) how important the issue at stake is considered by the decision-makers.

In terms of a decision-maker's behavior in crisis situations, the Psychological Model suggests the following observations: 1) decision-makers make the tautological argument that since they perceive themselves to be under a great threat, they must be in a crisis, otherwise they would not perceive themselves as being threatened, 2) decision-makers do not see many alternatives, 3) the alternatives seen by decision-makers are oversimplified, and 4) decision-makers feel great pressure to arrive at a

---

[52]Brecher, op. cit., pp. 11-12.

consensus, and dissent, if undertaken, is done so at great personal cost.

The cybernetic paradigm seems to allow the decision-maker to adapt to the environment by dividing a phenomenon into manageable components and deal with each one sequentially. However, a complex environment, by definition, does not seem to allow for separating the various dimensions into stable and manageable components. "The absence of stable decomposition and the concomitant presence of enormous uncertainty present what would appear to be staggering problems for the decision maker."[53]

Because of the difficulty of subdividing a complex phenomenon, the process of incremental adjustment and the basing of these decisions on accumulated experiences does not seem to be analytically useful. Complex decisions, despite a high level of uncertainty, do not seem to paralyze a decision-maker. Quite the contrary, complex decisions may be characterized by dramatic instances of decision.

A psychological explanation for a decision-maker's ability to resolve the uncertainty associated

---

[53]Steinbruner, op. cit., p. 88.

with a complex phenomenon may be the decision-maker's general structures of belief. Rules may be constructed by the human mind by inductive inferences from observed data. "To the cognitive theorist, this inferential capacity of the mind which is actively involved in imposing structure on otherwise highly ambiguous data is a fundamental force in the decision process."[54]

The cognitive theorists seem to have reached some basic agreement regarding the operations of the human brain. The search is for regularities in the way the human brain deals with values and uncertainty, that is, the structure of cognitive operations. Furthermore, "<u>a great deal of information processing is conducted apparently prior to and certainly independently of conscious direction and that in this activity the mind routinely performs logical operations of considerable power.</u>"[55]

The mind's process of inference may allow it to build reliable and structured perceptual images out of

---

[54]Ibid., p. 90.
[55]Ibid., p. 92.

ambivalent data. Perception of the complex problem may also determine the degree to which stored memory is brought to bear on a problem and/or inductive inference is used. In the following chapters we will seek to analyze the "mind set" and repertoire of beliefs that Nixon, Kissinger, and other involved decision-makers possessed and applied to the South Asia middle-level crisis.

Summary

The application of decision-making theory has been largely confined to crisis situations, although with the increased attention paid to Bureaucratic Politics and more general foreign policy formulation studies, there have been works undertaken of foreign policy formulation that do not involve the "pure" crisis situation (High Threat/Short Time/Surprise) as focus. Brecher's The Foreign Policy System of Israel and Newhouse's Cold Dawn are examples of this type of work, although these studies do not specifically deal with what has been here defined as a middle-level crisis.[56]

---

[56] Brecher, op. cit.; Newhouse, op. cit.

Crisis decision-making theory also seems applicable to a middle-level crisis from the three different perspectives of the Rational Man, Incremental, and Psychological Models. Similar assumptions are made in applying these models to the middle-level crisis as to a crisis. The basic difference in applying these models to a middle-level crisis is in the difference regarding the factors of 1) threat, 2) time, 3) surprise, and the emphasis to be placed on the concept of 4) priority. Since a prolonged middle-level crisis also "moves" along a continuum, it seems reasonable to suggest that the three models can be useful in explaining the different stages of the process. However, we will not undertake this effort in this study. We raise the issue in order to emphasize the <u>dynamic</u> nature of an event and to suggest the possible utility of these models for an understanding of the various stages involved.

We have examined such concepts as risk and uncertainty from the perspective of organizational behavior. Group decision-making has also been analyzed from the perspective of the three models we have outlined. The purpose of this undertaking is to provide different approaches and explanations for the phenomenon

we are dissecting. We are particularly concerned with
the process whereby decision-makers handle complex
issues. We have touched on those factors that allow
a decision-maker to simplify the complex variety of
stimuli that confront him. By utilizing his prior
experiences and analogizing to simple models, a decision-
maker is able to eliminate much of the uncertainty he
faces due to lack of information.

The next three chapters are organized according
to the categories of the Rational Man, Psychological,
and Incremental Models as means for examining the U.S.
foreign policy decision-making process in relation to
the decisions toward the 1971 South Asia events. The
Rational Man Model examines the probabilities and
desirabilities assigned by individual U.S. decision-
makers to the events in South Asia. The Psychological
Model analyzes the elite images and belief sets of
U.S. decision-makers in order to derive the "desirabilities"
they attached to alternative outcomes. The Incremental
Model suggests the process whereby changes in priorities
may occur through group decision-making and/or
restructuring of a problem from a regional to a global

issue. Through the derivation of the "desirabilities" and probabilities within the framework of the Rational Man Model, we will attempt to establish in Chapter IX a methodology for the systematized statement or formula for the calculation of an individual decision-maker's preference ranking.

VI: THE RATIONAL MAN MODEL: THE RATIONALE OF THE NIXON APPROACH

In the previous chapter we examined several assumptions inherent in the Rational Man Model. A focus on the outcome is one the major characteristics of the Rational Man Model. By focusing on the outcome and the probabilities attached to each of these outcomes, the Rational Man Model makes a significant contribution to the concept of priority formulation. The process delineated by the Rational Man Model will be utilized as the framework for the analysis of the process of priority formulation. Within that framework, the Psychological Model contributes to an analysis of the value that a decision-maker attaches to an outcome. While the economic Rational Man is able to assign a numerical payoff to an outcome, the political Rational Man is not dealing with a phenomenon that can be measured in such precise terms. In our later discussion of priority formulation, we will label "desirabilities" the subjective numbers or values assigned to an outcome by a decision-maker.

In this chapter we will examine the assumptions that led to the outcomes preferred by decision-makers in the Nixon Administration according to the rationale provided by the 1971 and 1972 versions of <u>A Report to The Congress</u> (henceforth, Nixon Report). The Nixon Reports of 1971 and 1972 are helpful for this examination because they provide a reflection of Nixon's and Kissinger's thoughts regarding their conceptual framework of international relations. The establishment of a legitimate world order and the attainment of peace constitute the vision of the world that is propounded in these documents. We will also examine the probabilities that Nixon and Kissinger attached to the outcomes they sought to achieve. We will be particularly interested why Nixon and Kissinger adopted the "tilt toward Pakistan" policy, notwithstanding their awareness of the very low or zero probability for the achievement of success.

The Nixon Reports deal explicitly with the importance of the global and regional balance of power. The 1971 Nixon Report provides a brief sketch of U.S.

interests in South Asia while recognizing the legitimate interests of the USSR and China. The 1972 Nixon Report attempts to explain the rationale for American foreign policy in South Asia toward the 1971 events. This explanation is of particular interest in examining the political Rational Man because of the framework utilized to interpret and process the events. By examining the framework and assumptions of the Nixon Reports, we will seek to understand the outcomes, desirabilities, or goals which the Nixon Administration argues it was striving to accomplish.

In the post-World War II period South Asia has been considered an area of relatively little importance for U.S. foreign policy. U.S. political and strategic interests were not viewed to be dependent on developments in the region, although during the 1950's and early 1960's Pakistan's role as U.S. ally, U.S. observation center on the Soviet Union, and link between CENTO and SEATO served to place the region within the Cold War context. With the waning of the Cold War era, Pakistan's utility in terms of U.S. strategic and political interests decreased. But the U.S. was concerned about Soviet penetration efforts into the region[1] and sought to counter them. "... we recognize that the unmet needs of South Asia, and its unresolved enmities, could make the area vulnerable to an undesirable level of foreign influence."[2]

In President Nixon's 1971 Nixon Report, the stated U.S. objective in South Asia was "to help these nations deal with their own problems, and to bring our activity into a stable balance with that of the other major powers with interests in the area."[3]

In contradistinction to the Dulles period, the Nixon-Kissinger view of the world presumed the unlikelihood that Third World countries could or would constitute a threat to U.S. security. The balance of power in a perceived multipolar world called for utilizing the Sino-Soviet rift and dealing directly with China in order to

---

[1] Norman D. Palmer, "Recent Soviet and Chinese Penetration in India and Pakistan: Guidelines for Political-Military Policy" (McLean, Va.: Research Analysis Corporation, February 1970).

[2] Richard Nixon, U.S. Foreign Policy for the 1970's: Building for Peace: A Report to the Congress (Washington, D.C.: USGPO, February 25, 1971), p. 112.

[3] Ibid., p. 111.

counter the Soviets.[4] The significant aspect of the 1971 Nixon Report with respect to South Asia is its recognition of the legitimate interest of the Soviet Union and, even more impressively, of China in the subcontinent.

Nixon's concern with Communist China, despite his anti-Communist position, is reflected in his article in Foreign Affairs in October 1967.

> Any American policy toward Asia must come urgently to grips with the reality of China ... Taking the long view, we simply cannot afford to leave China forever outside the family of nations, there to nurture its fantasies, cherish its hates and threaten its neighbors. There is no place on this small planet for a billion of its potentially most able people to live in angry isolation.... The world cannot be safe until China changes. Thus our aim, to the extent that we can influence events, should be to induce change. The way to do this is to persuade China that it must change: that it cannot satisfy its imperial ambitions, and that its own national interest requires a turning away from foreign adventuring and a turning inward toward the solution of its own domestic problems.[5]

---

[4]William J. Barnds, "India, Pakistan & American Realpolitik," Christianity and Crisis, June 12, 1972, p. 144.

[5]Richard Nixon, "Asia After Viet Nam," Foreign Affairs, October 1967, p. 121.

A Triangular Relationship: U.S., Pakistan, and China

In the delicate jockeying that was undertaken between the U.S. and China, although Rumanian leaders played a significant role, the principal interlocutor and courier between the two sides was Yahya Khan, who was in China between November 9 and 14. Pakistan served as the conduit for a secret exchange of messages between American and Chinese leaders during December 1970 and January 1971. Kissinger characterized the exchange as "the first serious, nonsparing exchange" in over twenty years.[6] The substance of the message was deliberately kept vague and ambiguous in case the Pakistanis read the contents. While no secret exchanges occurred between the United States and China by way of Pakistan for six weeks following Nixon's approval of the February 1971 incursion into Laos by the South Vietnamese military which was supported by the United States, the process of reconciliation was, nevertheless, underway.

The 1971 Nixon Report discusses South Asia's place within a global context and seems to indicate that

---

[6] As quoted in Marvin Kalb and Bernard Kalb, *Kissinger* (Boston: Little, Brown and Company, 1974), p. 234.

the area's importance is derived from the struggle for power between the global powers. The Nixon Administration sought to establish "rules of the game" as the principles for the conduct of U.S. foreign policy that were to be accepted by the other global and regional actors.

The Chinese invitation that an "American envoy" visit Peking was delivered to Kissinger by Agha Hilaly, the Pakistani Ambassador to the United States. Kissinger flew into Islamabad on July 8 on his way to Peking. Yahya hosted a state dinner for Kissinger that night and the following day the press was informed that Kissinger was suffering from a stomach ailment and would be staying at a mountain retreat.[7] This was the scheme arranged between Kissinger and Yahya as the cover for Kissinger's trip to China.[8] Some have argued that Nixon's "tilt toward Pakistan" can be explained as a repayment for the interlocutor and courier services rendered by Yahya,[9] although

---

[7] For an interesting exchange between Yahya and Kissinger, see Henry Brandon, The Retreat of American Power (Garden City, N.Y.: Doubleday and Company, 1973), pp. 247-248.

[8] For details of the "disappearing act," see Kalb and Kalb, op. cit., pp. 243-246.

[9] For example, see ibid., p. 244.

this explanation hardly seems credible as the primary factor for explaining American actions in South Asia. The fact that Pakistan served this role, however, was not accidental and its intermediary role may be viewed as a manifestation of a more important explanatory factor.

The White House candidly admitted that the American posture in South Asia should be in line with the restraint that the Nixon Doctrine professed. Examining the regional relations, the Nixon Report suggested that the welfare of the area could be substantially improved by the normalization of relations between India and Pakistan. The Administration emphasized that while it would encourage the two leading regional powers in the subcontinent to arrive at an accomodation, the U.S. would not dictate or seek to impose the terms of the establishment of normal relations.

Concerning the competition of the global powers in the region, the 1971 Nixon Report noted the Administration's recognition of the shifting patterns of alignments between the major states in South Asia with the global powers. Pakistan is depicted attempting to balance her relations between the Soviet Union, China, and the U.S., while India's non-alignment is viewed as having been eroded as a consequence of the Sino-Indian War of 1962.

A Triangular Affair: U.S., USSR, and China

The Nixon White House was prepared to accomodate itself to a complex triangular relationship among the three major global powers in South Asia. The Soviet Union's efforts were viewed as an attempt to achieve stability on its southern border by maintaining close relations with India and thereby protecting its southern flank while simultaneously checking Chinese influence and maintaining counter pressure on China. The Chinese were perceived to be building strong bonds with Pakistan as a counter to India at the regional level and a check on a Soviet drive for predominance in the subcontinent. The Administration was prepared to attempt to codify the regional and global balance of power rules in South Asia. The Nixon White House was opposed to the hegemony of any one power, whether global or regional, over the region because such a development was considered destabilizing. This traditional balance of power objective may account for the Administration's objection to the Indian attack.

> We will do nothing to harm legitimate Soviet and Chinese interest in the area. We are equally clear, however, that no outside power has a claim to a predominant influence, and that each can serve its own interests and the interests of South Asia best by conducting its activities in the region accordingly.[10]

According to the 1972 Nixon Report, the U.S. objective in South Asia in 1971 was "to prevent a war... and to encourage a political solution."[11] While the actions taken by the U.S. toward the region can be analyzed at different levels of explanation, the 1972 Nixon Report propounds the Administration's defense of its actions and argues with a high degree of forcefulness that the course of action chosen was correct.

Interviews with numerous U.S. Government officials who were participants in the American decision-making process regarding the South Asia crisis revealed a deeply-helf belief on the part of one school of thought (those within the White House circle) that President Nixon's 1972 A Report to the Congress is an accurate and complete explanation of America's policy and actions. A second

---

[10] Nixon, A Report to the Congress (1971), op. cit., p. 114.

[11] Richard Nixon, U.S. Foreign Policy For the 1970's: The Emerging Structure of Peace: A Report to the Congress (Washington, D.C.: USPGO, February 9, 1972), p. 141.

school of thought, primarily those outside the White House circle, views the Nixon Report as a rationalization after-the-fact.

The importance of the pronouncement in the Nixon Report is in the indication it provides of the context within which President Nixon and his national security advisor, Henry Kissinger, viewed the events in South Asia. The major matters of concern for the Administration during the period were its relations with the Soviet Union and, even more importantly, its emerging relations with China. Thus, foreign policy concerns of a higher degree of priority were to impinge on the Administration's ability to manage the South Asian crisis. Furthermore, once the Administration attached significance to the crisis it did so in terms of its priorities for global considerations.

The importance of the China connection in terms of the leverage that the U.S. would be able to exert on the Soviet Union by means of this new relationship was not openly discussed by the Administration. Upon his return from China on July 16, Kissinger emphasized that the United States was not seeking to take advantage of the Sino-Soviet rift in order to use one state against the other. Kissinger publicly stated that "[n]othing that has been done in our relations with the People's Republic of China has any purpose or is in any way directed against any other countries, and especially not against the Soviet Union."[12]

On October 12, 1971, Nixon announced his upcoming visit to Moscow in May 1972. The Soviets realized the importance of the new Sino-American connection despite Nixon's statements that neither the Moscow nor the China visit was being taken in order to take advantage of the Sino-Soviet conflict. The Soviets preferred a bipolar world to the complex triangular balance-of-power arrangement being constructed by the Nixon-Kissinger team. The Soviets were also probably aware that, notwithstanding Nixon's denials, the U.S. would not only take advantage of the Sino-Soviet rift but was nurturing relations with China in order to counter increased Soviet power.

The Nixon Report's Explanation of the 1971 South Asia Events

The 1972 Nixon Report takes the position that the "crisis [the Indo-Pakistani War] began as an internal

---

[12] As quoted in Kalb and Kalb, op. cit., p. 256.

conflict in Pakistan"[13] and that as a result of the process outlined in an earlier section, the "crisis quickly acquired an international character."[14] The Administration argues that the "United States did not support or condone"[15] the military action taken by Pakistan's central government in East Pakistan and emphasizes the cut-off of U.S. military supplies to Pakistan. The Report fails to mention the Nixon Administration's opposition to the arms cut-off in addition to Kissinger's anti-embargo remarks at various WSAG meetings.

The Nixon Report traces the international character of the South Asian developments to the Bengali refugees who became an unacceptable burden to the Indian Government. Therefore, the refugee problem became a regional controversy between India and Pakistan. As the regional conflict intensified, the global actors, the U.S., USSR, and China, sought to support their respective client states. The Report emphasizes the continuing American effort to deal with the Pakistani political crisis after the March 25

---

[13]Nixon, A Report to the Congress (1972), op. cit., p. 142.

[14]Ibid., p. 142.

[15]Ibid., p. 142.

crackdown. With the outbreak of the war between India and Pakistan what had been a regional conflict became a global issue that involved the web of inter-relationship of the U.S., USSR, and China.

> It was a foregone conclusion that if war broke out, India would win. But in our view war was neither inevitable nor acceptable.
> We realized full well that there were objective limits to what the United States could do. South Asia was a region in which we had no pre-eminent position of influence...[16]

In other words, Nixon and Kissinger were aware that there was little if any likelihood that their policy would prove successful. This realistic awareness is also reflected in the WSAG meetings. Nevertheless, the "tilt toward Pakistan" policy was implemented in order to achieve other objectives.

The Administration's account of its actions naturally places its actions in a light most favorable to its response. The U.S. response to events in South Asia focused on 1) the humanitarian emergency, 2) a search for a political settlement between East and West Pakistan,

---

[16] Ibid., pp. 142-143.

and 3) the prevention of war between India and Pakistan.[17] In addressing each of the problems, the Administration points to the aid it provided the refugees. The Administration's thesis is that the search for a political settlement of the Pakistani domestic crisis was the key to the solution. Accordingly, the Report argues that under U.S. insistence Yahya agreed not to execute Sheikh Mujib. The U.S. also undertook to establish negotiations between Yahya and Bengali representatives in Calcutta. But the Nixon Administration places the blame for the failure of this effort at a regional settlement on India.

With the outbreak of the Indo-Pakistani War, U.S. policy, according to the Nixon Report, had as its objective the achievement of a ceasefire. The U.S. sought to attain the cooperation of the Soviet Union in achieving this objective but the USSR vetoed UN Security Council Resolutions calling for a ceasefire and withdrawal of foreign forces. "The Soviet Union blocked international action until the capture of East Pakistan was a *fait*

---

[17]*Ibid.*, pp. 144-146.

accompli."[18]

The Nixon Administration's Considerations

Once the outbreak of the war had occurred, the Administration explained its policy as having been dictated by global considerations. Thus, the issue was no longer confined to the Pakistani domestic political crisis or the regional issue of Bengali refugees as a source of further conflict between India and Pakistan. With the outbreak of the war between India and Pakistan, U.S. policy focused on global concerns of the precedent that the event would have for other regions. To repeat Kissinger's considerations during the WSAG meeting:

> We must consider what other countries may be thinking of our action... We must consider what would be the impact of the current situation in the large complex of world affairs... We must look at the problem in terms of Security Council guarantees in the Mid-East and the impact on other areas.[19]

Moreover, American inaction during an attack on an ally would be a sign of weakness to the USSR and the People's Republic of China. This consideration became

---

[18]Ibid., p. 147.

[19]Anderson Papers, see Marta R. Nicholas and Philip Oldenburg, Bangladesh: The Birth of a Nation (Madras: M. Seshachalam and Co., 1972), p. 129.

particularly important when Kissinger felt that the threat presented by India was its intent to dismember West Pakistan.[20] Barnds reads the Anderson Papers and Nixon's 1972 foreign policy address to Congress as indicating primary concern with the destruction of West Pakistan.[21]

> ...during the week of December 6, we received convincing evidence that India was seriously contemplating the seizure of Pakistan-held portions of Kashmir and the destruction of Pakistan's military forces in the West. We could not ignore this evidence. Nor could we ignore the fact that when we repeatedly asked India and its supporters for clear assurances to the contrary, we did not receive them. We had to take action to prevent a wider war.[22]

The "convincing evidence" was a CIA report. The report served to confirm the suspicion that Kissinger had been expressing during the WSAG meetings. The suspicion was that India was planning to invade West Pakistan. However, even before receiving this CIA report of December 9, Sisco had stated at the December 6, 1971 meeting "that from a political point of view our efforts would have to be directed at keeping the Indians from

---

[20] Kalb and Kalb, op. cit., p. 259.

[21] Barnds, in Christianity and Crisis, op. cit., p. 147.

[22] Nixon, A Report to the Congress (1972), op. cit., p. 147.

'extinguishing' West Pakistan."[23]

The Enterprise Episode

The Enterprise episode followed as an American response to the developments in South Asia. The Enterprise episode is one of the more perplexing aspects of U.S. policies and actions in the Indo-Pakistani War. The officially stated purpose for the Enterprise's entry into the Bay of Bengal was the evacuation of the American community from Dacca. That a nuclear aircraft carrier of the Enterprise's size would hardly be necessary for such a task did not seem to trouble the Administration. Many still support the evacuation thesis.[24] As with many other aspects of U.S. foreign policy and actions in South Asia during 1971, alternative explanations for the Enterprise episode abound. One school of thought argues that the Enterprise episode fits very well within the Nixon-Kissinger frame-set that advocates the utility of

---

[23] Anderson Papers, see Nicholas and Oldenburg, op. cit., p. 126.

[24] Interview with U.S. Government official, March 1975.

force and favors a show of force.[25] Moreover, the U.S. also sought to project an image of a global power. Accordingly, the purpose of the show of force was not to convey a threat to India against proceeding to attempt to dismember West Pakistan but, more importantly, to convey to the Chinese leaders the seriousness and vital concern with which the Nixon Administration viewed the South Asia events. Moreover, the Nixon Administration had to demonstrate the serious possibility of success in the upcoming efforts to establish U.S.-Chinese relations and used the convergence of interests concerning Pakistan for that purpose. The Enterprise maneuver was simply another move in that effort. If this was indeed the objective, it was apparently successful. The U.S. seems to have convinced China that the Enterprise episode saved West Pakistan from India, and the Chinese leaders in turn convinced Bhutto that the U.S. saved the integrity of West Pakistan from Indian attack.[26]

Jack Anderson argues that the Enterprise was used

---

[25] Interview with U.S. Government official, March 1975.

[26] See Bhutto interview with Sulzberger in The New York Times, February 13, 1972.

primarily to divert Indian attention and to signal the Soviet Union to restrain India. The Enterprise, according to this thesis, was intended to divert the Indian Air Force away from Pakistani targets, cause the Indian aircraft carrier Vikrant to move from its position off the East Pakistan coast, and, possibly, force the Indians to lift their blockade of East Pakistan's ports. Furthermore, the Nixon Administration sought to ensure that the Enterprise task force would be sighted at the Strait of Malacca by alerting both the Indians and Russians of the task force's approach.[27]

Many of those who rule out the thesis that the Enterprise was used as a signal to China argue for the acceptance of the evacuation thesis and suggest that the Enterprise was first moved from the Far East simply for contingency purposes. Only once the ship was in the area was it used for its political impact according to this school of thought.[28] The message of the Enterprise was not directed at China but rather at India and the

---

[27] Jack Anderson with George Clifford, The Anderson Papers (New York: Random House, 1973), p. 263.

[28] Interview with U.S. Government official, March 1975.

Soviet Union. The U.S. Government apparently received a CIA report that purportedly indicated that India had the intent to attack West Pakistan, although it is not clear whether the CIA report indicated that this was an adopted decision by the Indian Government or only proposed by Indian officials at a cabinet meeting. One U.S. official who had access to this intelligence report argues that the information came from high Indian sources that the Indian cabinet was about to deliberate on the issue of initiating an attack on West Pakistan.[29] Kissinger's argument, according to this account, was that it would be preferable to signal the Indians through use of the Enterprise prior to the Indian cabinet's decision to attack West Pakistan rather than to wait for the Indian decision to be made and the attack begun. His reasoning was that at that point it would be too late for an American decision to have an effect.[30] Furthermore, at one WSAG meeting Kissinger lamented the fact that the U.S. had not signaled India prior to the attack on

---

[29] Interview with U.S. Government official, May 1975.

[30] Interview with U.S. Government official, May 1975.

East Pakistan arguing that perhaps such a signal would have prevented that Indian attack as well.

Many high level American officials believed that once finished with the mission in East Pakistan, India would turn her attention to an attack on West Pakistan. This view by the American officials may have been reinforced by the projection that situated in Mrs. Ganghi's position, they would attack. In addition, there were intelligence reports of Indian troop movements in preparation for an attack on West Pakistan following the operation in East Pakistan. Therefore, the Enterprise is viewed as a signal to India and her supporter the Soviet Union of the serious consequences attached to such an attack and the readiness of the U.S. to defend West Pakistan. This is essentially the thesis of the traditional gun boat diplomacy and showing the flag on the part of an Administration that liked to move ships around and believed in the sending of signals.[31]

In conclusion, the Enterprise may have been sent to the crisis area as a contingency plan to evacuate the Americans in Dacca. However, it is unlikely that this

---

[31] Interview with U.S. Government official, March 1975.

was its purpose. Evidence from interviews with participating U.S. decision-makers suggests that the Enterprise was moved into the area in order simply to see what would happen. This action would conform to a belief set that favored a showing of the flag and sending signals. Once in the area the Enterprise was utilized for its symbolic and signaling value. The question arises, however, to whom the message was directed and what the signal was. One observer even suggests that the entire U.S. policy toward the Indo-Pakistani War of 1971 and the "tilt toward Pakistan" can be viewed as one grandiose signal.[32] If the explanations provided above for the Enterprise's mission are unsatisfactory then one official's tongue in cheek observation that the incident can be explained as "little boys playing with big ships in a bathtub" may provide a simplistic counter-thesis.[33] Nevertheless, this simplistic statement provides some insight into attitudes that decision-makers had toward the 1971 South Asian events. As we will examine in the next chapter, it is certainly plausible, and indeed

---

[32] Interview with U.S. Government official, May 1975.

[33] Interview with U.S. Government official, March 1975.

likely, that decision-makers may in fact treat crisis management as a game. Obviously, however, it is a game with high degrees of risk and uncertainty. Decision-makers frequently analogize to a chess game where action-reaction is a key. Gun boat diplomacy is a traditional method of sending signals when verbal communications do not seem to have an impact. Furthermore, this type of signal also indicated American resolve to China. Consequently, the Enterprise does indeed seem to have been utilized as a signal, although its original move into the area was probably due to the absence of other effective American alternatives for attempting to exert influence on the USSR and India during the Indo-Pakistani War.

The Nixon Report: Taking Action

The Nixon Report suggests that once the war erupted the United States had the option of being neutral and doing nothing or taking a stand against the war. "Acquiescence had ominous implications for the survival of Pakistan, for the stability of many other countries in the world, for the integrity of international processes for keeping the peace, and for relations among the great powers."[34] Were it not for the Anderson Papers, these considerations would be considered after-the-fact justifications. Some still insist that they are windowdressing for Nixon's anti-India prejudice.[35] However, the Administration seems to have taken the notion of balance of power in a new multipolar world seriously.

> The global implications of this war were clear to the world community. The resort to military solutions if accepted, would only tempt other nations in other delicately poised regions of tension to try the same. The credibility of international efforts to promote or guarantee regional peace in strife-torn regions would be undermined. The danger of war in the Middle East, in particular, would be measurably increased. Restraints would be weakened all around the world.[36]

In addition to the effect which American policy is seen to have in other regions, the Nixon Report also stresses the importance of the new rules of the game to be established for the era of détente and the great power relations of the U.S., USSR and China. In discussing the

---

[34] Nixon, A Report to the Congress (1972), op. cit., pp. 148-149.

[35] Anderson, op. cit.

[36] Nixon, A Report to the Congress (1972), op. cit., pp. 148-149.

implications for great power relations, the Nixon Report focuses on Soviet behavior. Soviet policy is criticized by the Administration for the proclivity which it has manifested "to allow events to boil up toward crisis in the hope of political gain."[37] The Soviet Union conveyed the message to the White House that the Indo-Soviet Treaty of Peace, Friendship and Cooperation would serve to restrain India and provide for stability and peace. In reality, however, the announcement of the treaty was accompanied by the news that the Soviet Union would provide India with arms. The Treaty served to provide India with political support from the Soviet Union during the crisis, and the parties entered into the agreement with that specific intent. This treaty of August 9, 1971 may have been the turning point in Soviet behavior toward the developing events in South Asia. For example, in July 1971 an American intelligence report had stated that the Soviet Union did not want war on the subcontinent and emphasized Soviet cooperation in peace efforts aimed at preventing hostilities between India and Pakistan.

---

[37] Ibid., p. 149.

U.S.-USSR Relations

By keeping American commitments in line with her capabilities and calling for a greater degree of self-help from American client-states, the Nixon Doctrine had acknowledged that the U.S. would have a lower profile in international politics. Simultaneously, the U.S. had embarked on building better relations with the Soviet Union. But the barometer for measuring the Soviet commitment to the new era of U.S.-Soviet relations, labeled détente, would be Soviet actions in the international arena.

> It would be dangerous to world peace if our efforts to promote a detente between the superpowers were interpreted as an opportunity for the strategic expansion of Soviet power. If we had failed to take a stand, such an interpretation could only have been encouraged, and the genuine relaxation of tensions we have been seeking could have been jeopardized.[38]

This was the manifestation of the paradox apparent in the Nixon-Kissinger détente formulation. Successful détente would achieve a lasting easing in tensions between

---

[38] Ibid., p. 149.

the U.S. and the Soviet Union but the process of achieving this -- also called détente by the Administration -- might be marked by periodic "regression" into tension, or even confrontation. By 1973, the President's State of the World Message had already concluded that the earlier-- and more tense -- stage of détente had been passed successfully and that a new structure for peace had been securely laid. This structure or "web" of U.S.-Soviet interests, in the Administration's view, made reversion to the earlier period less likely. The irony is that the era that witnessed U.S.-Soviet confrontations in regional conflicts was dubbed the era of détente by the Administration.

Kissinger's disappointment with the Soviet failure to restrain India from attacking East Pakistan did not hinder his efforts to exercise influence over the Soviet Union to utilize its "leverage" on India. Despite Indian denials of an intention to dismember West Pakistan, Kissinger was convinced that such an intent existed. During an interview aboard Air Force One on December 14, 1971, Kissinger told reporters that Nixon would take a "new look" at his summit plans if the Soviets did not restrain India within the next few days and that the "entire US-Soviet relationship might well be reexamined."

Kissinger's explanation for the motive behind Soviet behavior was the Soviet desire to humiliate China by showing the international community China's lack of power to prevent the Indian attack on Pakistan.[39] After the news concerning the possible reconsideration of the Moscow summit was broadcast and published, the White House denied that Nixon was considering canceling the trip to Russia.

Nevertheless, after the war, Kissinger argued that his warnings to the Soviets served to pressure the Soviets to utilize their leverage on India to refrain from dismembering West Pakistan. By claiming that he had "saved" West Pakistan, Kissinger could take the credit for rescuing an ally of the United States and the state that had served as the conduit for the American initiatives to China. Bhutto has given credence to Kissinger's thesis by stating that the Chinese leadership told him that American actions saved West Pakistan.[40] However, the December 9, 1971 CIA report notwithstanding, it seems

---

[39] Kalb and Kalb, op. cit., pp. 261-262.

[40] Bhutto interview with Sulzberger in The New York Times, February 13, 1972.

unlikely that India had the specific intent to dismember West Pakistan.

At the December 6, 1971 WSAG meeting General Westmoreland pointed out the limited logistics capabilities of the Indian military. Based on intelligence reports, he estimated that it would take India up to a month to move most or all of her troops from the East to the West. General Westmoreland indicated that the "Indian position in the West was not unadvantageous." However, he felt that Indian military initiatives in the south were of a diversionary character with the purpose of relieving Pakistani pressure from Kashmir. At the December 8, 1971 WSAG meeting Kissinger expressed his belief that India might be attempting "to render Pakistan impotent." Later during the same meeting when he began a discussion of contingencies should India seek to dismember West Pakistan, Sisco expressed his doubts that this was the objective of the Indians. Moreover, American intelligence reports indicated that despite the widespread fighting in East Pakistan, neither side had committed major ground units in the West.

The China Factor

The Nixon Report also notes the importance of the China factor within the global context of U.S. policy in South Asia. The correct significance to be attached to the China factor remains the most puzzling issue in the complex web of interrelationship among the global and regional powers involved in the 1971 South Asian events.

> ... it was our view that the war in South Asia was bound to have serious implications for the evolution of the policy of the Peoples Republic of China. That country's attitude toward the global system was certain to be profoundly influenced by its assessment of the principles by which this system was governed whether force and threat ruled or whether restraint was the international standard.[41]

The Administration's concern with the effect that its action in the South Asian war would have on its developing relations with the People's Republic of China can be seen from the above citation and from interviews with participants in the American governments's decision-making process.[42] However, there are those government

---

[41] Nixon, A Report to the Congress (1972), op. cit., p. 149.

[42] Interviews with U.S. Government officials, March and May 1975.

officials who argue that the China factor was only used after the fact as a justification for a policy that is otherwise devoid of any merit.[43]

The Nixon White House emphasized several times that the U.S. was not participating in either the Moscow or Peking summit meetings in order to align itself against another state. The Administration labeled "fanciful speculation"[44] the notion of an alignment between the U.S. and China during the 1971 South Asia crisis. Such repeated denials may only have served to arouse the Soviet suspicion of a Sino-American alignment. The significance of renewed Sino-American relations after more than twenty years was coupled with the American effort to establish a triangular global relationship with the U.S. and China having the common objective of checking and countering Soviet expansion.

> A more constructive approach to great-power relations in South Asia -- and elsewhere -- will be one of the goals I hope to further in any discussion in both Peking and Moscow.
> A tragic irony of 1971 was that the conflict

---

[43] Interviews with U.S. Government officials, March 1975.

[44] Nixon, A Report to the Congress (1972), op. cit., p. 151.

> in South Asia erupted against a background
> of major developments, global and regional,
> which has offered unprecedented hope:
> --Globally, we could see the beginnings
> of a new relationship between the
> United States and the Peoples Republic
> of China; concrete progress on
> important issues in U.S.-Soviet
> relations; a maturing relationship
> between the United States and
> East Asia as the Nixon Doctrine
> took effect and the United States
> sharply reduced its military
> involvement in Vietnam...[45]

The world view of the Nixon Doctrine called for a multipolar world and placed a high premium on the participation of the People's Republic of China as a stabilizing force and counter to the Soviet Union generally, and especially in Southeast Asia following the American withdrawal from the area. On the one hand, defenders of the Administration's 1971 South Asian policy argue that the priority of U.S. policy was global and that the policy was dictated by considerations of the U.S.-Soviet-Chinese relationship. Critics, on the other hand, suggest that the U.S. South Asian policy was misguided since it not only failed to take account of the merits

---

[45] Ibid., p. 151.

of respective positions of India and Pakistan, but that there was no necessary linkage between U.S. policy in South Asia and the forthcoming attempts to establish U.S.-Chinese relations. In the alternative, the argument is also made that the establishment of direct relations with China could have been undertaken without bringing to the forefront the strain in relations with India to such a high degree.[46]

Nixon's and Kissinger's view of the new global relations were in harmony. The key for the stability of the global system was viewed in terms of the relations of the major powers and their relationship to be established was labeled détente. With the increased importance of the relations among the major powers, regional conflicts were to be muted in order not to interfere with the improved relations of the major powers. Cooperation with the major power, in this case the Soviet Union, was to be judged according to its behavior in regional crisis in order to be able to observe whether it was in fact placing

---

[46]Rudolph and Rudolph, op. cit., pp. 47-58 and Barnds, op. cit., in Christianity and Crisis, p. 149.

its improved relations with the United States ahead of the possible political and strategic gains that it might be able to reap by exacerbating the local conflict.

The Nixon Report: The Unmentioned Factors

The factors not mentioned involving U.S. foreign policy in the Indo-Pakistani War are also of particular interest. Quite naturally, the 1972 Nixon Report does not mention the possibility that the Administration's pro-Pakistani policy can be explained by the better personal rapport between U.S. and Pakistani leaders than between U.S. and Indian leaders.[47] This possibility was discussed by Kissinger at the December 7, 1971 briefing and is considered more fully in the next section.

Moreover, Pakistan's role in the establishment of the U.S.-Chinese relationship is also not discussed.

> Given the post-war history of bitter antagonism between Washington and Peking, considerable preliminary probing and testing would have been essential to convince each of the other's seriousness, and to convey a preliminary sense of the shape of the new relationship. Thus an interlocutor

---

[47]Barnds, op. cit., in Christianity and Crisis, p. 146.

trusted by both sides, and with whom each felt it could communicate, was essential.[48]

The U.S. efforts to establish relations with the People's Republic of China occurred in a period of history when the Administration had made the decision to limit its overseas commitments. Chinese interests in South Asia had been in conflict with those of India. Following the 1962 Sino-Indian War and the Indo-Pakistani War of 1965, China provided Pakistan with substantial military aid. Thus, U.S. and Chinese interests coincided and converged in their support for Pakistan, the country that came to serve the role of intermediary in arranging the U.S.-Chinese rapprochment.

The opening of relations between the U.S. and China was undertaken by means of unilateral acts by the U.S. primarily in the economic sphere. With the recognition of the Sino-Soviet schism, Nixon, who viewed the Soviet Union as the primary adversary of the U.S., realized the leverage he would be able to utilize over the USSR in a multipolar world where U.S. and Chinese interests did and could converge.[49] The Chinese interest in welcoming the

---

[48] Ibid., pp. 145-146.

[49] Kalb and Kalb, op. cit., pp. 215-220.

American initiative toward China emanated from the perceived Soviet threat and desire to utilize the U.S. as a counter to the Soviet Union.[50]

Accordingly, the stage was set to apply the Nixon Doctrine's three pillars: 1) strength, 2) partnership, and 3) negotiations. Thus, the explanation that is given by defenders of the Administration's policies is that India as an "ally" of the Soviet Union was not to be allowed to change unilaterally the status quo in South Asia. Furthermore, the U.S. position and support for an ally had to be demonstrated both to the Soviet Union and China as well as to the rest of the world.

The importance of the establishment of the China connection in relation to U.S. foreign policy in the Indo-Pakistani War of 1971 is derived not only from the framework in which the issue was cast but also in terms of the time that Kissinger spent on the matter during the months of November and December 1971.

> Personal diplomacy, the trademark of the Nixon-Kissinger team, had its price. On the Asian subcontinent a brutal war was

---

[50] Ibid., p. 231.

brewing; but, for a good part of the year Kissinger simply did not have time to deal with it, and, of course, he did not trust the bureaucracy to manage it. The turn of developments was catastrophic for American policy in the area.[51]

Although among the arguments of this work is that 1) South Asia has traditionally had a low priority in American foreign policy, 2) Kissinger and other high-ranking Administration members had little or no time to deal with South Asia, 3) Kissinger did not trust the bureaucracy to manage South Asia and that a schism emerged between the area experts and non-experts, and 4) U.S. policy toward the emerging war was in substantial part a function of the emerging U.S.-USSR-China relations, it is doubtful, that the developments were "catastrophic for American policy in the area."[52]

Summary

Notwithstanding the reservations concerning the Nixon Report's version of the Administration's management of the South Asia middle-level crisis of 1971, the Report

---

[51] Ibid., p. 257.
[52] Ibid., p. 257.

does provide a cogent explanation for a conceptual framework through which the events were processed. A key element in this conceptual framework is the linkage it provides between global and regional international politics.

The outcome preferred by the Nixon Administration was not confined to regional considerations. Rather, the strength of the global triangular relationship and the legitimacy of the world order could be tested in this regional conflict. A major goal was to prevent a global power, the USSR, from taking unilateral advantage of the situation and along with its ally, India, acquiring what the Nixon Administration perceived to be hegemony in South Asia. According to this explanation, the Administration's actions were politically rational and should be understood in terms of their aim for arriving at the objectives which the Administration had determined to be the priorities. Therefore, the Administration's actions had several objectives, including the support of an American ally and demonstrating this support to the rest of the world at a time of American retrenchment. Other objectives included balancing the Soviet Union in South Asia, preventing Indian hegemony in South Asia, assuring successful opening of relations with China, and establishing a strong foundation for the "rules of the game" in global and regional politics.

The Nixon Report and the WSAG meetings do reveal that Nixon and Kissinger were evaluating the South Asian events in terms of the objectives they were seeking to accomplish and the probability of achieving their preferred outcome. Accordingly, the contribution made by the Rational Man Model to the concept of priority formulation is on the emphasis it places on the examination of alternative outcomes. Furthermore, the Rational Man Model also focuses on the probability of achieving success by choosing a particular alternative. In the next chapter we will examine the contributions provided by the Psychological Model to an assessment of the preferred outcome or desirabilities of a decision-maker. In deriving a systematized statement of an individual decision-maker's priority formulation, we will utilize the concepts of expected value and expected utility to determine his preference ranking.

VII: THE PSYCHOLOGICAL MODEL: THE PIQUE THEORY

In contradistinction to the Rational Man Model, the Psychological Model emphasizes the motivations of the individual decision-makers in an organizational context. The field of psychology focuses on the study of the individual's behavioral characteristics by examining individual drives and motivations.[1] The Psychological Model, therefore, focuses on the decision-makers' background characteristics, cognition, individual beliefs, and personality characteristics. Accordingly, we are interested in the mental process whereby an individual acquires knowledge, and how he applies this knowledge to stimuli that confront him. Therefore, such factors as an individual decision-maker's perception, reasoning, and intuition will play a major role in determining the "desirabilities" or value that he attaches to a particular outcome.

The Psychological Model examines the dynamics of international relations by focusing primarily on the behavior of elites. Such variables as national and elite self-images, perceptions of history, perceptions of other nations

---

[1] See Raymond Tanter, "Crisis Management: A Critical Review of Academic Literature," in *The Jerusalem Journal of International Relations*, Fall 1975, Vol. 1, No. 1, pp. 71-101.

and their leaders, the belief set dealing with necessary and proper means of acting during conflict situations, and attitudes about the specific problem in the conflict are some of the factors involved in explaining leadership behavior from a psychological perspective. An individual decision-maker will develop a belief set and response set. This response set contains a few, simple models that allow a decision-maker to respond effectively to the complex stimuli that he confronts. By choosing a basic paradigm from among those in his response set and applying it to a complex problem, a decision-maker is able to eliminate much of the uncertainty associated with a complex phenomenon.

A psychological approach has traditionally been used to analyze conflict. Studies undertaken at the interpersonal, intergroup, and international levels demonstrate that the resolution of the conflict may be distinguished between cooperative or competitive outcomes. The outcome depends on whether or not the parties are at least minimally satisfied with the outcome. We will examine the interaction among the preferences of individual decision-makers in the next chapter which deals with the Incremental Model. There we will analyze the concept of agenda-building and the process of reaching a consensus.

Elite Images

Brecher's framework stresses the importance of the "psychological environment" which includes the "attitudinal prism" and "elite images."[2] The "attitudinal prism" includes the factors of ideology, historical legacy and personality predispositions. The "elite images" consist of perceptions of the "operational environment" which in turn encompasses the external and internal environments. The former includes the global system, subordinate regional systems, and bilateral relations, while the latter consists of military capability, economic capability, political structure, interest groups, and competing groups. Steinbruner's work on belief sets and value formation supplements Brecher's framework. The work done by Steinbruner was preceded by the work of Shapiro and Bonham.[3] They focused on the relationship between cognitive complexity and the complexity of policy recommendation. In particular, their emphasis was on the effect of historical events on

---

[2] Brecher, op. cit., pp. 11-13.

[3] Michael J. Shapiro and G. Matthew Bonham, "Cognitive Process and Foreign Policy Decision-Making," International Studies Quarterly, June 2, 1973, pp. 147-176.

the images and perceptions of the foreign policy decision-makers. They suggest the importance of the impact of history on current attitudes and behavior as a consequence of the tendency that decision-makers have to analogize from the past.[4] George has taken the notion of the leaders' belief system a step further by examining several cognitive constraints on rationality.[5]

The psychological approach seems to allow some generalization in terms of what factors an analyst might examine. However, it seems that the shared images or beliefs may by no means encompass the views of all the decision-makers and the findings may be idiosyncratic to a large extent. Nevertheless, there may be a core of shared images and beliefs that remain constant despite changes in leadership.

Jervis and White have focused on perceptions of the enemy as a key explanatory variable for foreign policy

---

[4] R. Jervis, "Hypotheses on Misperception," World Politics, April 1968, pp. 454-479.

[5] Alexander George, "The 'Operational Code': A Neglected Approach to the Study of Political Leaders and Decision-Making," International Studies Quarterly, June 2, 1969, pp. 190-222.

decision-making.[6] For example, Jervis has argued that previously held theories and images, perhaps shaped by previous experience, as well as the ambiguity of the data which create a situation of uncertainty, are among the sources of misperception.[7] Furthermore, such concepts as projection of one's self-image have been advanced to explain certain attitudes held by decision-makers toward others.

On the one hand, Nixon's 1972 State of the World Message presents the arguments associated with the Rational Man Model. The Nixon Report emphasizes the global factors and the weighing of alternatives that were considered during the deliberations as the method by which U.S. policy was formulated during the 1971 South Asia crisis. On the other hand, Vinod Gupta's Anderson Papers: A Study of Nixon's Blackmail of India equates what he delineates as Nixon's values, beliefs, and actions with U.S. foreign policy in South Asia during 1971.[8]

---

[6] Jervis, op. cit.; Ralph K. White, Nobody Wanted War: Misperception in Vietnam and Other Wars (New York: Doubleday, 1970).

[7] Jervis, op. cit.

[8] Vinod Gupta, Anderson Papers: A Study of Nixon's Blackmail of India (Delhi: ISSD, 1972).

Gupta, despite the vitriolic tone, awkward style, and simplistic thesis of his owrk, is not alone in arguing that Nixon's bias in favor of Pakistan and his antipathy for India and Indians accounts for American foreign policy during the 1971 war and the events that preceded it. Thus, for example, one Nixon Administration official suggests that Nixon has a "thing," that is, a tender spot, for Pakistan.[9] Another former Nixon Administration official argues that the Anderson Papers do indeed reveal that the Administration's decisions regarding the South Asian events were made in pique and the lack of importance that has traditionally been attached to the region may be a plausible explanation for the way the decision was made.[10] An additional factor stressed by the advocates of the psychological explanation is the importance of the personal relationship between U.S. and Pakistani leaders. This group argues that the U.S. would have adopted the same policy toward the events in South Asia regardless of the China factor.

---

[9] Interview with U.S. Government official, March 1975.

[10] Interview with U.S. Government official, March 1975.

The background of Nixon's bias for Pakistan may be important in having predisposed Nixon to support Pakistan during her confrontation with India in 1971. Nixon's "thing" for Pakistan can be traced to his actions and beliefs relating to Pakistan's security and defense needs when he was Vice-President. During his visit to Pakistan in 1953 Nixon pledged his support to Pakistan's leaders and apparently backed that country's request for U.S. arms at a National Security Council meeting. Nixon's support for Pakistan during the 1950's had the dual purpose of defending Pakistan from the Soviet Union within the American security system and establishing a counter to Nehru's neutralism. "No other American leader is loved more in Pakistan than Nixon, and his personal feelings for Pakistan might, apart from the new China policy, help explain U.S. policy during the Bangladesh crisis of 1971."[11] In August 1969 Nixon pointed out to Yahya his past role in establishing a "special relationship with Pakistan" and added that "Pakistan's friendship with the U.S. will be dearer" to

---

[11] G.W. Choudhury, India, Pakistan, Bangladesh, and the Major Powers (New York: Free Press, 1975), p. 86.

him as President.[12] By October 1970 U.S. arms shipments to Pakistan were resumed.

In focusing on Nixon's "thing" for Pakistan, the argument has been advanced that Nixon's "love for Pakistan"[13] is matched by his antipathy for India because of the snub he received from Indian officials during his 1953 visit as Vice-President and especially his 1964 visit as a private citizen when he was ignored by the Indian Foreign Ministry. The lavish reception accorded to Nixon in Pakistan was diametrically opposed to the treatment he had been subjected to in India.

> Although these personal things should and must not influence the national policy of a country but (sic) the fact remains that Mr. Nixon's inimical attitude towards India emanates from such trivial matters. Besides, Mr. Nixon suffers from misplaced egotism of 'power superiority.' He likes strong men. Field Marshal Ayub Khan was known as a strong man.[14]

Furthermore, argues Gupta, another important factor is

---

[12] As quoted in ibid., p. 202, from unpublished records of the Nixon-Yahya talks, Lahore, Pakistan, August 1969.

[13] Gupta, op. cit., p. 22.

[14] Ibid., p. 25.

Nixon's cold warrior past which prompted him to regard Pakistan as a U.S. ally during his tenure as Vice-President in response to Indian neutralism.

Nixon's personality traits are particularly difficult to establish as revealed by his behavior during his turbulent political career. Gupta states that Nixon's "rhetoric for peace essentially springs from the wanton search for power."[15] However, this characteristic hardly seems to distinguish Nixon from other political leaders. Nixon's conflicts with the liberal intellectuals as a result of the Hiss case and his penchant for secrecy, which became known as a credibility gap, also characterized Nixon's political career.

Those who look to the psychological explanations as a key factor tend to view a nation-state's foreign policy as embodied in the beliefs and actions of its national leaders.

> In 1969, when Nixon went to Pakistan on a state visit, it is understood, feelers were thrown to the Pakistani President to arrange a dialogue between the U.S.A. and China.

---

[15]Ibid., p. 31.

> Yahya Khan was too glad to offer his services to bring his two friends [Nixon and Mao] together. It is understood that Nixon agreed in his talks at Lahore to provide bombers and fighters to the General, in spite of embargo in lieu (sic) of his services to arrange the invitation. The General had personal contacts with Chairman Mao. The Chinese leadership for obvious reasons was also keen to start a dialogue with Nixon. General Yahya Khan assumed the role of a broker between the two.[16]

This personalized thesis of foreign policy is also clearly revealed in the following statement.

> The 'Enterprise episode' will go down in the U.S. history as the most absurd military decision taken at the highest level. Mr. Nixon wanted to test our nerves at the most difficult time of Indian history but he miserably failed to scare India. He wanted to bully us, but his monstrous aircraft carrier had to beat a hasty retreat in humiliation.[17]

The thesis that Nixon's decisions stemmed from his prejudices is at the core of the argument that U.S. foreign policy in the 1971 South Asia crisis can be explained in terms of Nixon's personal preference for Pakistan and antipathy toward India. In other words, according to this thesis, the "tilt toward Pakistan" was adopted as U.S. policy because of Nixon's bias which was imposed on other

---

[16] Ibid., p. 86.

[17] Ibid., p. 112.

U.S. decision-makers and not because of U.S. national and global interests.

> President Nixon, apparently because he liked Pakistan's strong man General Yahya Khan and disliked India's Prime Minister Indira Gandhi placed the U.S. on the side of a minor military dictatorship against the world's lagest democracy.
> The President overrode the advice of the State Department's professionals who urged him to use his special influence with Yahya to stop the Pakistani persecution and to grant the Bengalis a measure of autonomy. When the Indian Army finally came to the aid of the Bengalis, the professionalists (sic) pleaded with Mr. Nixon to remain neutral if for no other reason than that Pakistan looked like a sure loser.
> Instead he supported the repressor.
> In a fit of petulance, the President sent a naval task force to the Bay of Bengal and risked a military confrontation with Soviet warships...[18]

Jack Anderson's thesis also fits most readily into the Psychological Model as the key explanatory factor. His suggestion that Nixon brought the U.S. to the brink of a world war seems to border on hysterics. Anderson argues that

> Kennedy's handling of the Cuban confrontation made a deep impression on Richard Nixon. He spoke admiringly of the cold courage Kennedy had demonstrated when he faced an imminent

---

[18]Ibid., pp. 163-164.

nuclear holocaust. In December 1971 President Nixon had an opportunity to stage his own nuclear showdown in the Bay of Bengal.[19]

But Nixon tended to exhibit indecisiveness during Superpower confrontations and the South Asia 1971 events were not an exception. Those who use the Psychological Model to explain Nixon's behavior are also those who were in opposition to U.S. policy in the subcontinent in 1971. The argument is made by this school of thought that Nixon overreacted in attempting to deal with the crisis.[20]

In suggesting the importance of the Psychological Model and its focus on Nixon, various analysts have made the assumption that Nixon was in total control of U.S. foreign policy in South Asia and could dictate the policy and the actions to be undertaken. Nixon's penchant for secrecy and his desire to decide issues alone after having received information from his staff has been indicated previously.[21] Consequently, the Nixon Administration's officials came in contact not with Nixon but with Kissinger.

---

[19] Jack Anderson with George Clifford, The Anderson Papers (New York: Random House, 1973), p. 208.

[20] See, for example, ibid., p. 259.

[21] Johnson, op. cit., p. 210.

Because Nixon and Kissinger did seem to operate as a team, it is difficult to separate Kissinger's beliefs and values from Nixon's with respect to South Asia. The possibility exists that their attitudes and beliefs in this case were identical.

> Kissinger's anti-India zeal troubled some subordinates. 'Sometimes Kissinger acted like a wild man,' a source on Kissinger's staff told me. 'His animus toward India seemed irrational.'[22]

The advocates of the Psychological Model argue that Nixon's penchant for secrecy was utilized in order to implement a "tilt toward Pakistan" policy while simultaneously maintaining to the American public and Congress that the Administration was absolutely neutral regarding the Indo-Pakistani conflict. Nixon had, however, struck a warm friendship with Yahya Khan. Furthermore, he sought to establish and demonstrate to China a common interest with China in the region. But Nixon's anti-India sentiment had also predisposed him to aid Pakistan.

The anti-India policy, moreover, was premeditated. As early as August 1971, four months before the

---

[22]Anderson, op. cit., p. 210.

outbreak of the war, Nixon told his foreign policy planners that he intended to back Yahya in his conflict with India.[23]

In dealing with the thesis that the Nixon Administration sought to repay Yahya Khan for having acted as the interlocutor between the U.S. and China, the argument has been made that Nixon's personal feelings toward the Pakistani and Indian leadership reinforced the tendency to "tilt toward Pakistan."[24]

> As the price for Yahya's friendship, Nixon turned away from India, the world's largest democracy. It was a decision Nixon made easily. Like other American leaders, the President had been irritated by India's frequent carping about the international conduct of the United States. Further, Nixon harbored deep resentment against India's prime minister, Mrs. Gandhi. She is a brilliant politician who, our sources say, outmaneuvered him in their private encounters in New Delhi and Washington. Nixon not only finds it difficult to regard women as statesmen, but resents being upstaged by foreign leaders who are more adroit than he is. Mrs. Gandhi annoyed him, both as a leader and as a woman.[25]

Those emphasizing the personal bonds that solidified U.S.-Pakistani relations point to the Yahya Khan-Farland

---

[23]Ibid., p. 212.

[24]Barnds, op. cit., in *Christianity and Crisis*, p. 148.

[25]Anderson, op. cit., p. 217.

in addition to the Yahya Khan-Nixon ties. "Yahya Khan had an extraordinary relationship with American Ambassador Joseph Farland; they met almost daily and sometimes shared a bottle of Scotch."[26] Anderson argues that Farland played the role of confidant for Yahya Khan, although Farland denies it. According to Farland, he and Yahya Khan "had a normal diplomatic relationship. We have met twice socially.... Normally, I met Yahya Khan on official business in the morning."[27]

The antipathy which Nixon apparently felt for India and Indira Gandhi was further exacerbated by the apparent misunderstanding that resulted from their November 1971 meeting in Washington. Many of the Administration's senior officials apparently shared the President's intense aversion to the Indians with whom they were negotiating. The prevailing view by the American officials was that the Indian negotiators were not only "cantankerous" in their negotiating style but also "hypocrites" who were coming to Washington for "windowdressing" as the Indian Army was

---

[26] Ibid., p. 220.

[27] As quoted in ibid., p. 222.

preparing to invade East Pakistan.[28] U.S. Government officials who were involved in these negotiations suggest that Nixon believed that he had succeeded "in buying time" during which to attempt further negotiations between the regional parties. The Indian invasion of East Pakistan convinced Nixon of Mrs. Gandhi's treachery and may account for the intensity of the Administration's anti-India sentiment. Kissinger stated that during the Nixon-Gandhi negotiations "we were not given the slightest inkling that such a military operation was in any way imminent...."[29] U.S. Ambassador to India Keating opposed the coloration which the Administration sought to add to its explanation of the events.[30]

Nixon did not want the U.S. to be neutral toward the events in the subcontinent. At the WSAG meetings Kissinger was persistent in attempting to open up a source or arms supplies for Pakistan in order to circumvent the American arms embargo. The question raised involved the

---

[28]Interview with U.S. Government official, March 1975.

[29]Nicholas and Oldenburg, op. cit., p. 140.

[30]See text of Keating's cable "U.S. Public Position on Road to War," in Anderson, op. cit., pp. 237-239.

legality of having third parties, such as Jordan, transfer arms to Pakistan. Kissinger's role as it related to Nixon's anti-India bias is somewhat unclear. Nevertheless, WSAG participants suggest that although Kissinger was utilizing the President's office and authority in order to impose the policy that had already been decided upon, Kissinger exhibited an anti-India bias as well.

> Those who worked closely with Kissinger throughout the India-Pakistan crisis thought there was a personal animosity toward India in his attitude. But he was usually careful to attribute any anti-India actions directly to the President.[31]

During his December 7, 1971 "background briefing," Kissinger sought to convey the Administration's approach to the South Asia problem.

> First of all, let us get a number of things straight. There have been some comments that the Administration is anti-Indian. This is totally inaccurate. India is a great country. It is the most populous free country. It is governed by democratic procedures.[32]

Kissinger stated that the U.S. "in many respects has had a love affair with India"[33] and argued that the

---

[31]Anderson, op. cit., p. 254.

[32]Nicholas and Oldenburg, op. cit., p. 135.

[33]Ibid., p. 135.

U.S. should not hesitate to support Pakistan simply because India has a population five times greater than Pakistan's.

One reporter asked Kissinger why he had not mentioned the China factor or the Nixon-Kissinger personal preference for Pakistan in his opening remarks. Kissinger replied as follows:

> With respect to the first question, we do not have the impression that the Peoples Republic of China considers agreement with us a prerequisite for a successful visit on other issues... we do not consider that the Peoples Republic of China has a veto over our policies....
> Secondly, speaking first about myself, the first time I visited the Indian subcontinent I was the subject, in 1962, as can easily be checked in newspaper files, to the most violent newspaper criticisms in Pakistan for my allegedly Harvard-produced preference for Indians, and so much so that I even suggested that I might cancel my visit to Pakistan.
> There is no personal preference on my part for Pakistan, and the views that I expressed at the beginning, of the American position-- that is, about the critical importance of India as a country in the world and in the subcontinent-- have always been strongly held by me, and I, therefore, enthusiastically support those as an expression of bipartisan American policy in the postwar period.
> As for the President, I was not aware of his preference for Pakistan leaders over Indian leaders, and I, therefore, asked him this morning what this might be based on. He pointed out-- as you know, I was not acquainted with the President before his present position-- but he pointed out to me that on his trip in

1967, he was received very warmly by the Prime
Minister and by the President of India; that
the reports that he was snubbed at any point
are without any foundation, and that in any
event, the warmth of the reception that we
extended to the Indian Prime Minister two weeks
before the attacks on Pakistan started should
make clear what enormous value we attach to
Indian friendship.
While I can understand that there can be
sincere differences of opinion about the wise
course to take, I do not think we do ourselves
any justice if we ascribe policies to the
personal pique of individuals.[34]

The Psychological Model in this case looks to Nixon's personal motivations for seeking to impose his "tilt toward Pakistan" policy on the Administration's officials. Most of the officials involved in the WSAG deliberations were not sure whether the policy was dictated by Kissinger or Nixon. Some have suggested that both men were in agreement regarding the "tilt toward Pakistan" position. One official has disclosed that at one WSAG meeting Kissinger stated that the explanation for the U.S. policy adopted by Nixon was a matter of Nixon's personal loyalty for Yahya that couldn't be reversed by WSAG.[35] Nixon and Kissinger sought to "lecture" Indira Gandhi not to attack, but when she did,

---

[34] Ibid., p. 139.

[35] Interview with U.S. Government official, March 1975.

the Nixon-Kissinger team felt betrayed and pursued its pro-Pakistan tilt in a more discernible fashion. The Anderson Papers depict a decision made in pique, and Kissinger's remark that we do not do ourselves "any justice if we ascribe policies to the personal pique of individuals" notwithstanding, the pique theory may be a plausible explanation in light of the small degree of importance attached to South Asia.

Nixon's "gut feeling" favoring Pakistan was intensified by the increasing importance of the China connection.[36] Combined with Nixon's ego problems when challenged by others,[37] the President apparently increased his effort to assure that the pro-Pakistan policy be implemented by the bureaucracy.

Kissinger and Nixon were very disturbed by the resistance to their policy on the part of the bureaucracy. Kissinger was angered by what he considered to be the disloyalty to the President by those who did not carry

---

[36]Interview with U.S. Government official, March 1975.

[37]William L. Safire, Before the Fall: An Inside View of the Pre-Watergate White House (Garden City, N.Y.: Doubleday, 1975).

out his plans and orders.[38] Therefore, if it is true that the policy had been made as a result of the President's pique with India and the WSAG and NSC members were told that the reason for the "tilt" policy was a matter of the President's personal preference, then perhaps the resistance exhibited by the bureaucracy may be viewed more sympathetically.

Belief Sets

The cognitive aspect of the Psychological Model also deals with decision-making process in an organizational context. The theory examines the organizational hierarchy, the background and beliefs of the individuals involved, and the sources and channels of the inputs. Steinbruner distinguishes among three different models of thinking: 1) Grooved, 2) Uncommitted, and 3) Theoretical.[39] "Grooved thinking" is essentially equivalent to Allison's characterization of the application of Standard Operating Procedures, which will be examined in the next chapter dealing with

---

[38]Interview with U.S. Government official, May 1975.

[39]Steinbruner, op. cit., pp. 125-136.

the Incremental Model. Steinbruner argues that the President of the United States manifests behavior typical of "Uncommitted Thinking." He argues that such a decision-maker will fluctuate between competing belief patterns because Steinbruner assumes that high-level political leaders do not possess sufficient past experience which would allow them to have an opinion on the issue. Consequently, he argues that such decision-makers utilize a "larger, theoretical belief structure" and may "adopt different belief patterns for the same decision problem."[40]

However, these assumptions do not seem to apply to an individual such as Nixon, for example, who considered himself an expert on foreign policy. Furthermore, the observations seem to be equally, if not more, inaccurate as they relate to Kissinger. These general comments do not appear to be supported by the Nixon-Kissinger foreign policy formulation for U.S. policy in the Indo-Pakistani War of 1971, even though Nixon and Kissinger did indeed appear to share "larger, theoretical belief structures." Sharing the theoretical belief structure did not preclude

---

[40] *Ibid.*, p. 129.

these two decision-makers from having sufficient past experiences to have formulated <u>one</u> <u>definite</u> belief pattern that was imposed on the events.

The objections raised above to the "Uncommitted Thinking" mode seem to be answered by the notion of "Theoretical Thinking." This decision-maker is characterized by the adoption of "abstract and extensive belief patterns."[41] This is the decision-making mode that seems to explain Nixon's approach toward the South Asian events of 1971:

> The theoretical decision maker is an aggressive thinker who is very active in imposing an extensive pattern of meaning on immediate events. In the decision situation this means that he will connect concrete alternatives to an extensive pattern of calculations about the environment. Typically he is committed to one alternative which he invests with substantial significance in terms of very general values. In accord with the general cognitive pattern, his beliefs are organized around a single value.[42]

This type of decision-maker will connect his general value with the specific objective he seeks to accomplish.

---

[41]Ibid., p. 131.

[42]Ibid., pp. 131-132.

The "chain of inference" which the specific event has triggered, rather than the particular event itself, will be the basis for this decision-maker's behavior.

Cognitive theorists argue that foreign policy decision-makers have a belief set which they use in order to process incoming information. We have previously examined the advantages and disadvantages inherent in utilizing such a belief system. Halperin and Allison have listed a set of widely shared images of the bulk of the American public and its officials.[43] Among the shared images they have emphasized, the following seem significant for an understanding of U.S. foreign policy during the 1971 South Asian events.

> --The preeminent future of international politics is the conflict between Communism and the Free World.
>
> --The surest simple guide to U.S. interests in foreign policy is opposition to Communism.
>
> --The United States -- and only the United States-- has the power, ability, responsibility, and right to defend the Free World and maintain international order. The rest of the Free World must contribute as much as possible to the U.S. effort to defend against aggression.

---

[43]Morton H. Halperin, Bureaucratic Politics and Foreign Policy (Washington, D.C.: The Brookings Institution, 1974); Graham T. Allison, "Cool It: The Foreign Policy of Young America," Foreign Policy, Winter 1970-1971, pp. 144-160.

--The United States has an obligation to aid any Free Peoples resisting Communism at home or abroad.

--Peace is indivisible. Therefore collective defense is necessary. The new international order is based primarily on U.S. assumption of responsibility for other states' security, in support of which the United States must show itself ready to resist aggression. Thus any expansion of Communist influence must be resisted.

--Concessions made under pressure constitute appeasement which only wets the appetite of aggressors.

--The Third World really matters, because (a) it is the battleground between Communism and the Free World; (b) Western capital will generate economic development and political stability with a minimum of violence; and (c) instability is the great threat to progress in the Third World.[44]

American policy toward a regional area may be affected by changes in personnel within the Administration. In the chapter entitled "The Indo-Pakistani Conflict and The Cold War," we traced changes in American policy toward South Asia. Many of these changes were caused, as was pointed out, by changes of Administration. For regional areas, the set of shared images which are used to process information and conduct policy are held by a relatively few individuals who are involved in the decision-making process. As a result, changes in personnel may

---

[44]Halperin, op. cit., pp. 11-12.

result in sudden changes in policy. However, despite the changes of Administration during the post World War II period, American foreign policy toward South Asia remained relatively stable.

A decision-maker is likely to process an issue according to the stakes he believes to be involved and the position he occupies. However, many decision-makers are likely to look to the President for guidance because of his central position and authority in the foreign policy arena.

> His perception and judgment of what is in the national interest are dominant in the system. A strong President -- with a clear sense of direction and leadership -- can have a very strong influence on the images shared by bureaucratic participants, by Congress, and by the public.[45]

However, Nixon's images of the South Asia middle-level crisis were not shared by many members of the bureaucracy and Congress. Consequently, resistance and friction developed within the system during the advisory and implementation stages of the process. This resistance aspect will be examined in greater detail in the next

---

[45] Ibid., p. 17.

chapter dealing with the Incremental Model.

Despite a specified belief set, a President may wish to expand his information prior to making his decision. Halperin provides nine possible ways that a Chief Executive can obtain more information under conditions of uncertainty. However, in the case of Nixon's behavior during the South Asia middle-level crisis, Nixon did not utilize several of these methods. For instance, he did not send any representative to the region to examine the situation. He also sought to quash divergent views rather than encourage them to be expressed. Furthermore, Nixon did not seek to establish divergent channels of information. In short, Nixon applied his belief set to the events, knew that at the minimum he wanted an anti-Indian policy, and concerned himself with assuring the implementation of that policy.

Summary

The Psychological Model focuses on an individual decision-maker's drives and motivations. We have argued that decision-makers possess belief sets and response sets acquired through their past experiences as well as their reasoning, perception, and intuition. By utilizing one of the simple models in his response set, a decision-maker can function effectively by reaching decisions quickly. This adaptive procedure is accomplished through the application of a basic model that eliminates the uncertainty in a complex issue that otherwise confronts a decision-maker. An examination of a decision-maker's belief set provides an assessment of his "desirabilities." In other words, an individual decision-maker's "desirabilities" are derived from his image of the event and the belief and response set that he utilizes to process the event.

The first part of the psychological analysis focused on an examination of the thesis that Nixon's reputed antipathy for India as a country and for its leader Mrs. Gandhi explains the Nixon Administration's pro-Pakistan "tilt" policy. Even though this thesis seems simplistic, the high "desirabilities" scores attached by key U.S. decision-makers to such objectives as the establishment of the China connection, the prevention of an Indian attack on a U.S. ally, and the antipathy to India seem to explain the intensity of the Administration's pursuit of its "tilt" policy. Furthermore, the negative references to Mrs. Gandhi during the WSAG deliberations are also consistent with this thesis, as are such Kissinger remarks as "Dr. Kissinger inquired what the next turn of the screw [against India] might be."[46]

However, Nixon was by no means alone among U.S. decision-makers who harbored a pro-Pakistan and anti-India bias. As pointed out in other chapters, the Nixon Administration was also concerned about relations with the USSR and China and adjusted its behavior in South Asia accordingly. Moreover, U.S. foreign policy behavior in South Asia during 1971 can also be explained by the shared images of U.S. decision-makers. These are generalized beliefs that make up a world view which aid the decision-maker by providing him with simple assumptions. These basic premises constitute a framework utilized to process events.

These shared images may also account for the consistency of U.S. policy in a region. However, because very few decision-makers are involved in formulating U.S.

---

[46]Anderson Papers, Nicholas and Oldenburg, op. cit., p. 129.

policy toward a region, a change in Administration may also yield a change in policy. In the next chapter we will examine the Incremental Model and analyze those factors that resist change and tend to maintain a consistent foreign policy. Furthermore, we will seek to describe and explain the process whereby a decision-making group arrives at a consensus. Whether each of the participants is satisfied with the decision reached has important implications regarding the implementation of the decision.

VIII: THE INCREMENTAL MODEL: CHANGE OR NO CHANGE

Incrementalism has been advocated as an appropriate alternative model to explain decision-making under time pressure and lack of complete information. In the previous chapter we observed how the Psychological Model utilizes the concepts of values and beliefs to cope with events and attach desirabilities to possible outcomes. The Incremental Model argues that under such conditions a decision-maker may be expected to prefer an acceptable rather than the optimal outcome.

The Incremental Model explains decision-making behavior as characterized by "satisficing" as opposed to the Rational Man Model's "maximizing." As an organization confronts an issue it will process it through its Standard Operating Procedures. A series of ad hoc decisions may be made by the various governmental organizations involved in coping with the issue being faced. Accordingly, because of these limitations, a decision-maker will direct his energies toward resolving short-term rather than long-term issues. Whereas in isolation each step of the decision process may be rational, when the policy is examined as a whole, the result may be "disjointed incrementalism." "Disjointed incrementalism" means that only those policies that vary only slightly or incrementally from the <u>status</u> <u>quo</u> will be given serious consideration.

Therefore, emphasis will be placed on considering marginal differences in outputs rather than undertaking a full examination of a problem. Because only marginal differences in policy are seriously considered as appropriate alternatives for decision-makers, only a few alternatives will actually be up for debate during deliberations. The Incremental Model posits that the policy decisions that emerge from an organization will be minor modifications of what had previously been the organization's position. As a result, major or revolutionary change is unlikely to occur.

While the Rational Man Model looks to the outcome, the Incremental Model adjusts the perceived objectives to the available means. Under the Incremental Model's analysis, a decision-maker may prefer to examine the means available at his disposal to implement his preferred outcome. As certain outcomes are ruled out as impractical because of the serious problems associated with their implementation, decision-makers will change the goals they seek to achieve. Once the issues are presented, decision-makers will tend to resolve their differences through "mutual adjustment" during group deliberation.

As pointed out in the discussion concerning organizational behavior, we are particularly interested in two facets of group decision-making behavior for their contribution to the concept of priority formulation. These two facts are: 1) the process whereby a decision-making group arrives at a consensus concerning the issue being confronted, and 2) the adjustments that an individual decision-maker adopts in order to be in harmony with the consensus reached by the group. We will be interested in examining the interaction among the individual preferences of the participating decision-makers according to the authority possessed by these individuals. The purpose for doing this is to describe and analyze the process whereby a group arrives at a consensus regarding the appropriate decision to be adopted. The Incremental Model will also be utilized to analyze the implementation and feedback phases of decision-making. We will examine means, such as invoking presidential authority, used by Kissinger to assure that all the participants were on the same wave length. In addition, we will observe the process whereby a participating decision-maker changes his conceptual frame of reference and, hence, his priority formulation through restructuring the problem in global terms. This process is likely to occur to a decision-maker who has been a regional expert and is subsequently exposed to a global world view by becoming a staff member of an agency such as the NSC under Kissinger's leadership.

The Incremental Model also suggests that there may be no overall coherence to the policy of the governmental unit or to the policy that has been aggregated from the numerous steps of all the governmental units that made their inputs into the policy. To the degree that policy requires a definite course or method of action selected from among alternatives and in light of given conditions to guide and determine present and future decisions, one could suggest that there may at times be no policy.

Having examined the Nixon Report within the framework of a Rational Man Model approach and having considered "Nixon's pique," belief set, and response set in terms of the Psychological Model, we can also inspect the process of arriving at consensus. We can then proceed to examine the degree of change required in the Nixon White House as well as within the Executive Branch as a whole in undertaking a pro-Pakistan "tilt" policy and the opening to China through a consideration of the Incremental Model.

Contrasting the China and Pakistan Policies

As has been pointed out previously, the opening to China, symbolized by Nixon's visit to that country, was orchestrated by Nixon and Kissinger. The veil of secrecy that shrouded the entire China question during 1971 indicates the mistrust which the White House had toward the State Department and other bodies, and the uncertainty associated with whether the venture would prove to be successful. As a result, U.S. change in its China policy was not incremental on the part of Nixon but was a rather clean break from his past anti-China views.

The Nixon Administration made various gestures to the People's Republic of China beginning in 1971 which indicated that the break with previous U.S. policy had been made. But because of possible U.S. domestic repercussions, a strong foundation had to be laid to assure the success of an opening to China objective. In 1971 the U.S. began to eliminate its travel restrictions to China. In addition, the U.S. eased its restrictions on trade with China. The Chinese reciprocated by purchasing some American-made products and inviting a U.S. ping-pong team to tour China. Thus began what came to be dubbed "ping-pong diplomacy."[1]

The opening to China was taken through small steps that amounted to probing and testing techniques by both the U.S. and China. Nixon's strategic decision, however, to go ahead with a new China policy had been made and only the tactical implementation remained to be determined. It is within this framework that the various reciprocal arrangements between the U.S. and China unfolded during 1971.

---

[1] Michael Oksenberg, "The Strategies of Peking," Foreign Affairs, October 1971, Vol. 50, No. 1, p. 16. See also Jerome Alan Cohen, "Recognizing China," Foreign Affairs, ibid.

The decision to proceed with a new China policy was not a matter that the bureaucratic agencies of the U.S. Government processed. Therefore, the type of compromise that characterizes bureaucreatic interactions was not found in the U.S. Government's new China policy. The decision was made by a President whose image of himself was his strength in foreign affairs and who enjoyed acting as his own Secretary of State. As the holder of a reputation as staunch Cold Warrior and anti-communist, Nixon did have a constraint presented by the right-wing elements of the Republican Party who supported Taiwan and would oppose his new China policy. But the change in the U.S. policy toward China was embodied in one man-- Nixon. His view of the USSR as the primary American adversary and the need for the U.S. to take advantage of the Sino-Soviet conflict during America's retreat from her previous role dictated to him the necessity for involving China in the international arena as a counter to Soviet attempts to extend her power further.

Nixon's "tilt toward Pakistan" policy may have been part of the China connection policy of attempting to use China as a counter to Soviet efforts to expand her influence in South Asia through India as a proxy. However, Kissinger himself realized the independence of India and her leader from the Soviet Union.

> We are trying to get across the idea that India has jeopardized relations with the United States. Dr. Kissinger said that we cannot afford to ease India's state of mind. "The Lady" is cold blooded and tough and will not turn into a Soviet satellite merely because of pique.[2]

The U.S. Government's decision to "tilt toward Pakistan" was made by Nixon and was transmitted to the NSC and WSAG by Kissinger. That Nixon's pro-Pakistan position is a natural flow from his previous pro-Pakistan position can also be seen from the previous Psychological Model. While Kissinger does in fact emerge as Nixon's messenger boy, it is possible that his invoking of the President's status and wrath was done in order to impose on the dissenting WSAG members the solution which Kissinger had been instrumental in recommending to Nixon.

By invoking the President's wrath, Kissinger was attempting to assure that the WSAG participants would all be on the same wave length regarding the "tilt" policy

---

[2] Anderson Papers, Nicholas and Oldenburg, op. cit., p. 132.

that Nixon wanted to implement. However, not all the participants were content with this outcome. In other words, the desirabilities of several participants differed from those of Nixon and Kissinger. They felt that their views had not been taken into account in the formulation of the "tilt" policy. Consequently, these decision-makers felt that Kissinger was not attempting to reach a consensus but was only imposing his and Nixon's preferences on the members of WSAG. The lack of consensus among the decision-makers explains the problems the Nixon Administration had in coordinating and implementing its policy.

Furthermore, as we have previously pointed out, several Administration officials have suggested that the "tilt toward Pakistan" policy would have been adopted as U.S. policy toward the South Asia events of 1971 even without the China connection factor, Nixon's preference for Pakistan, and the previous pro-Pakistan record of the U.S. Thus, with the exception of the State Department, the other U.S. governmental units have tended to favor Pakistan. This is especially true of the Defense Department and the intelligence community whose ties with Pakistan go back to the 1950's when Pakistan served as an important U.S. defense base and intelligence-gathering center against the Soviet Union.

While one former State Department official argues that the Department is pro-Pakistan,[3] the consensus of the other officials is that the Department had tended to favor India, especially in comparison with the other U.S. governmental organizations such as the Department of Defense and the CIA. During the WSAG deliberations, the State Department's representatives, Sisco, Williams, and Van Hollen, were the most vocal in resisting Nixon's pro-Pakistan "tilt" policy.

However, except for Kissinger, no other member of WSAG pressed for the adoption of an anti-India or pro-Pakistan policy. David Packard of the Defense Department emphasized that the U.S. should do nothing if it could not do anything effective. Therefore, the argument that a "tilt toward Pakistan" policy would have been generated by the bureaucracy is not necessarily self-evident, despite the fact that on balance the U.S. bureaucracy was pro-Pakistani.

---

[3] Interview with U.S. Government official, March 1975.

In the absence of the value that Nixon attached to the China objective and his personal preference for Pakistan, it seems highly unlikely that the Nixon White House's "tilt" in favor of Pakistan would have been so intense. However, it seems equally unlikely that the bureaucracy would have adopted a pro-India policy in support of Indian military intervention in East Pakistan. The best that the Indians could expect from the American bureaucracy was the State Department position. The Department's recommendation was essentially American silence as a response to the Indian military action. The Nixon White House reacted to this prescription by insisting that the U.S. make its position toward India unmistakably clear regardless of the utility of such a step.

The State Department was, therefore, in conflict with the White House on the proper steps to be taken. Each was proposing a step which flowed from its previously held position. The State Department's past involvement with India through AID was balanced by the Nixon's White House involvement in favor of Pakistan. Had the President of the United States been one who believed in the continuation of what Kissinger labeled the American love affair with India, it is likely that the State Department view, recommending American silence as the proper policy, would have prevailed. The change of President in the U.S. does seem to result in changes in American policy toward certain countries, and India and Pakistan present a good example. During the Kennedy Administration, China was considered the major threat to U.S. interests in Asia, and India was supported by the U.S. as a counter to the Chinese. During the Nixon Administration, the Soviet Union was considered to constitute the primary threat to U.S. interests in Asia, and China was supported by the Administration as a counter to the USSR and India, which the Nixon Administration considered a Russian proxy. However, in the 1971 Indo-Pakistani War the American ability to affect the outcome was negligible. Moreover, the Nixon Administration realized its inability to influence events in South Asia, and in the alternative, decided to make its position a matter of public record even though it would have no bearing on the result.

However, because of the secrecy imposed by the Nixon Administration concerning the establishment of the

China connection, many of the State Department officials were not privy to the linkage that Nixon and Kissinger perceived between the China factor and the events in South Asia. The conceptual frame of reference employed by Kissinger's associates was the global world view that Kissinger had formulated. They were able to take account of the China factor in arriving at their preferences and in integrating the importance of the China connection into their belief set.

A Bureaucratic Perspective

In the previous chapter which dealt with the Psychological Model, we emphasized the notion that decision-makers have belief sets which are in large part reflected by the shared images that we presented. The consistency of these shared images tends to yield policies that are unlikely to change other than to a marginal degree.

As we have pointed out above, a decision-maker's image of critical variables is shaped by his organizational affiliation. A decision-maker may be able to maintain a consistent belief system by restructuring the problem he faces. By being exposed to a different perspective and restructuring the problem, a decision-maker may change his priorities, thereby allowing him to maintain his consistent belief system. If participating decision-makers change their priorities in the direction of a common policy, the group can achieve a consensus and agree on a preferred outcome as their decision.

    A few shared images tend to contribute to the programmed response held by these decision-makers. SOPs (Standard Operating Procedures) combined with these shared images comprise the programmed response which is utilized to focus on a few key factors thereby resulting in what both Halperin and Steinbruner have labeled grooved thinking. However, grooved thinking is not confined to the Incremental Model. In fact, Halperin and Steinbruner characterize it as part of the cognitive process, although they do suggest that it can also be utilized to understand the incremental process. Grooved thinking aids decision-makers in not having to undertake a complete analysis of each issue they confront. By responding to particular issues in pre-determined ways, decision-makers tend to adopt the SOPs and values of their respective organizations. Thus, from this perspective it is not surprising that the State Department representatives expressed opposition to the White House pro-Pakistan "tilt" position. The State

Department has traditionally been considered pro-India, while the Nixon White House was pro-Pakistan. Each of these organizations behaved as expected and the conflict described in greater detail in the chapter entitled "U.S. Decision-Making: organization and Policy" arose.

Under the incremental analysis the rules or SOPs that are utilized to process the problem will play a large role in determining the outcomes. The position occupied by the decision-makers involved in processing the problem will also play a significant role in determining the degree of change in policy that he is ready to recommend or undertake. Furthermore, the amount and type of information at a decision-maker's disposal will also affect the variance reflected in the outcome. Information concerning the South Asian events of 1971 was available but was interpreted differently by various decision-makers.

Non-incremental changes in U.S. foreign policy behavior is likely to be generated by circumstances such as "attention-getting" behavior or sudden changes in the behavior of other states, changes in the American personnel dealing with the issue, and changes in the shared images of the society or bureaucracy.[4] Changes in the output of the decision process are, however, constrained by rules of the game concerning how an issue is processed. Accordingly, it is clear that the NSC system will play a major role in dealing with foreign policy issues, especially when an individual such as Kissinger is at the helm of that system. As Halperin points out, the rules of the game will dictate how and who will deal with particular problems, including which issues will call for the President's attention and action.[5] With changes in Presidential leadership styles, the rules of the game concerning how issues are to be processed may also change. An adviser's reputation with the President may vary both according to issue areas as well as over time. But the President and different sets of advisers may undertake to change the rules concerning such matters as information flows and access to the President. A President's circle of advisers may expand or contract depending on the issue he faces and his personal preferences. Nixon preferred to deal with very small groups or just one adviser per

---

[4]Halperin, op. cit., pp. 101-104.

[5]Ibid., pp. 105-108.

issue who would present him with the options and make the recommendation. Nixon would then make the ultimate decision. Nixon's personal preference did not encourage divergent views to be debated in his presence, as had been the case during the Truman and Nixon Administrations. Therefore, the individual decision-maker who possesses the institutional authority is likely to be decisive in establishing the agenda and preference toward which others in the group decision-making process will converge if the group desires consensus.

The bureaucratic process itself poses a constraint which combines the concepts of priority formulation and incrementalism. Allison has dealt with this theme as follows:

> Information does not pass from the tentacle to the top of the organization instantaneously. Facts can be "in the system" without being available to the head of the organization. Information must be winnowed at every step up the organizational hierarchy, since the number of minutes in each day limits the number of bits of information each individual can absorb. It is impossible for men at the top to examine every report from sources in 100 nations (25 of which had as high a priority as Cuba). But those who decide which information their boss shall see rarely see their bosses' problem.

> Finally, facts that with hindsight are clear
> signals are frequently indistinguishable
> from surrounding "noise" before the
> occurrence.[6]

Information flows are indeed a key factor in the decision-making process. Each decision-maker is likely to process the information he receives according to his values and beliefs. This aspect of information monitoring has been discussed in the Psychological Model and its cognitive aspect. However, as Allison notes, this decision-making factor has implications for the Incremental Model. In other words, the system is likely to generate incremental alternatives and decisions because of the hierarchical processing. Nevertheless, during the deliberations there is the possibility that divergent views will be expressed and non-incremental alternatives proposed. If a decision-maker feels strongly enough about a rejected position that he has propounded, he does have the recourse of leaking information to the press. The dissatisfaction with the WSAG meetings and the Nixon Administration's policies and actions led some participants to leak information about the meetings to newsmen. During one WSAG meeting Kissinger

---

[6]Allison, op. cit., p. 120.

stated to the participants that the leaks were provoking the President's wrath. When Kissinger denied Jack Anderson's column which had passed the leaked information on to the public, Anderson published a participant's notes of several WSAG meetings.

The President may make a decision and assume that its implementation by the bureaucracy will necessarily follow. However, as Halperin points out, presidential orders are not automatically implemented for three basic reasons: "(1) officials at the operations level may not know what it is that senior officials want them to do; (2) they may be unable to do what they believe they have been ordered to do; (3) they may resist doing what they have been ordered to do."[7]

During the South Asia middle-level crisis of 1971 the difficulties faced by the Nixon Administration in terms of the formulation and implementation of policy were twofold. The Nixon Administration failed to build consensus for support of the policy it wanted pursued. Furthermore, the White House failed to coordinate effectively the

---

[7]Halperin, op. cit., p. 238.

implementation of its policy. The implementation of the South Asian policy may be compared and contrasted with Kissinger's mission to China. The implementation of a South Asian policy required the building of consensus and coordinating a large number of complex organizations. However, the Nixon Administration faced a high degree of resistance to its South Asian policy from certain elements in the bureaucracy. The Nixon Administration faced resistance both at the deliberation and the implementation stages. For example, in protest to the Administration's policy, one State Department official refused to do any work on South Asia. When Nixon decided to open relations with China, he sent Kissinger to Peking in order to circumvent the SOP constraints of the State Department.

Kissinger's remarks one year prior to the South Asian policy of 1971 seem to apply to those events as well.

> The outsider believes a Presidential order is consistently followed out. Nonsense, I have to spend considerable time seeing that it is carried out in the spirit the President intended. Inevitably, in the nature of bureaucracy, departments become pressure groups for a point of view. If the President decides against them, they are convinced

some evil influence worked on the President: if only he knew all the facts, he would have decided their way.[8]

Halperin argues that government career officials tend to view themselves as the fixed decision-makers in the government while the political leaders are viewed as transient. This may explain the resistance that some officials exhibited to Nixon's South Asia policy in 1971. Several officials disregarded presidential orders concerning the policy and refused to respond to presidential requests. Many of these officials did offer their divergent opinions during the first few WSAG deliberations which have not been published in the Anderson Papers. These officials also presented a struggle at the implementation stage and the U.S. policy that emerged was characterized by a high degree of confusion. For example, the implementation of the arms supply policy for South Asia was characterized by total confusion in the system as an on-again, off-again military supply flow sputtered along. As a result, the Nixon Administration

---

[8] Saul Pett, "Henry A. Kissinger: Loyal Retainer of Nixon's Svengali?" The Washington Post, August 23, 1970.

felt there was sabotage somewhere in the system.[9]

The Nixon Administration faced serious coordination problems for its policy not only in Washington but also in the field. We have mentioned the conflict between Arch Blood and Joseph Farland concerning the policy they recommended for the Administration to adopt. Once Farland's view was adopted by the Nixon Administration, Ambassador Keating offered his objections as well. The resistance by some elements of the bureaucracy to Nixon's policy served to intensify the Administration's effort to impose its decision on those organizations which were needed to implement the policy. In addition, the Administration withdrew from the bureaucracy those functions which had been assigned to it and transferred those functions to the White House. As the locus of decision was concentrated within the White House, the preference ranking or priorities of Nixon and Kissinger became a key factor in determining U.S. policy in South Asia.

---

[9]Interview with U.S. Government official, March 1975.

Summary

The Incremental Model provides us with an additional perspective for understanding the priority formulation involved in U.S. foreign policy decision-making in the 1971 South Asia middle-level crisis. We have examined decision-making behavior that is characterized by "satisficing" as opposed to the Rational Man Model's "maximizing." This model has helped us focus on the constraints imposed by the bureaucracy on the outcomes that the Nixon Administration sought to achieve. This perspective has also aided us in the understanding of the conflicts that occur during the decision-making process. The consequence may be the "science of muddling through."

The Incremental Model contributes to the concept of priority formulation by examining 1) the process whereby a decision-making group arrives at a consensus concerning the issue being confronted, and 2) the adjustments that an individual decision-maker adopts in order to be in harmony with the consensus reached by the group. Once the participating decision-makers arrive at their individual preference ranking or priorities, the group will seek to arrive at a consensus regarding the decision to be adopted. The leader of the group will attempt to assure that the participants agree to implement the decision reached.

In order to arrive at a consensus, we have examined the process whereby a decision-maker's conceptual frame of reference is modified and his priorities adapted. For example, a decision-maker may adapt his priorities by restructuring the problem he confronts. A decision may also be achieved by the leader of the group imposing his preferences on the other participants. However, where each of the participants is not satisfied with the decision, the group may have serious difficulties formulating and implementing the decision. Those members of the group who are dissatisfied with the decision may resist its implementation. Consequently, the output that results is not necessarily one decision. The arms supplies policy disputes and the contradictions and confusion that were generated during the attempt to implement a "tilt" policy exemplify this problem.

In processing regional foreign policy issues through governmental units, each of the units focuses on its goal as it attempts to cope with the issue. The unit may have no overall objective whatsoever. Furthermore, it may process each issue in isolation and as an end in itself. If there is a framework within which the issue will be cast, it is important to appreciate the assumptions and values of that framework as a means to understand the priorities that are sought. Conflicts that emerge will be resolved by reaching a consensus. If, however, the units fail to converge on a preferred outcome, the unit possessing the necessary authority is likely to attempt to impose its preference.

In the next chapter we will present the concept of priority formulation as an approach for integrating the various decision-making models we have presented. We will suggest that the contributions made by the decision-making models to the concept of priority formulation can be expressed in a systematic fashion.

IX: THE GLOBAL-REGIONAL CONTROVERSY
A PROBLEM OF FOCUS AND DESIRABILITIES

In examining the structure of decision-making, we concentrated on those governmental institutions and agencies most directly concerned with processing U.S. foreign policy problems. Those bodies that are mobilized to deal with the issue will make their major impact on the problem in terms of their ability to structure the problem, or as Cobb and Elder label it, agenda-building.[1] Those governmental institutions, agencies, and personalities who have the greatest authority and take the most initiative to cope with the problem will play the predominant role in structuring the issue. Consequently, the preferences of that actor are likely to provide the agenda. The interaction among the preferences of these actors will yield a preferred outcome through means ranging from the development of consensus to the imposition of the dominant actor's preference. Cobb and Elder deal with two types of political agendas. The first type is the systemic

---

[1] Roger W. Cobb and Charles D. Elder, Participation in American Politics: The Dynamics of Agenda-Building (Boston: Allyn and Bacon, 1972).

agenda which "consists of all issues that are commonly perceived by members of the political community as meriting public attention and as involving matters within the legitimate jurisdiction of existing governmental authority."[2] The second type of agenda is the formal agenda which is defined as "that set of items explicitly up for the active and serious consideration of authoritative decision-makers."[3]

The personal and subjective process whereby a decision-maker determines to make an issue an item for prior consideration, the determination of the attention to be given the issue, and the processing of the item by a rank order is what we have chosen to label the process of priority formulation. Through an examination of a decision-maker's derivation of his probabilities and desirabilities regarding an outcome, we will introduce the Rational Man approach to the concept of priority formulation. This will be followed by an examination of the process of an individual's preference ranking of the issues he thinks merit prior attention. We will

---

[2] Ibid., p. 85.
[3] Ibid., p. 86.

attempt to express this process in a series of systematized statements. During the course of this chapter, we will deal with the contributions made by the Psychological Model in determining the cognition, belief set, and values held by various types of decision-makers. The purpose of such an analysis is to acquire an understanding of the perceptions that decision-makers have regarding the desirabilities of certain outcomes. A decision-maker's belief set and perception of an event he confronts are likely to determine the simple model within his response set that he will utilize in structuring and approaching an issue.

     A major problem of focus for U.S. foreign policy decision-makers was whether the 1971 South Asian events were to be interpreted as a global or regional conflict. On the one hand, Nixon and Kissinger viewed the primary significance of the issue in terms of its possible global implications for U.S. relations with the USSR and China. An additional factor was the precedent-setting value of a Soviet-client state waging war on a U.S.-client state and ally. On the other hand, the regional experts tended to view the South Asia conflict as a continuation of the Indo-Pakistani struggle that was truly a regional and not

global issue. These and other divergent belief sets led
individual decision-makers to attach different values to
alternative strategies, thereby yielding variances between
individual preference rankings.

The Rational Man, Expected Value, Utility Theory, and Bayes' Theorem

In the discussion that follows we will examine
means of describing and analyzing the decision-making
process systematically. Some readers will, no doubt,
argue that such an analysis is not necessary and, in any
event, does not reflect the thought process of an
individual decision-maker. In response to such an
argument, we maintain that, at a minimum, the analysis
that follows is an ideal model of the process whereby an
individual derives his preferences or priorities. Despite
the arguments made by various writers critical of the
assumption of rationality in a decision-making model, we
have already observed that the Rational Man Model provides
what appears to be the most satisfactory approach to an
understanding of U.S. foreign policy behavior during the
1971 South Asia events. The thrust of the argument
presented here is that the following approach toward the

analysis of an individual's priority formulation does describe many decision-making situations. Moreover, the approach takes the subjective and personal perspective of the decision-maker by accepting the value that he attaches to his desirabilities and probabilities. Finally, as a tool of analysis, the priority formulation approach forces a decision-maker to make his assumptions and values explicit.

The Rational Man Model depicts the decision-making process as a problem that can be broken down into its major component parts and then aggregated to arrive at a decision. The decision-maker will attempt to maximize the value he can attain within the constraints imposed by the environment. However, in order to be able to maximize the value, the decision-maker is presumed to have assessed his preferences and rank-ordered them. This is a crucial assumption for determining the process of priority formulation.

> Lacking an objective and independent means of establishing utility values, the analytic paradigm leaves to the discretion of the decision-maker the matter of determining relative value. The analysis of the paradigm cannot begin until the assignments have been made. By allowing this discretion and assuming the product to be a utility assignment (or a preference

ordering, such that a utility assignment c\
be objectively derived which reflects the
ordering), the analytic paradigm assumes
that the individual decision-maker makes the
assessment of relative value.[4]

The analytic decision-maker is presumed to proc\ competing claims on his values by examining the trade-off relationship after attaching a weight factor to each of the values and outcomes. For example, a manager of a firm may be considering two alternative investment possibilities. The Rational Man Model argues that he first examines each alternative and posits a value for each possible outcome. In other words, the manager estimates the various net profit figures. His next step is the assignment of a probability score to the realization of that outcome. This probability score may be determined either through objective or subjective criteria. The third step is to multiply the probability by the value of the outcome. The fourth step is to sum the values in order to determine the expected value and, finally, choose the highest expected value. Suppose that an analysis of Project A reveals that the net profits will be $10,000,

---

[4]Steinbruner, op. cit., p. 29.

20,000, or $30,000 with subjective probabilities of .1, .2, and .3 respectively. Project B is thought to provide a 50-50 chance of a successful investment with $100,000 net profits or an unsuccessful investment with $0 net profit. If each project requires the same amount of dollar investment, the issue is which one is preferable in terms of expected value.

$$E(A) = (\$10,000)(.1) + (\$20,000)(.2) + (\$30,000)(.3) = \$14,000$$

$$E(B) = (\$0)(.5) + (\$100,000)(.5) = \$50,000$$

The manager would maximize his expected net profit by adopting Project B.[5]

Utility theory goes beyond the concept of expected value by suggesting that each individual has a measurable preference among various alternatives available in situations of uncertainty. This is posited to be the individual's utility function and is measured in units labeled "utiles."[6] We will be utilizing the approach of utility theory in our formulation of preference ranking.

---

[5] See Morris Hamburg, *Statistical Analysis for Decision-Making* (New York: Harcourt, Brace & World, 1970), pp. 210-223.

[6] For a more detailed discussion of utility theory, see Ralph O. Swalm, "Utility Theory-- Insights into Risk Taking," *Harvard Business Review*, November-December, 1966, pp. 123-136.

A decision tree approach is also used in risk analysis for business decisions when a manager estimates the probability of various events occurring. Thus, for example, the risk analysis approach can be utilized to estimate the chances of expropriation with or without compensation, under various assumptions regarding political control. In Stobaugh's decision tree a .5 probability is attached to the event that the government will be overthrown and the assumption is made that a .81 probability exists that the plant will not be nationalized.

The rational decision-maker will seek to expand his analysis beyond the prior analysis which is based on expected outcomes multiplied by the prior probabilities. He will also be interested in integrating expected payoffs on the basis of posterior probabilities which are changes in the prior probabilities based on additional information. In deliberating a decision, one evaluates possible courses of action in terms of their consequences, which, because of uncertainty, may depend on circumstances the decision-maker cannot control or predict.[7] Bayes' theorem is the method utilized in order to revise the prior probabilities.

---

[7] R.C. Jeffrey, The Logic of Decision (New York: McGraw-Hill, 1965), p. 1.

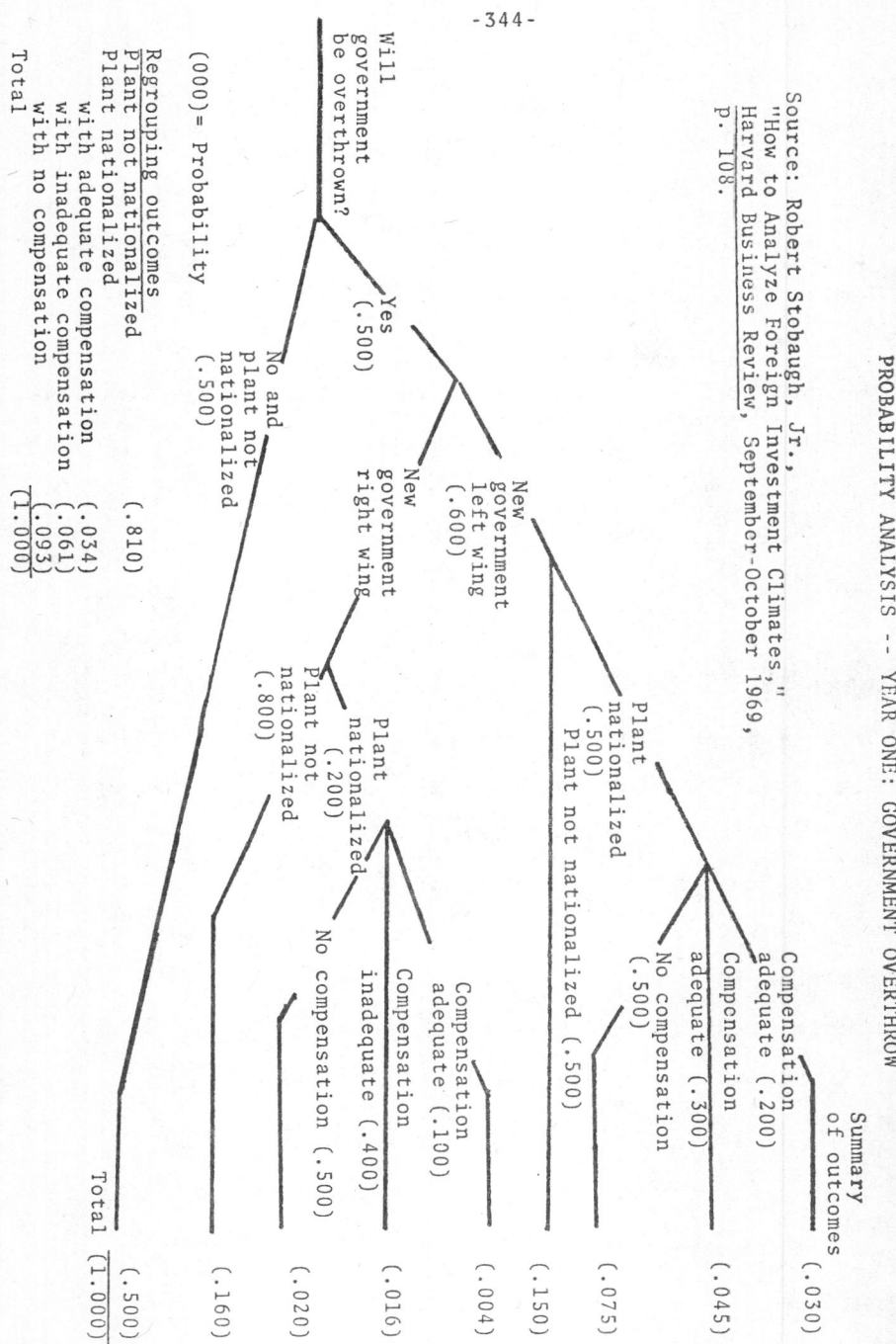

PROBABILITY ANALYSIS -- YEAR ONE: GOVERNMENT OVERTHROW

Source: Robert Stobaugh, Jr., "How to Analyze Foreign Investment Climates," *Harvard Business Review*, September-October 1969, p. 108.

Since the 1973 Arab-Israeli War, Bayesian analysis has been used by the CIA in the monitoring of Middle East events.[8] This technique is used to provide decision-makers with revised evaluations based on information indicating changed circumstances. Despite its limitations, this method of analysis has the advantage of forcing the group of experts who are monitoring the events to make their assumptions explicit.

Bayes' rule is a restatement of the rule for conditional probability:

$$P(A \cap B) = P(B/A) \times P(A) = P(A/B) \times P(B)$$

Divided by $P(A)$ yields:

$$P(B/A) = \frac{P(A/B) \times P(B)}{P(A)}$$

or if there are numerous B events

$$P(Bi/A) = \frac{P(A/Bi) \times P(Bi)}{\sum_{i=1} P(A/Bi) \times P(Bi)}$$

Bayes's rule can be utilized to reflect experience and calculate the new probability $P(Bi/A)$. Thus,

$$P(Bi/A) = \frac{P(A/B1) \times P(B1)}{P(A/B1) \times P(B1) + P(A/B2) \times P(B2)}$$

---

[8]Nicholas Schweitzer (CIA, Office of Political Research), "Bayesian Analysis for Intelligence: Some Focus on the Middle East," paper presented at the International Studies Association Convention, Toronto, Canada, February 28, 1976.

Bayes' rule is perhaps easier to visualize as a decision tree, although in the example that follows intersection probabilities rather than conditional probabilities are used. Gupta and Cozzolino give an example of an oil company that is considering drilling for oil.[9] The chief geologist thinks that the probability of a dry well is 80 per cent while the probability of finding oil is 20 per cent. More information can be received by seismographic recording. The evidence will be provided for one of three conditions:

    Event R_1: no subsurface structure

    Event R_2: open subsurface structure

    Event R_3: closed subsurface structure

Past experience reveals that the probabilities of these three events are .30, .36, and .34 respectively, while the probabilities of the outcomes are .68, .28, and .04 respectively if there is no oil. The three possible outcomes of the test will yield a revised probability that there is oil at the site. The revised probability can

---

[9]Shiv K. Gupta and John M. Cozzolino, <u>Fundamentals of Operations Research for Management</u> (San Francisco: Holden-Day, Inc., 1974), pp. 186-187.

be depicted as follows:

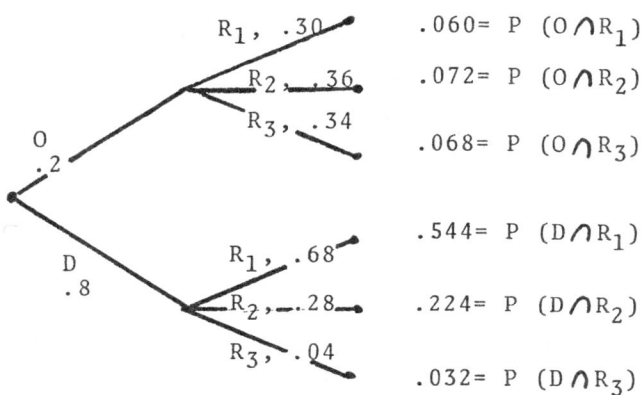

Three applications of Bayes' rule are made:

$$P(O/R_1) = \frac{P(O \cap R_1)}{P(O \cap R_1) + P(D \cap R_1)} = \frac{.060}{.060 + .544} = .099$$

$$P(O/R_2) = \frac{P(O \cap R_2)}{P(O \cap R_2) + P(D \cap R_2)} = \frac{.072}{.072 + .224} = .243$$

$$P(O/R_3) = \frac{P(O \cap R_3)}{P(O \cap R_3) + P(D \cap R_3)} = \frac{.068}{.068 + .032} = .680$$

The first and third outcomes would have a great effect upon the probability of oil. In assessing whether or not to undertake the experiment, it is important to find the probabilities of these three outcomes. These are the denominators of the three applications of Bayes' rule.[10]

---

[10] The decision whether or not to drill for oil given each of the three possible outcomes of the seismographic recording is examined in ibid., pp. 192-198.

We have presented Bayes' theorem in order to examine how a decision-maker may establish his probability estimates and revise these probabilities as he obtains more information. We will now proceed to use the probability estimates and the desirabilities in order to establish an individual's preference ranking.

Preference Ranking

William Bundy has suggested that U.S. policy during the South Asia events of 1971 seems to have been "a classic case of doing the wrong thing in a regional situation for the sake of wider relationships..."[11] Because regions have their own dynamics, global policy as a guide for a Superpower's actions within a regional issue may be inappropriate for the region.

The formulation of the foreign policy objectives seems to differ, as seen in the previous section, depending on the model being utilized. While we have shown that both the Rational Man and Psychological Models can be used to develop a preference ranking, Steinbruner

---

[11] William Bundy, "International Security Today," Foreign Affairs, Vol. 53, No. 1, October 1974, p. 38.

argues that the cybernetic paradigm has a different focus from that of the analytic paradigm and provides a substitute means by which to understand a decision. Servomechanism is the crucial notion in cybernetics and is illustrated by a thermostat, for example, which will keep the temperature within a specified range by closing and opening the system. Cybernetics proceeds on the basis of a few very simple assumptions rather than trying to account for the reality and deal with preference formation. The actors who participate in the decision-making process have their respective priorities and the priority that is chosen for implementation will be that held by the actor who predominates in the deliberations. The issue of priority arises because the decision-making unit may not be able to process all the demands made on it by providing each with the attention it needs. The inputs may arise simultaneously and be beyond the human and organizational capacities to allocate the necessary attention, resources, and action. The challenge is how to order priorities among the problems that are confronted and how to evaluate the alternatives.

In evaluating possible courses of action in terms of their consequences, a decision-maker may not be able to control or predict circumstances that affect those consequences. Earlier we discussed the utilization of Bayes' theorem to calculate new probabilities by reflecting past experiences or additional information. Jeffrey uses the Bayesian model to introduce the notion of "expected desirability." The "expected desirability" is computed from the probabilities of the relevant circumstances involved and the desirabilities of the possible consequences. We have dealt with each of these concepts in both the Rational Man and Psychological Models. "The Bayesian principle for deliberation is then to <u>perform an act which has maximum expected desirability</u>."[12] Furthermore, "two or more of the possible acts may have the same, maximum expected desirability."[13]

Jeffrey defines the desirability and probability in terms of the actor's preference ranking.[14] The analyst

---

[12] R.C. Jeffrey, <u>The Logic of Decision</u> (New York: McGraw-Hill, 1965), p. 1.

[13] <u>Ibid.</u>, p. 1.

[14] <u>Ibid.</u>, p. 63.

may assume that the subjective probability and desirability are known or he may determine the preference ranking and the proceed to "deduce the probability and desirability assignments from the preference ranking."[15]

Suppose that we are dealing with the following three propositions:

    A= that it is important to support Pakistan.
    B= that is is important to align with China.
    C= that it is important to have good relations with India.

There exist eight possibilities for the joint truth or falsity of the three propositions. In Table I ttt represents the case where all three propositions are true and fff where all three propositions are false. The probabilities ('prob') that an actor assigns to the eight cases consist of eight numbers none of which can be negative and that their sum be equal to one. The desirabilities ('des') can be represented by any number which the actor wants to assign to the eight cases.

---

[15] Ibid., p. 63.

TABLE I

	A	B	C	prob.	des.
1	t	t	t	.1	2
2	t	t	f	.1	1
3	t	f	t	.2	-1
4	t	f	f	.1	0
5	f	t	t	.2	1
6	f	t	f	.1	1
7	f	f	t	.1	-1
8	f	f	f	.1	-2
				1.0	

The probability of a proposition is the sum of the probabilities in each of the cases in which it is true. For example, the prob A= .1 + .1 + .2 +.1= .5 The desirabilities of each of the eight cases can also be computed. The rule for the computation of the desirability of a proposition is given by the weighted average of the desirabilities of the cases in which it is true, where the weights are in proportion to the probabilities of the cases.[16] This computation can be

---

[16]Ibid., p. 67.

done in three steps: (1) the desirability of each case in which the proposition is true is multiplied by the probability of that case; (2) the products are summed; (3) this sum is divided by the probability of the proposition, that is, by the sum of the probabilities of the case in which the proposition is true.

Using the probabilities and desirabilities given in Table I, we can calculate the des A which is true in the first four cases. Step (1) results in the following:

$(.1)(2) = .2$

$(.1)(1) = .1$

$(.2)(-1) = -.2$

$(.1)(0) = 0$

Step (2) results in the sum

$(.2) + (.1) + (-.2) + (0) = .1$

Step (3) calls for dividing this sum by the probability of A which is the sum

$(.1) + (.1) + (.2) + (.1) = .5$

of the cases in which A is true. The result is

des A = $(.1) \div (.5) = \frac{1}{5}$

The entire computation can be represented by a single formula,

$$\text{des } A = \frac{(.1)(2) + (.1)(1) + (.2)(-1) + (.1)(0)}{.1 + .1 + .2 + .1} = \frac{1}{5}$$

The calculation for $\bar{A}$[17] which is true in the last four cases yields

$$\text{des } \bar{A} = 0$$

The computations for other desirabilities yield the following results: $\text{des } B = \frac{6}{5}$, $\text{des } \bar{B} = \frac{-4}{5}$, $\text{des } C = \frac{1}{6}$, $\text{des } \bar{C} = 0$, $\text{des } T = .1$, $\text{des } A \lor B = .5$[18]

We can also determine the desirabilities of each of the cases ttt, ttf, ..., fff whose desirabilities are equivalent to the propositions ABC, $AB\bar{C}$, ..., $\overline{ABC}$.

From these results a more complete preference ranking with the appropriate computed desirabilites would appear as follows:

---

[17] Where $\bar{A}$ as opposed to A indicates that the proposition is false.

[18] $A \lor B$ denotes the case where either A or B is true and T is the proposition that is true in all cases.

2	A B C
1.2	B
1	$\bar{A}$ B $\bar{C}$, A B $\bar{C}$, $\bar{A}$ B C
.5	A v B
.2	A
.1$\bar{6}$	C
.1	T
0	A $\bar{B}$ $\bar{C}$, $\bar{C}$, $\bar{A}$
-.8	$\bar{B}$
-1	$\bar{A}$ $\bar{B}$ C, A $\bar{B}$ C
-2	$\bar{A}$ $\bar{B}$ $\bar{C}$

This provides a decision-maker with his individual preference ranking. In identifying his preference ranking, the actor is passive in the sense that he has not sought to take action that would make one of the propositions come true. Jeffrey ties an act to a proposition by suggesting that the "necessary proposition" would correspond to allowing events to proceed without the actor's interference, whereas an act is a "proposition which is within the agent's power to make true if he pleases."[19]

---

[19] Jeffrey, op. cit., p. 73.

However, the desirabilities of the propositions that the actor considers constitute a reflection of his preferences. These preferences, in turn, are constructed on the basis of a normative framework whereby the decision-maker imposes his beliefs and values on the phenomena. Nevertheless, this approach to preference ranking accepts the decision-maker's value system and beliefs as given and only deals with the results that his values and beliefs generate. "... it provides a framework within which one can study the relations among various possible belief, value, and desirability functions, and between these and policies for decision-making."[20]

Contradictory historical precedents can be used by decision-makers to explain a current event. Thus, for example, Soviet and Cuban involvement in Angola during 1976 may be viewed by U.S. decision-makers as calling for a Munich or Vietnam response. Those using the Vietnam analogy will argue that the United States should not get involved in Angola because of the danger of becoming entangled in another quagmire. Those arguing

---

[20]Ibid., p. 199.

for some form of U.S. intervention will suggest that the United States must show its resolve not to allow the Soviets to change unilaterally the status quo and use a Munich analogy. These decision-makers suggest that the Soviets be required to show restraint in the Third World in order to maintain the global structure of peace and U.S.-Soviet détente.

A decision-maker's belief structure may yield a negative image of an alternative which, consequently, will not be considered and will aid him in maintaining consistency. Belief strength is also provided by the process of small group interactions. "...one of the prime characteristics of human beings under uncertainty is that they bolster their judgments by the concurring opinions of other people."[21]

Therefore, in contradistinction to the analytic paradigm that deals with uncertainty by attaching a probability score to alternative outcomes, cognitive theory looks to the decision-maker's belief set. Thus, the decision-maker will impose his belief set on events

---

[21]Steinbruner, op. cit., p. 121.

such that high payoffs will be attached to the outcome he prefers and low payoffs for those he dislikes. In this manner the decision-maker is able to impose the image he has on the events and maintain his original view. The inputs that do not fit the preconceived image are rejected and the decision-maker deals with the uncertainty aspect of complexity by utilizing his preconceived value set to process the inputs.

Value Formation

Priority is an important concept in two aspects of foreign policy formulation. Decision-makers in confronting an issue must decide the importance of the issue itself in comparison to other issues in order to determine the amount of attention the issue warrants. In addition, the priority will be a function of how a decision-maker structures the problem. A decision-maker may view the issue in isolation or regional outlook, or he may consider it in terms of global factors or overriding world view. Another dimension of the priority concept is involved when the decision-makers enter into the considerations of the alternatives. Thus, if the decision-makers do in fact consider the alternatives, each decision-maker is likely to consider the alternatives in terms of the priority he attaches to the objective he seeks to accomplish. Priority in this latter context is the consideration of the advantages and disadvantages of each option such that the alternatives are rank-ordered.

The major argument of the cognitive theorists is that the "structure of beliefs" serves to process stimuli and information. The regularities of the beliefs constitute a set of beliefs, consequently, a structure, despite the variances in the substantive content of beliefs, attitudes, and perceptions, for example.

Steinbruner emphasizes the "hierarchical" relationships in memory. That Munich is associated with appeasement is characteristic of hierarchical relationships whereby the general concept, but not the details, is the key. In addition to the importance of inferences in the establishment of sets of beliefs, the cognitive theorists emphasize the constraint imposed by the notion that a decision-maker's sundry internal beliefs must be consistent in their relationship to each other. Conflicts occur when the particular objective reality is in contradiction to the perceptions of the mind and the inferences drawn based on past experience. The major issue is how the conflict is resolved, that is, whether the attitude will shift or a further search conducted for information to justify the original attitude which is then reinforced and kept.

Furthermore, the human mind will be constrained by reality. However, since the human mind may be incapable of dealing with the complex reality, the brain may process stimuli by means of selective perception. This process maintains a simple and stable set of beliefs whereby the decision-maker is predisposed through his past experience to select those stimuli that reinforce his prior attitudes.

The question of trade-offs involving two or more values may be especially relevant in connection with the process of priority formulation. The connection between values and priorities may be made by arguing that each set is rank ordered and that the resolution of conflicts in determining the value hierarchy will yield a set of rank-ordered priorities. How this process unfolds is subject to debate, however.

> The complex decision problem has been defined in part as a problem of trade-offs involving two or more values. The first task, then, in extending cognitive processing principles to policy questions is that of specifying how the mind, operating in the manner described, goes about handling

incommensurate values. The applicable
assumption of the analytic paradigm holds
that a process of limited value integration
occurs whereby one value is weighed in
relation to another, even if this cannot be
done explicitly or made logically compelling.
For cognitive theory the question is whether
the inference mechanisms which compromise
the information-processing system of the
mind operate in such a fashion. Given the
fact that much of the human information-
processing system operates outside of
consciousness, it is possible that value
integration occurs even when the decision-
maker is unaware of it and does not
consciously try to do it.[22]

Value integration is not necessarily the result that emerges from trade-offs when the mind processes values that are in conflict. In fact, in cases of high uncertainty, value integration apparently does not take place. Moreover it is possible that at high uncertainty levels, decision-makers are likely to pursue separate and inconsistent values without realizing or else denying the conflicts that exist.

The analytic paradigm's assumption of value integration is challenged by the cognitive theory. The cognitive theory argues that the mind will process the incoming stimuli such that conflicts in the trade-off

---

[22]Ibid., p. 103.

relationship will be avoided unless the external situation poses a constraint that does not allow the mind to accomplish such an evolution.

> Cognitive principles thus suggest the contrary assumption of value separation. According to this assumption, the two values of a complex problem will not be related to one another in the mind of the decision maker, but divided and pursued separately, as if they were independent considerations. The information-processing operations of the human mind strain to set up single-value decision problems.[23]

Moreover, the mind may seek to establish separate decision problems whereby each issue is ruled by one value or a set of values that are rank ordered. This notion of value separation may also account for the way complex issues are decomposed and the cybernetic process applied.

The cognitive theory challenges both the analytic and cybernetic paradigms in explaining how beliefs are established when a decision-maker confronts uncertainty. The cybernetic paradigm posits the prior existence of a decision rule which guides a decision-maker's actions as he processes incoming information. However, the analytic paradigm emphasizes the determination of outcomes by means

---

[23] Ibid., p. 108.

of calculating probabilities and applying them to the available information. The challenge posed by the cognitive theory is "the assumption that structure will be imposed on uncertain situations, and uncertainty thereby resolved, not by probabilistic judgments, but by categorical inferences."[24]

Thus, under the cognitive theory a decision-maker will seek to impose a general, overall meaning to the events he witnesses. A decision-maker will rely even more on categorical inferences under conditions of complexity when the uncertainty needs to be resolved. He will seek to impose a structure on the incoming information by utilizing his beliefs to resolve the uncertainty. "The essential assertion of the cognitive paradigm is that human beliefs are given strength from sources other than the weight of objective evidence and that these partially independent sources of belief are important in imposing structure on complexity (and thereby resolving uncertainty)."[25]

---

[24] Ibid., p. 110.
[25] Ibid., p. 113

The conceptual framework of American foreign policy has been a global strategy with the focus on the process and structure of Superpower relations and not on a particular state. "U.S. foreign policy toward India is merely the local application of a global strategy, which has little to do with India specifically except insofar as India is seen as an available instrument or an unnecessary obstacle in the execution of that strategy."[26] Nayar distinguishes states into those that are subjects and those that are objects of international relations and argues that India, having been a past object of actions by the Superpowers, aspires to be a subject in the international arena. However, Indian aspirations run counter to American security interests based on realpolitik considerations calling for a regional balance of power without the establishment of a predominant and independent regional power. As indicated previously, the Nixon Administration was angered by what is had acknowledged would be a foregone conclusion of the outcome of the Indo-Pakistani War. India succeeded in confirming the White House's fear by

---

[26] Baldev Raj Nayar, "Treat India Seriously," Foreign Policy, No. 18, Spring 1975, p. 134.

establishing a new power structure in South Asia. This approached India's hegemony of the subcontinent in opposition to the American support for a regional balance of power based on equality between India and Pakistan.

American foreign policy has been oriented toward global and bilateral relations rather than toward regional policy.[27] This orientation has occurred despite the organizational structure of the State Department into regional divisions. The combination of the Near East and South Asia within one division may account for the lack of attention that South Asia has received. But because international crises tend to emanate most frequently from regions, one school of thought argues that the focus for action and policy should be directed at the regional level.[28]

Looking at the Events in 1971

The U.S. Government's monitoring of the events from December 1970 through December 1971 was undertaken by numerous agencies and the locus of decision-making

---

[27] Rudolph and Rudolph, op. cit., p. 35.

[28] Louis J. Cantori and Steven L. Spiegel, The International Politics of Regions: A Comparative Approach (Englewood Cliffs, New Jersey: Prentice-Hall, 1970).

depended on the intensity and magnitude of the crisis. As a noncrisis developed into a middle level crisis, the locus of the decision shifted to the White House from the field and the bureaucracy.

> When crises occur there is a general tendency for the action to move up and out of those levels of the State Department that are country and regionally informed. Action moves from roughly the embassy and country director level beyond the assistant secretary to the seventh floor policy planning levels and out to the White House and National Security Council.[29]

As a result, area experts tend to be cut off from the decision-making process once the situation has reached the crisis level. The President's men, who tend to deal with the global balance of power, gain control over the process. This process was verified by the 1971 South Asia middle-level crisis. Consequently, different organizations and individuals were involved in the latter stages of the crisis and they analyzed the situation according to a global rather than regional outlook. In short, each of the two schools of thought imposed its respective belief and value sets on the events. A conflict between the area experts and the President's men often

---

[29] Rudolph and Rudolph, op. cit., p. 39.

accompanies this shift in control over the action to be implemented. In short, those who have the power to decide are not the area experts and the area experts do not have decision-making power.

The regional experts in the U.S. Government focused on India's national security interests and her regional aspirations as a means of framing the 1971 South Asia events. These experts viewed the millions of refugees for whom India had become a sanctuary as a burden that would compel India to take action in East Pakistan. The characterization that an American regional official provides of Indira Gandhi's dealings with the Soviet Union indicates the low priority he assessed to the global factors. "She told the Russians she was going ahead and they said okay, if you must."[30] The belief set of a regional decision-maker tended to allow him to downplay the importance of global dimensions of the regional war, even if he was aware of the Nixon Administration's world view.

Under the Nixon-Kissinger NSC system foreign policy decision-making was extremely centralized from a

---

[30] As quoted in ibid., p. 52.

managerial perspective. This structure made the shift to the White House likely to occur at an earlier stage than under different organizational schemes. During the early phases of the South Asia events, the monitoring within the U.S. Government was done primarily by the State Department bureaus, CIA, and Department of Defense bureaus. Monitoring was done in the field and decisions could be made either in the field or by low-level decision-makers in the bureaucracy. In short, the agenda was set and resolved by the embassies and State Department. As the events unfolded, WSAG meetings were held during those periods that the Nixon Administration perceived to constitute a "crisis." Thus, for example, a few Senior Review Group meetings were held following Sheik Mujib's election victory and after the March 25, 1971 crackdown in East Pakistan.

However, during 1971, when the South Asia events were unfolding, the major focus or priority of the Administration in foreign policy was on U.S. relations with the Soviet Union and, more significantly for the Nixon White House, on the opening of relations with China. In its China initiative and détente with the Soviet Union, the Nixon White House was attempting to reorient the relationships among the great powers in an effort to structure the balance of power at the global level.[31] Other areas of major concern were Vietnam and the Middle East. The decision-makers connected most directly with the White House were aware of the China connection and its importance. The desirability and value score which they attached to this factor seems to explain their focus on the global issues regarding the South Asia events.

Within the Nixon Administration's frameworks South Asia continued to be a low priority area in comparison to Southeast Asia and the Middle East. U.S. foreign policy decision-makers had become absorbed in the Vietnam conflict which had propelled Southeast Asia into a top-priority area. The expansion of Soviet activities in the Arab Middle East following the 1967 Arab-Israeli War, the Six-Day War, also preoccupied U.S. foreign policy decision-makers. South Asia remained a region to which relatively little importance was attached by the American decision-makers. The Deputy Assistant Secretary of Defense for Near Eastern, African and South Asian

---

[31] Ibid., p. 38.

Affairs, James H. Noyes, testified:

> No critical U.S. security interests are involved in South Asia.... Those interests the United States does have in the subcontinent are primarily political... They include a basic interest in peace and stability of the region and in insuring that no outside power achieves dominance over any of the regional nations.[32]

The time that Nixon and Kissinger could devote to dealing with South Asia as events were unfolding was extremely limited. The desirability of having good relations with India had probably never been particularly high for the United States. Before mid-November 1971 American policy in South Asia was largely one of non-action. With the more rapid than anticipated establishment of contacts with China and the July 15 announcement of Nixon's upcoming trip to China in February 1972, the importance of the South Asian events during the Fall of 1971 was primarily due to the framework in which the Nixon Administration cast the emerging events. Thus, the desirability of opening a China connection increased dramatically for the key U.S. decision-makers. The Nixon

---

[32] Hearing before the Subcommittee on Near East and South Asia of the Committee on Foreign Affairs, House of Representatives, March 12, 15, 20, and 27, Washington, D.C. 1973, p. 82.

Report provides the Rational Man approach in arguing that global considerations should be given priority over regional factors. That the Administration's desirability score for having good relations with China was very high while this score for India was low largely explains the Nixon-Kissinger policy.

The importance of the China connection is argued by the generalists. The U.S.-USSR-China triangular relationship was being brought to the forefront by the Nixon Administration. South Asia was one of the first regions in which this global relationship was being implemented while the regional arena was witnessing overt hostility. The White House attributed South Asia's importance to China from a vantage point of China's desire to prevent the USSR from encircling China through India. The global-regional interaction can be depicted as follows:[33]

---

[33] Richard Porth, "A Study of the United States 1971 Intervention in Bangladesh," unpublished paper, University of Pennsylvania, 1975.

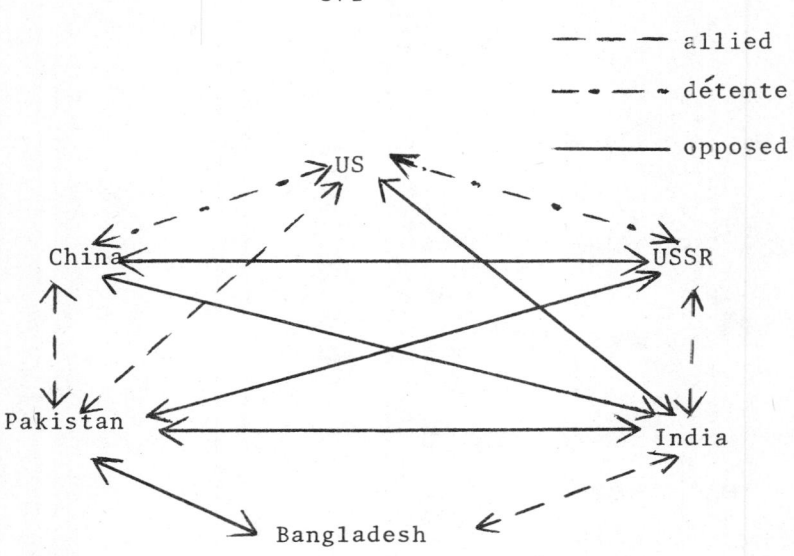

Because of the importance of establishing relations with China, the generalists were sensitive to the image the U.S. would project to China by the American handling of the Pakistani ally. The Rudolphs quote an official familiar with Kissinger's generalists:

> If the Chinese were looking to the U.S. as an ally what kind of an ally would the U.S. be? They might learn something from how the U.S. treated its ally Pakistan.... How we treated our ally Pakistan and how we stood up to India, the Soviet Union's ally, would indicate how we would act with respect to our allies generally. The U.S. did not go in for a pro-Pakistan tilt per se but rather engaged in behavior consistent with these kinds of concerns.[34]

---

[34] As quoted in Rudolph and Rudolph, op. cit., p. 50.

This perception explains, in part, the behavior of certain U.S. decision-makers in attaching such a high value to the China connection and the relation of the South Asian events to that value.

In his 1971 Message to the Congress, President Nixon said:

> We have a deep interest in insuring that the subcontinent does not become a focus of great power conflict... We will try to keep our activities in balance with those of the other major powers concerned... No outside power has a claim to a predominant influence...[35]

A similar thesis is expressed in the 1972 Nixon Report and is also reflected in a 1973 report by the Subcommittee on the Near East and South Asia of the House Committee on Foreign Affairs entitled <u>The United States Interests in and Policies Toward South Asia.</u>

> U.S. strategic interests in the area today relate primarily to regional stability and the avoidance of any situation or presence in South Asia or the adjoining Indian Ocean and Persian Gulf areas which attract a large scale presence, involvement or intervention by any outside power.[36]

Choudhury points out that even though the Nixon-Kissinger team did not consider South Asia a priority area, they

---

[35] Nixon, <u>A Report to the Congress</u> (1971), op. cit., pp. 112-114.

[36] U.S. House of Representatives, Committee on Foreign Affairs, Subcommittee on the Near East and South Asia, <u>Hearings</u>, March 12, 15, 20, and 27, 1973 (Washington, D.C.: <u>GPO, 1973</u>).

had not totally written off the area.[37]

The Nixon Administration also had difficulties formulating and implementing its decisions because of the conflicts among the American Government's representatives in South Asia. The U.S. Consul-General in Dacca, Arch Blood, wanted the Nixon Administration to condemn the Pakistan Government immediately for its brutal massacre in East Pakistan. Ambassador Farland's advocacy for a "quiet diplomacy" approach in dealing with Yahya was approved by Nixon. In India, however, Ambassador Keating attached a higher priority to maintaining good U.S. relations with India especially since the Administration's "quiet diplomacy" approach was not bearing any results and was alienating the Indians.

The generalists argue that in late August 1971 the Soviets had stopped urging the Indians not to go to war and the signal for this was the Indo-Soviet Treaty. Moreover, the events were also cast in terms of the triangular U.S.-USSR-China relationship and the need to show China a convergence of interest in Pakistan and the

---

[37]Choudhury, The Major Powers, op. cit., p. 219.

containment of India. The conflict between Sisco and Kissinger and the different formulations of the priorities and recommended courses of action or nonaction can be explained on the basis of the differing perspectives and weight attached to the global as opposed to regional factors.

The Nixon Doctrine admitted the limitations of U.S. power and announced the American intent to lower its profile and reduce its commitments in Asia. In order to keep its primary role in the international arena, the U.S. sought a rapprochement with China in order to counter the Soviet Union. China had joined the nuclear club and was viewed by the Nixon White House as having the potential to become a major global power. With the emergence of the U.S.-USSR-China triangle, the Nixon Administration realized that the U.S. would be the holder of the balance of power in the relationship because of the Sino-Soviet conflict.

The U.S. pursuit of rapprochement with China eliminated the rationale for the previous American policy of supporting India in order to contain China. Henry Kissinger gave expression to this new policy as distinguished from the 1962 American aid to India when he reportedly told Indian officials that "if China entered the fray between India and Pakistan, India must not expect any help from the U.S."[38] The Nixon Administration sought to counter Soviet influence by way of Indian hegemony of South Asia through U.S. support for Pakistan and China. U.S. conduct and policy during the Bangladesh crisis can be viewed as consistent with previous U.S. global realpolitik policy in the subcontinent. "Its chief aim was to safeguard developing U.S. relations with China."[39]

Under the Nixon-Kissinger system the establishment of priorities and the actions undertaken in the regional subsystem were a function of foreign policy objectives on a global level. The major objective of the global policy was the opening and improvement of U.S. relations with China. Pakistan's President, Yahya Khan, performed a key role in acting as an intermediary between the U.S. and China. Thus, the primary objective or priority was the global framework in which U.S. policy was to be initiated. Regional subsystemic conflict was to be used

---

[38]*Time*, August 23, 1971, p. 7.

[39]Nayar, op. cit., p. 149.

as a bellweather to measure the degree to which global détente had been achieved or to indicate what were to be the permissible amounts of lower level conflict.

A Superpower that is acting to implement its goals in a regional subsystem, whether or not its objectives are dictated by global priorities, will behave in accordance with its previous commitments. Previous U.S. commitments in South Asia were directed in favor of Pakistan despite the arms embargo following the 1965 Indo-Pakistani War. Pakistan, moreover, was a U.S. ally and this consideration was emphasized repeatedly by Kissinger during the WSAG deliberations. For Nixon and Kissinger there was no conflict between their personal preferences between Pakistan and India and their global priority of establishing relations with China. Thus, the previous commitments toward Pakistan, Nixon's and Kissinger's antipathy to India, the objective of establishing relations with China, the perceived need to contain the Soviet Union and its client state in South Asia, as well as Nixon's and Kissinger's personal bias in favor of Pakistan combined to direct U.S. policy toward the "tilt to Pakistan."

Congressional Concerns

The role of Congress in the 1971 South Asia events was peripheral in comparison to the White House's structuring of the problem. Furthermore, the Administration had the authority, ultimately took the initiative, and established the priorities regarding the events. Congressional sentiment may have been a better barometer of the public's sentiments regarding the South Asia crisis. A Louis Harris survey revealed that despite the fact that the American public had not shown much interest in South Asia, a ratio of two-to-one disapproved of Nixon's management of the crisis.

Several Congressional members seem to have focused on the refugee issue and were critical of the Administration's pro-Pakistan policy as being in alignment with a military dictatorship and brutal regime. Senator Kennedy was one of the outspoken Congressional critics regarding U.S. policy during the crisis. Serving as the Chairman of the Subcommittee on Refugees and Escapees, Kennedy utilized this position to criticize the Administration and charge that Nixon "watched this crisis in silence."[40] However, the interaction between Congress and the Executive Branch was limited to Congressional hearing in which members of the Executive Branch were asked to explain American actions in South Asia. Secretary of State Rogers dealt with Congressional members concerning the refugee issue and the American violation of the arms embargo against Pakistan. Kissinger, however, could not be called upon to testify or explain American policy before Congress.

  Congressional pressure on the issue of the arms embargo toward Pakistan did have an impact. Between 1954 and 1965 the United States supplied Pakistan with approximately $2 billion worth of arms. The purpose of these arms, as stated in the U.S.-Pakistani Mutual Defence Assistance Agreement of May 19, 1954, was to contain the Communist bloc, and particularly the Soviet Union. However, these arms had been used in the Indo-Pakistani War of 1965. In response to this development, the United States imposed an arms embargo on both countries, although the Nixon Administration made an exception to the embargo in

---

[40] William Millinship, "Has Nixon Paid a Smuggler's Debt to Pakistan?" <u>Observer Foreign News Service</u>, December 10, 1971.

October 1970 by selling arms to Pakistan. The U.S. arms supplies to Pakistan became a major source of conflict between India and the United States during 1971. Furthermore, the U.S. arms supplies to Pakistan also became an area of conflict between those, such as Senator Kennedy, who linked the U.S. arms supplies to the use of the arms by the Pakistanis in their effort to suppress and kill the Bengalis. As of April 6, 1971, the U.S. State Department had an arms embargo on supplies for Pakistan but during the period between May and October 1971 the Pentagon, according to Kennedy, had signed contracts valued at $10 million with the Pakistani Government. Moreover, he charged, the State Department had provided licenses to U.S. companies that were shipping arms purchased from the USSR and East European countries to Pakistan.[41]

As far as Indians were concerned, the arms supplies to Pakistan revealed American, and particularly the Nixon Administration's, deceit. During his Washington visit in June 1971, Swaran Singh had apparently been assured by the Nixon Administration that U.S. arms would

---

[41] Time, October 25, 1971.

not be supplied to Pakistan. The State Department later stated that an "administrative oversight" was the reason that the arms were delivered to Pakistan after the assurances had been made to Singh. As late as August 1971, the State Department admitted that $4 million worth of American arms destined for Pakistan were still in the pipeline.[42] However, there was in fact a great deal of confusion regarding a policy as well as the implementation of a policy dealing with U.S. arms supplies to Pakistan.[43] The U.S. arms were being utilized for purposes which the U.S. Government had not authorized. Notwithstanding that fact, the Nixon Administration continued to send U.S. arms to Pakistan.[44] Secretary of State Rogers felt very strongly that the small amount of arms shipments to Pakistan was not worth the Congressional antipathy being generated. As a result, the arms embargo was eventually fully implemented, despite Kissinger's lamenting this development during the WSAG discussions in which he queried

---

[42] For an account of this see Time, August 23, 1971.

[43] Interview with U.S. Government official, March 1975,

[44] For an account of the arms supply issue see Subrata Roy Chowdhury, The Genesis of Bangladesh: A Study in International Legal Norms and Permissive Conscience (Bombay: Asia Publishing House, 1972), pp. 260-281.

the possibility of transferring American arms from third countries to Pakistan.

Congressional concern with the refugee issue did involve certain members of Congress in the South Asia events. The American involvement became channeled in the form of humanitarian aid to the refugees. Thus, these members of Congress and the regional experts in the State Department, including those in AID, had a convergence of interest on the refugee issue which both groups regarded as the possible source of a regional war. Consequently, several State Department officials who were indignant with the Administration's policy and actions in South Asia utilized Congressional committees and certain Congressional members as an outlet for their information and criticism. In the formulation of policy and implementation, however, Congressional objectives played a small role in comparison with the priorities established within the White House and NSC staff.

Summary

Notwithstanding the establishment of priorities within the various groups and institutions, decision-making is undertaken by human beings. Despite the organizational structures within which decisions are made, the human dimension in decision-making is the key. The difficulty of determining the thought processes of a decision-maker are acknowledged; yet the hypothesis has been proposed that the establishment of priorities is directly linked to the cognition, beliefs, and previously held values of the decision-makers. Accordingly, we have observed the arguments that Nixon, Kissinger, and other U.S. decision-makers attached little importance to South Asia in comparison to regions such as the Middle East and Southeast Asia. In addition, we have examined the Nixon-Kissinger preference for and high value attached to the opening of U.S. relations with China. Finally, we have probed the Nixon-Kissinger world view with its emphasis on global matters as the framework for understanding the importance they attached to South Asia, but only insofar as U.S. global relations were affected.

  We have suggested that the Rational Man Model presents an approach with a high degree of explanatory power concerning U.S. foreign policy behavior in South Asia. We have utilized a number of "rational" approaches in order to focus on the elements of probabilities and desirabilities that are at the heart of the concept of priority formulation. We have emphasized the subjective and personal approach inherent in our analysis of priority formulation. The Psychological Model has been used to derive a decision-maker's desirabilities. Variations among decision-makers regarding the desirabilities they attach to particular outcomes are the result of their different cognition, beliefs, and values. Consequently, the framework within which decision-makers cast an issue may differ and yield divergent desirabilities. Earlier we suggested the possible utility of the Incremental Model to determine the possible convergence of preferences in order to arrive at a consensus. We also pointed out, however, the difficulties in terms of resistance associated with group decision-making situations that do not generate a consensus and a preference is imposed.

We are quite aware of the difficulty associated with demonstrating that preference ranking is in fact a process that explains the way decision-makers establish their priorities. Some may even argue that there is no such process as priority formulation. We are not advocating a thesis that a decision-maker undertakes the type of exhaustive calculations in terms of the preference ranking process that we examined above. However, we are advancing an argument that preference ranking and the more general concept of priority formulation are at the core of the general decision-making process. A decision-maker, in other words, does make decisions concerning which issues he will seek to resolve, how much time he will devote to a particular issue, how important he thinks the problem is, what he would like that outcome to be, and how crucial he believes it is to reach that outcome.

The concept of priority formulation has been the key tool used in the preceding chapters to help explain U.S. foreign policy decision-making during the 1971 South Asia middle-level crisis. We have found this concept to be a useful device for foreign policy analysis. During the past several years, decision-making theory for foreign policy analysis has been largely confined to the three models: the Rational Man, Psychological, and Incremental Models, which we have also employed. As useful of this type of analysis has been, decision-making theory has also been constrained in its explanatory power by this trilogy approach. Hopefully, priority formulation will prove to be a useful concept and tool of analysis that can be used to transcend the limitations imposed by the persistent focus on three models.

CONCLUSION

The South Asia events of 1971 culminated in a two week war that changed the regional make-up of South Asia. The war began on December 3, 1971 with Pakistan's air attacks on several airfields in the western part of India. India counter-attacked against Pakistan and concentrated its efforts in the east. By December 16 the two week war had come to an end with the unconditional surrender by the Pakistani army in East Pakistan, which India had recognized as the Peoples Republic of Bangladesh on December 6. On the western front, the fighting had not resulted in significant border changes and a cease-fire took effect on December 17.

The stages of U.S. foreign policy in the Indo-Pakistani War of 1971 may be divided as follows: 1) the election period, November 1969- February 1970, 2) March 1971, the crackdown period, 3) the refugee period-- April- June 1971, 4) the period of Indian intervention in guerrilla action-- July- November 1971, 5) November- December 7, 1971-- the "crisis" period, 6) December 1971--

the war period. The application of the three models and the concept of priority formulation provide differing perspectives for analyzing the phases of the middle-level crisis. Even though the time periods have been designated stages of a middle-level crisis, it is, nevertheless, crucial to emphasize that the process is properly viewed as <u>dynamic</u> in terms of movements along a continuum from noncrisis to crisis. Moreover, the actions of the decision-makers are also dynamic and susceptible to change.

From a theoretical perspective this study has argued that the 1971 Indo-Pakistani War is not a unique phenomenon for U.S. foreign policy. The argument has been presented that there exists a category of crises that can be labeled middle-level crisis. A crisis may be viewed as a continuum ranging from noncrisis at one pole to crisis at the other. We found that the South Asia events of 1971 may be characterized as a middle-level crisis because of the low priority attached to the area by U.S. decision-makers. These crises, it has been suggested, have characteristics that differentiate them from crises such as the Cuban missile crisis. The heart of the distinction seems to be the degree of priority and threat that U.S.

foreign policy decision-makers attach to the issue area being considered.

From the perspective of U.S. foreign policy decision-makers the 1971 events in South Asia may be characterized as a middle-level crisis. However, from the perspective of the regional powers involved in the war, the events constituted a pure crisis. Rather than studying an event solely as a unique case study of U.S. foreign policy, it is suggested that other phenomena that seem to fall within the framework of what we have here labeled a middle-level crisis be examined in terms of the propositions that we have advanced. Thus, for example, the conflict in Cyprus may be analyzed in light of the findings advanced in this study in order to examine whether U.S. foreign policy decision-makers processed those events in an analogous fashion.

This study was undertaken for the purpose of determining and explaining U.S. foreign policy decision-making in the Indo-Pakistani War of 1971. However, a conscious effort has been made not to allow the work to become a case study in diplomatic history. While this project is in fact a case study, it has sought to serve the more general purpose of contributing to an understanding of the formulation of U.S. foreign policy objectives and priorities. In analyzing U.S. policy formulation toward the 1971 Indo-Pakistani War from different perspectives, an attempt has been made to utilize theoretical models as a means of examining the formulation of policy and priorities.

This study has suggested that decision-makers process stimuli by their respective belief sets. These beliefs and values bear on the desirabilities subjectively attached to the outcomes they seek to achieve. This process explains, in part, how decision-makers rank order their preferences and then proceed to concentrate their attention and energies on the issue which they consider of greatest importance.

We have sought to contribute to an understanding of a decision-maker's formulation of foreign policy objectives and priorities. During the course of the study, decision-making theories were utilized to analyze U.S. policy formulation. We have presented the argument that the concept of priority formulation is the core of the decision-making process.

We have attempted to develop a systematic approach

toward priority formulation. The examination of priority formulation was undertaken through the subjective and personal priority scale of an individual decision-maker. An individual decision-maker's preference ranking was developed from his assessment of the probabilities of the occurrence of his preferred outcomes and the derivation of the value that he attaches to attaining that outcome.

In developing the concept of priority formulation, we relied primarily on the Rational Man Model for focusing on the probabilities and desirabilities of an individual decision-maker. The Psychological Model was used primarily in order to determine the intensity or value that an individual decision-maker attaches to achieving an outcome. We examined such concepts as cognition, values, belief sets, and response sets in order to determine an individual decision-maker's desirabilities. Furthermore, we examined the proposition that an individual decision-maker possesses simple paradigms in his response set. We urged that in dealing with a complex issue characterized by uncertainty, a decision-maker will utilize, from the repertoire of his response set, a model that he perceives to be appropriate. By doing so, a decision-maker simplifies the environment in which he is operating.

However, government is not composed of a single decision-making unit with a clear cut objective. Consequently, various decision-makers, probably from different governmental units, are likely to possess divergent priorities and as a result, conflicts may emerge. Conflicts among the participants concerning the proper objectives and the means to be utilized should not be surprising. The conflicts among the decision-makers over the priorities contribute to an Administration's difficulty in coordinating complexity. On the one hand, a decision may be successfully imposed by those who possess the power and authority to insist on a specific policy, although a consensus may be achieved through a pulling and hauling process. On the other hand, the actions generated by the government may be in conflict and confusion may be a characteristic of both the formulation and implementation stages if the bureaucracy resists the Executive's decision. This analysis was undertaken by means of the Incremental Model.

The policy sought to be explained in this project was the Nixon Administration's "tilt in favor of Pakistan."

This study has sought to emphasize how government functions and mobilizes in confronting regional middle-level crises. We pointed out that, despite its shortcomings, the Rational Man Model provides the most satisfactory explanation of U.S. foreign policy decision-making toward South Asia in 1971.

W. Norman Brown reached the following conclusion regarding U.S. policy in South Asia in 1971.

> One of the most damaging blows to American prestige in the subcontinent was self-inflicted in 1971-72 in connection with the revolt in East Pakistan, which led to the India-Pakistan War of December 1971... The recklessness of the American administration in relations with the world's largest democracy-- and a natural ally of America-- seems beyond explanation. Not even the secret minutes of the high-level Washington planning group, which the columnist Jack Anderson got hold of and published, reveal any basis for the action. They merely show that the President, though claiming to be even-handed, was really "tilting" his policy in favor of Pakistan. No explanation has been offered by the United States administration.[1]

However, the Rational Man Model has pointed out the role that a factor such as the opening of China had

---

[1] W. Norman Brown, The United States and India, Pakistan, Bangladesh (Cambridge, Massachusetts: Harvard University Press, 1972), pp. 414-416.

in the global view developed by Nixon and Kissinger. Furthermore, because of the low priority that key U.S. decision-makers attached to South Asia, they were able to undertake actions involving that region for global purposes. By restructuring the problem, they were attempting to accomplish goals, such as establishing precedents regarding U.S. reaction to unilateral military attacks, that were not to be judged solely by regional standards. In addition, we have examined how the Psychological and Incremental Models supplement our understanding of a complex decision-making process. An effort was made to explain this policy in terms of global considerations such as the China connection and traditional balance of power notions, psychological explanations such as Nixon's and numerous U.S. officials' antipathy for India and her representatives and bias in favor of Pakistan, and the bureaucratic explanation of past U.S. commitments to Pakistan and tendency to continue such ties even if the reasons for the original commitment were no longer germane.

We began with the proposition that the locus of a decision in the American government shifts to the Executive Office as a noncrisis develops into a middle-level crisis.

This is a characteristic of a middle-level crisis because a pure crisis, such as the Cuban missile crisis, tends to be processed by the Executive Office from its origin due to the elements of priority and surprise. The efforts to cope with the events in South Asia were traced from the attempts made by U.S. representatives in the field to the control sought to be exercised by the State Department and the eventual direction provided by the Executive Office through WSAG and the NSC. The conflict that emerged between the generalists and the regional experts and the shift of the decision-making power to the generalists as events evolved into a middle-level crisis was also confirmed by the study. We have found that the Nixon Administration's attitude toward the South Asian events was the wish that the entire proble would go away. As a result, the events in the region unfolded without receiving priority from the Administration and U.S. policy drifted.

The differences in the perspective of the foreign policy decision-makers in relation to the relative importance of the global as opposed to the regional factors were at the core of the struggle between the generalists and the regionalists at the extremes of the continuum. The generalists and the regionalists operated on the basis of different assumptions and values regarding the proper role for U.S. foreign policy in the area. While the latter believed that the U.S. should deal with the merits of the regional struggle between India and Pakistan in terms of India's refugee problem, the generalists cast the issue in a global context where the primary concern was the global balance of power and the regional South Asia conflict as a part of the global jockeying between the U.S., USSR, and China. Accordingly, if the argument is accepted that the Nixon Administration was concerned about the global balance of power and viewed India as a Soviet client state with the result that an Indian victory over Pakistan would be a harmful precedent for U.S. global interests, the "tilt toward Pakistan" may be explained as dictated by U.S. global considerations.

In examining the global approach argument, we have not neglected to undertake an examination of alternative explanations such as Nixon's personal bias in favor of Pakistan and his antipathy for India. In the 1971 Indo-Pakistani War there was no conflict between the President's personal preference and his policy objective of implementing a China connection policy. However, a different case study analyzed within the framework of a middle-level crisis may present the situation of a conflict existing between the President's personal preferences on the one hand and U.S. global interests on the other. In such a case, a conflict would likely emerge in terms of what the priorities of U.S. policy should be. In our case, the conflict was between U.S. regional interests on the one hand and U.S. global interests and the President's personal preferences on the other.

Numerous commentators who appraised U.S. policy in the 1971 Indo-Pakistani War suggested that the developments were "catastrophic for American policy in the area."[1] However, while U.S.-India relations were in fact strained for a period of time following the war, the U.S. posture in the area has not been irrevocably harmed. Perhaps the lack of harm done to the American position is due to the lack of priority attached to the region by U.S. decision-makers. The U.S. no longer concerns itself with South Asia in the same Cold War urgency of the 1950s. The U.S. has adjusted itself to the reality of the South Asian situation with a modified balance of power in

---

[1] Kalb and Kalb, op. cit., p. 257.

existence, despite the possibility of Indian hegemony. The U.S. has retreated from its past global role and its tendency to intervene in those situations that might adversely affect its interests.

However, the U.S. has not abandoned its South Asia posture completely, despite the reduced interest that is being shown in the area. Diego Garcia has become a major base for the U.S. in the Indian Ocean. The importance of the Indian Ocean for U.S. defense policy has brought South Asia into the American security system through another channel. Oddly enough, the Indian Ocean came into the limelight and began to be considered an important issue to the American national security by the summer of 1971.[2]

The American government's organizational structure for coping with events in South Asia may in part account for the low priority attached to the area and the small

---

[2] See "The Indian Ocean: Political and Strategic Future," Hearings Before the Subcommittee on National Security Policy and Scientific Developments of the Committee on Foreign Affairs, House of Representatives, Ninety-Second Congress, First Session, July 20, 22, 27 and 28, 1971 (Washington, D.C.: U.S. Government Printing Office, 1971).

amount of attention that the region receives. Some
suggest, however, that the low priority the area receives
accounts for the organizational arrangement. In any event,
South Asia has been and continues to be grouped with the
Middle East and often North Africa as one region. This
arrangement tends to be the case throughout the agencies
of the Executive Branch and within the Congressional
committee system. Since the heads of the Middle East
and South Asia organizational structure invariably tend
to be experts on the Middle East, they usually tend to
know little if anything about South Asia. Most have
rarely if ever even visited a South Asian state. Moreover, there seems to be no common denominator between
the Middle East and South Asia which would justify lumping
them in one bureau. Consequently, the Middle East expert
who heads the Middle East and South Asia bureau tends to
spend approximately nine-five per cent of his time on
the Middle East and five per cent on South Asia. A
possible and simple prescription for this situation is
to split the South Asia bureau from the Middle East
bureau.

  Nevertheless, American Government decision-makers
involved in the Indo-Pakistani War suggest that they

devoted a considerable amount of energy to this crisis. This was due to the China and other global factors that were occupying the attention of the top-level decision-makers. Furthermore, there were no serious competing events during the November-December crisis period for the lower-level decision-makers. In short, it was the only crisis in town.

The issue of whether U.S. policy in a region should be dictated by global considerations or examined in terms of the regional merits is difficult to establish with any degree of confidence.

> Coordinating organizations and procedures of the Johnson and Nixon administrations failed to sustain compatible policies at the global, regional and bilateral levels. By unnecessarily subordinating regional and bilateral to global considerations, gratuitous losses were suffered in regional and bilateral relations...[3]

Because of the low priority attached by the Nixon White House to South Asia as a region, the Nixon Administration viewed any importance in the region in terms of the role it played in the global context of the

---

[3] Rudolph and Rudolph, op. cit., p. 41.

U.S., USSR, and China triangle. South Asia was an area of conflict because the major powers had chosen to attempt to exercise their influence in the region. It was a region where each major power saw its position advanced or upset depending on the fortunes of its proxy. The U.S. was pursuing its détente policy with the Soviet Union and this meant that the U.S. would no longer compete with the USSR with the intensity that had characterized the Cold War. Restraint was supposed to characterize U.S.-Soviet relations in regional conflicts. China, moreover, was to be introduced into a triangular international realpolitik arena by the U.S. in order to act as a counter to the USSR.

Whether the "tilt toward Pakistan" policy makes sense as a necessary U.S. policy that helped to bring forth the structure of peace that Nixon envisaged will remain a subject of controversy. Several points seem clea, however. Because of the low priority attached to South Asia by the Nixon Administration, it was relatively easy to make the decision that the U.S. should make its position unmistakably clear even if the outcome of an Indian victory could not be prevented. Moreover, in making the "tilt toward Pakistan" decision, the Nixon-Kissinger team was not confronted by contradictory stimuli. The China connection factor, personal preference toward Pakistan and antipathy for India, and the previous U.S. commitment to Pakistan indicated a policy with an impetus toward one direction-- pro-Pakistan.

In contradistinction to Nixon's analysis and values, Senators Church and Kennedy came to different conclusions despite their agreement regarding the region's low priority.

Senator Frank Church made the following statement on December 6, 1971:

> The war that has erupted between India and Pakistan is no affair of ours. Whichever side prevails, we can live with the result. Our vital interests as a nation are not at stake on the Indian subcontinent, as long as the great powers refrain from direct intervention in the conflict.[4]

Senator Kennedy stated:

> This Administration has rightly taken pride in its efforts to re-establish contact with one-fifth of mankind's population in China. But

---

[4] India News, December 17, 1971, p. 3.

> are we going to simultaneously alienate one-sixth of manking in India-- a democratic nation with whom we have had years or productive relations?[5]

The South Asia events of 1971 were cast in either-or terms by U.S. foreign policy decision-makers. On the one hand, the Nixon-Kissinger view was apparently dictated by realpolitik considerations. After touring South Asia, both Congressman Gallagher and Senator Kennedy received some attention from the media, and they described the situation in the region in terms of a holocaust and genocide. Those who viewed the U.S. confronting a moral issue in South Asia argued that the appropriate American response would be to address the moral question. This school of thought opposed the Nixon Administration's support for Yahya's regime, especially following the March 25 crackdown.

The theoretical models we have used to analyze the events have revealed several interesting points. There are alternative means by which to examine and explain the decision-making process and result. Furthermore, there was no single U.S. policy. Different U.S. government agencies

---

[5] Ibid., p. 3.

and individuals had different positions and the results that emerged were often contradictory. There was also no clear consensus among the decision-makers and the Nixon White House had to impose its position on the agencies and individuals it needed to implement the decisions. As a result, the policy-making mechanism did not function smoothly. Confusion regarding the reasons for the adoption of the "tilt in favor of Pakistan" policy and what steps were to be implemented as the manifestation of the policy emerged during this middle-level crisis.

Nixon's policy was dubbed a "tilt" in favor of Pakistan by Kissinger. Joseph Sisco, Assistant Secretary of State for Near Eastern and South Asian Affairs, explained it was "a tilt toward peace and to achieve and help achieve the kind of peace and stability which we think is in the interest of all countries in the area as well as the major powers who have an interest in the area."[6]

Critics of the Nixon Administration's "tilt" policy argue that even though the U.S. was opening her

---

[6]Hearings Before the Subcommittee on Near East and South Asia of the Committee on Foreign Affairs, House of Representatives, March 12, 15, 20, and 27, 1973 (Washington, D.C.: USGPO, 1973), p. 82.

relations with China, that factor did not justify an American policy that entailed alienating India or aligning with a ruthless and oppressive Pakistani military regime. However, U.S.-Indian relations had become strained prior to Nixon's entry into the White House in 1969. One writer has described the tension in U.S.-Indian relations as "a broken love affair involving two acolescents in world politics that had never really known one another very well in the first place."[7]

The American position in South Asia was precarious. From an interest analysis perspective a fundamental reality of U.S.-Indian relations and the U.S. position in South Asia generally is the low priority that India and South Asia hold for U.S. strategic and economic interests when compared to other regions of the world. Despite the Nixon Administration's awareness of its limited influence and interest in South Asia, the White House sought to prevent India from unilaterally changing the status quo of the South Asian regional system by an armed attack on East Pakistan, while simultaneously attempting to convince

---

[7]Marcus F. Franda, "Indo-American Relations: A Year of Deterioration," Field Staff Reports, South Asia Series, Vol. XVII, No. 3, January 1973, p. 1.

Pakistan's central government to grant autonomy to the East wing. The Nixon Administration was concerned about the realpolitik balance of power issues in South Asia and the interests of the major powers in the region.

The Nixon Administration acknowledged the legitimate interest of the USSR and China in South Asia. Because of their proximity to South Asia and the intensity of their rivalry, the USSR and China seem to have a greater interest in South Asia than does the U.S. This does not mean that the U.S. has no role to play in the region, but it does suggest that the U.S. should maintain a low profile in the area. The key triangular geopolitical relationship in South Asia involves the USSR, China, and India. The shifts in alignments beginning in 1971 have seen the USSR and India aligning in opposition to China, the U.S. and China against the USSR, and on a regional level, the continuation of China and Pakistan against India.

The major impact of the 1971 South Asia War has been on the region itself. India has emerged as the dominant power in the subcontinent. The effect on the major powers has not been as dramatic but does have some significance. The Soviets have strengthened their position to the south and have implemented part of their goal of of encircling China. The U.S., in Indian eyes, was wholeheartedly committed to the support of Pakistan's military dictatorship. Accordingly, the Nixon policy alienated India without preserving the integrity of Pakistan. If the Chinese were the audience for the Administration's actions, it is doubtful that they were impressed by the effectiveness of the U.S. policy unless they really believed that the American actions saved West Pakistan from Indian attack.

Indirectly at least, the closer ties between India and the USSR have reinforced the previously developing Sino-American relations. The Chinese are keenly aware of the Soviet effort to encircle them and have found the interest shown by the U.S. to be a propitious means to counter the Soviet attempt. However, except for Pakistan, the Chinese may have been the biggest losers in 1971 as a result of "the shattering of its Pakistan ally, the rise of Indian prestige and power to counter Peking's 'gravitational pull,' and, most damaging in Chinese eyes, the furtherance of Soviet schemes to encircle China."[8]

---

[8] Fred Greene, "The Indian-Pakistan War and the Asian Balance of Power," Naval War College Review, January-February 1973, p. 22.

The strains in U.S.-Indian relations have continued since the 1971 South Asia War. The divergent world views held by each of these powers seem to account for a large part of their mutual misperceptions and policy differences concerning South Asia. These differences are not simply a matter of perception but have their roots in substantive issues as well. The Indian Ambassador to the United States, T. N. Kaul, has pointed to the different geopolitical factors that are matters of concern for each of these states. While he has expressed optimism regarding future U.S.-Indian relations, Ambassador Kaul does so by emphasizing equality, reciprocity, and non-interference as the basis for bilateral, regional, and even global relations involving the U.S. and India.[9] Even though the U.S. has maintained a low profile in South Asia, it is unlikely that the U.S. and India will conduct their relations based on the three premises that Ambassador Kaul has advanced. South Asia is likely to remain a low priority for the U.S. Furthermore, China will be

---

[9] T.N. Kaul, "The Tilt and After," India News, November 30, 1973, p. 3.

increasingly looked upon by the U.S. as the counter to the USSR at the global level and India at the regional level.

We have examined a middle-level crisis and its implications for the U.S. and a region. This study emphasizes the importance of values that decision-makers hold. These values have major consequences for the way decisions are made and implemented. In addition, actions whether implemented or not will have a major impact on people living thousands of miles away. These values and belief sets need to be and should be examined by the individual decision-makers in terms of the consequences they may bear.

BIBLIOGRAPHY

Akhtar, Jamna Das, *Saga of Bangla Desh* (Delhi: Oriental Publishers, 1971).

Ali, Tariq, *Pakistan: Military Rule or People's Power* (New York: William Morrow and Co., 1970).

Allison, Graham T., *Essence of Decision: Explaining the Cuban Missile Crisis* (Boston: Little, Brown and Co., 1971).

Allport, Gordon W., *The Nature of Prejudice* (Garden City, N.Y.: Doubleday, 1958).

Almond, Gabriel A., *The American People and Foreign Policy* (New York: Harcourt, Brace, 1950).

_____, "Comparative Political Systems," *Journal of Politics*, August 1956, pp. 391-409.

Alvi, Hamza and Amir Khusro, *Pakistan and the Burden of U.S. Aid* (Karachi: Syed and Syed, 1965).

Anderson, Jack with George Clifford, *The Anderson Papers* (New York: Random House, 1973).

Bangla Desh Documents (New Delhi: Ministry of External Affairs, 1971).

Barnds, William J., *India, Pakistan and the Great Powers* (New York: Praeger, 1972).

Bhutto, Zulfikar Ali, *The Myth of Independence* (London: Oxford University Press, 1969).

Bloomfield, Lincoln P., *The Foreign Policy Process: Making Theory Relevant* (Beverly Hills: Sage Publications, 1974).

Brandon, Henry, *The Retreat of American Power* (Garden City, N.Y.: Doubleday, 1973).

Brecher, Michael, *The Foreign Policy System of Israel: Setting, Images, Process* (New Haven: Yale University Press, 1972).

Brown, Norman W., *The United States and India and Pakistan* (Cambridge: Harvard University Press, 1963).

Brown, Roger, Social Psychology (New York: The Free Press, 1965).

Budruddin, S.G.M., Election Handbook 1970 (Karachi: Publishing and Marketing Associated Ltd., 1970).

Bundy, William, "International Security Today," Foreign Affairs, Vol 53, No. 1, October 1974.

Callard, Keith, Pakistan: A Political Study (New York: The Macmillan Co., 1957).

_____, Pakistan's Foreign Policy: An Interpretation (New York: Institute of Pacific Relations, 1957).

Campbell, John C., Defense of the Middle East: Problems of American Policy (New York: Praeger, 1960).

Cantori, Louis J. and Spiegel, Steven L., The International Politics of Regions: A Comparative Approach (Englewood Cliffs, N.J.: Prentice-Hall, 1970).

Cartwright, Dorwin and Alvin Zander, Group Dynamics: Research and Theory, 3rd edition (New York: Harper & Row Publishers, 1968).

Chittik, William O., State Department, Press and Pressure Groups: A Role Analysis (New York: Wiley-Inter-science, 1970).

Choudhury, G.W., India, Pakistan, Bangladesh and the Major Powers: Politics of a Divided Subcontinent (New York: The Free Press, 1975).

_____, The Last Days of United Pakistan (Bloomington: Indiana University Press, 1974).

_____, and Parvez Hasan, Pakistan's External Relations (Karachi: Pakistan Institute of International Affairs, 1958).

Chowdhury, Subrata Roy, The Genesis of Bangladesh: A Study in International Legal Norms and Permissive Conscience (Bombay: Asia Publishing House, 1972).

Cobb, Roger W. and Charles D. Elder, Participation in American Politics: The Dynamics of Agenda-Building (Boston: Allyn and Bacon, 1972).

Cohen, Bernard C. (ed.), Foreign Policy in American Government (Boston: Little, Brown and Co., 1965).

Cohen, Bernard C., The Public's Impact on Foreign Policy (Boston: Little, Brown and Co., 1973).

Cohen, Jerome Alan, "Recognizing China," Foreign Affairs, October 1971, Vol 50, No. 1.

Crisis in South Asia. A Report by Senator Edward M. Kennedy to the Subcommittee to Investigate Problems Connected with Refugees and Escapees of the Committee on the Judiciary, United States Senate, Washington, D.C.: U.S. Government Printing Office, November 1, 1971.

Destler, I.M., Presidents, Bureaucrats and Foreign Policy: The Politics of Organizational Reform (Princeton: Princeton University Press, 1972).

Deutsch, Karl W., The Nerves of Government (New York: The Free Press, 1964).

Dougherty, James E. and Pfaltzgraff, Robert L., Contending Theories of International Relations (Philadelphia, Penna.: Lippincott, 1971).

Deutsch, Karl W., Nationalism and Social Communication (Cambridge, Mass.: MIT Press, 1966).

Easton, David, A Framework for Political Analysis (Englewood Cliffs, N.J.: Prentice-Hall, 1965).

Feldman, Herbert, From Crisis to Crisis: Pakistan 1962-1969 (London: Oxford University Press, 1972).

Fox, Douglas M. (ed.), The Politics of U.S. Foreign Policy Making (Pacific Palisades, Calif.: Goodyear Publishing Co., 1971).

Frankel, Joseph, The Making of Foreign Policy: An Analysis of Decision Making (New York: Osford University Press, 1963).

Gandhi, Indira, *India and Bangla Desh* (New Delhi: Orient Longman, 1972).

Graubard, Stephen R., *Kissinger: Portrait of a Mind* (New York: W.W. Norton & Co., 1974).

Greene, Fred, "The Indian-Pakistan War and the Asian Balance of Power," *Naval War College Review*, January-February 1973, p. 22.

Gupta, Vinod, *Anderson Papers: A Study of Nixon's Blackmail of India* (Delhi: ISSD, 1972).

Haas, Ernest B., *Beyond the Nation State* (Stanford: Stanford University Press, 1964).

Halperin, Morton H., *Bureaucratic Politics and Foreign Policy* (Washington, D.C.: The Brookings Institution, 1974).

_____ and Arnold Kanter (eds.), *Readings in American Foreign Policy: A Bureaucratic Perspective* (Boston: Little, Brown and Co., 1973).

Hampton, David R., Summer, Charles E., and Webber, Ross A., *Organizational Behavior and the Practice of Management* (Glenview, Ill.: Scott, Foresman and Co., 1968).

Hare, A. Paul, *Handbook of Small Group Research* (New York: The Free Press, 1962).

Hermann, Charles F. (ed.), *International Crises: Insights From Behavioral Research* (New York: The Free Press, 1972).

Hilsman, Roger, *To Move a Nation* (New York: Dell Publishing Company, 1967).

Hilsman, Roger, *The Politics of Policy Making in Defense and Foreign Affairs* (New York: Harper & Row, 1971).

Holsti, K.J., *International Politics: A Framework for Analysis* (Englewood Cliffs, N.J.: Prentice-Hall, 1967).

Hussain, Arif, *Pakistan: Its Ideology and Foreign Policy* (London: Frank Cass and Co., Ltd., 1966).

"The Indian Ocean: Political and Strategic Future," Hearings before the Subcommittee on National Security Policy and Scientific Developments of the Committee on Foreign Affairs, House of Representatives, Ninety-Second Congress, First Session, July 20, 22, 27, and 28, 1971, Washington, D.C.: USGPO, 1971.

Jacob, Philip E. and James V. Toscano (eds.), The Integration of Political Communities (Philadelphia, Penna.: J.B. Lippincott, 1964).

Jahan, Rounaq, Pakistan: Failure in National Integration (New York: Columbia University Press, 1972).

Jain, A.P. (ed.), India and the World (Delhi: D.K. Publishing House, 1972).

Janis, Irving, Victims of Groupthink: A Psychological Study of Foreign-Policy Decision and Fiascoes (Boston: Houghton-Mifflin, 1967).

Johnson, Richard Tanner, Managing the White House: An Intimate Study of the Presidency (New York: Harper & Row, 1974).

Kalb, Marvin and Bernard Kalb, Kissinger (Boston: Little, Brown and Company, 1974).

Kaushik, Devendra, Soviet Relations with India and Pakistan (Delhi: Vikas Publications, 1971).

Keesing's Research Report, Pakistan: From 1947 to the Creation of Bangladesh (New York: Charles Scribner's Sons, 1973).

Kelman, Herbert C. (ed.), International Behavior: A Social-Psychological Analysis (New York: Holt, Rinehart & Winston, 1965).

Khan, Mohammad Ayub, Friends Not Masters: A Political Autobiography (New York: Oxford University Press, 1967).

Kissinger, Henry A., American Foreign Policy: Three Essays (New York: W.W. Norton & Co., 1969).

Kleinberg, Otto, The Human Dimension in International Relations (New York: Osford University Press, 1967).

Knorr, Klaus and Sidney Verba (eds.), *The International System: Theoretical Essays* (Princeton, N.J.: Princeton University Press, 1961).

Laundau, David, *Kissinger: The Uses of Power* (Boston: Houghton Mifflin, 1972).

Lindberg, Leon N. and Stuart A. Scheingold, *Europe's Would-Be Polity: Patterns of Change in the European Community* (Englewood Cliffs, N.J.: Prentice-Hall, 1970).

Luce, R. Duncan and Howard Raiffa, *Games and Decisions* (New York: John Wiley and Sons, 1957).

Millinship, William, "Has Nixon Paid a Smuggler's Debt to Pakistan?" Observer Foreign News Service, December 10, 1971.

Minogue, K.R., *Nationalism* (New York: Basic Books, 1967).

Moraes, Dom, *The Tempest Within* (New Delhi: Vikas, 1971).

Moraes, Frank, "India and Pakistan," *Pacific Community*, October 1971.

Morgenthau, Hans J., *Politics Among Nations: The Struggle for Power and Peace* (New York: Alfred Knopf, 1967).

Nayar, Baldev Raj, "Treat India Seriously," *Foreign Policy*, No. 18, Spring 1975.

Neustadt, Richard E., *Presidential Power: The Politics of Leadership* (New York: Wiley, 1960).

Newhouse, John, *Cold Dawn: The Story of SALT* (New York: Holt, Rinehart & Winston, 1973).

Nicholas, Marta and Oldenburg, Philip, *Bangladesh: The Birth of a Nation* (Madros, India: M. Seshachalam and Company, 1972).

Nixon, Richard M., "Asia After VietNam," *Foreign Affairs* October 1967, pp. 111-125.

_____, *Six Crises* (Garden City, N.Y.: Doubleday, 1962).

_____, U.S. Foreign Policy for the 1970's: The Emerging Structure of Peace, A Report to the Congress (Washington, D.C.: United States Government Printing Office, February 9, 1972).

Oksenberg, Michael, "The Strategies of Peking," Foreign Affairs, Vol. 50, No. 1, October 1971.

Paige, Glenn D., The Korean Decision (New York: The Free Press, 1968).

Palmer, Norman D., Recent Soviet and Chinese Penetration in India and Pakistan: Guidelines for Political-Military Policy (McLean, Va.: Research Analysis Corp., 1970).

_____, South Asia and United States Policy (Boston: Houghton Mifflin Co., 1966).

Payne, Robert, Massacre (New York: The Macmillan Co., 1973).

Porth, Richard, "A Study of the United States 1971 Intervention in Bangladesh," unpublished paper, University of Pennsylvania, 1975.

Pruitt, Dean G. and Richard C. Snyder, Theory and Research on the Causes of War (Englewood Cliffs, N.J.: Prentice-Hall, 1969).

Ra'anan, Uri, The USSR Arms the Third World: Case Studies in Soviet Foreign Policy (Cambridge, Mass.: MIT Press, 1969).

Rahman, Sheikh Mujibur, Bangladesh, My Bangladesh (New Delhi: Orient Longman, 1972).

Rosenau, James N. (ed.), Domestic Sources of Foreign Policy (New York: The Free Press, 1967).

Safire, William L., Before the Fall: An Inside View of The Pre-Watergate White House (Garden City, N.Y.: Doubleday, 1975).

Sharma, B. L., The Pakistan-China Axis (Bombay: Asia Publishing House, 1968).

Sherwani, Latif Ahmed, et. al., Foreign Policy of Pakistan: An Analysis (Karachi: The Allies Book Corp., 1964).

Siddiqi, Aslam, Pakistan Seeks Security (Lahore: Longmans, Green and Co., 1960).

Simon, Sheldon W., "The Kashmir Dispute in Sino-Soviet Perspective," Asian Survey, March 1967.

Singhal, Damodar P., Pakistan (Englewood Cliffs, N.J.: Prentice-Hall, 1972).

Snyder, Richard C., H. W. Bruck, and Burton Sapin (eds.), Foreign Policy Decision-Making (New York: The Free Press of Glencoe, 1963).

Spanier, John W., American Foreign Policy Since World War II (New York: Frederick A. Praeger, 1968).

_____, and Eric M. Uslaner, How American Foreign Policy is Made (New York: Praeger, 1974).

Spiro, Herbert J., World Politics: The Global System (Homewood, Ill.: Dorsey Press, 1966).

Steinbruner, John E., The Cybernetic Theory of Decision: New Dimensions of Political Analysis (Princeton, N.J.: Princeton University Press, 1974).

Stoessinger, John G., Why Nations Go to War (New York: St. Martin's Press, 1974).

Strausz-Hupé, Robert and Stefan T. Possony, International Relations (New York: McGraw-Hill, 1954).

Syed, Anwar Hussain, China and Pakistan: Diplomacy of an Entente Cordiale (Amherst: The University of Massachusetts Press, 1974).

_____, "Reflections of the Arabian Decade in Pakistan," Pakistan Administrative Staff College Journal, IX, December 1971.

Tanter, Raymond, "Crisis Management: A Critical Review of Academic Literature," The Jerusalem Journal of International Relations, Vol. 1, No. 1, Fall 1975.

U.S. House of Representatives, Committee on Foreign Affairs, Subcommittee on the Near East and South Asia, Hearings (Washington, D.C.: USGPO, 1973).

Van Doorn, Jacques, Armed Forces and Society (The Hague: Mouton, 1968).

Watt, Donald, "Pakistan From Within: A Threeway Split," Commonwealth Journal of International Affairs, No. 245, January 1972.

Wheeler, Richard S., The Politics of Pakistan: A Constitutional Quest (Ithaca, N.Y.: Cornell University Press, 1970).

White, Ralph K., "Misperception and the Vietnam War," The Journal of Social Issues, Vol. XXII, No. 3, July 1966.

White Paper on the Crisis in East Pakistan (Islamabad: Ministry of Information and National Affairs, 1971).

Wilcox, Wayne, The Emergence of Bangladesh: Problems and Opportunities for a Redefined American Policy in South Asia (Washington, D.C.: American Enterprise Institute for Public Policy Research, 1973).

_____, The Kashmir Problem and the Indo-Pakistani War of 1965, unpublished manuscript, Columbia University.

Yost, Charles W., The Conduct and Misconduct of Foreign Affairs (New York: Random House, 1972).

Zeigler, Harmon L. and Wayne G. Peak, Interest Groups in American Society (Englewood Cliffs, N.J.: Prentice-Hall, 1972).

INDEX

Afghanistan, 41
Ahmad, Ghulam, 91
Ahsan, S.M., 84
Ali, Mohammad, 48
Ali, Tariq, 31
All India Congress Committee Resolution, 34
Allison, Graham, 7, 8, 10, 25, 219, 229, 301, 328
Allport, Gordon, 38
Almond, Gabriel, 134, 215
Alvi, Hamza, 48-49
Anderson, Jack, 259-260, 291-292, 295, 329, 392
Anderson Paper, 125, 160, 161, 257, 265, 286, 300, 331
Arab World, 41, 44, 46
Awami League, 73, 78, 79, 80, 81-85, 87, 89

Baghdad Pact, 44
Bangladesh, 73, 376, 386
Barnds, William J., 257
Bayes Theorem, 343, 345-348, 350
Bhutto, Zulfikar Ali, 35, 81-85, 259, 269
Blood, Arch, 93, 94, 104, 332, 374

Bonham, Matthew, 283-284

Bowles, Chester, 43

Boulding, Kenneth, 233

Braybrooke, David, 224-225

Brown, Norman W., 392

Bundy, William, 348

Brecher, Michael, 3, 107-108, 217, 233, 237, 283

Bureaucratic Model, 229, 230, 231

Bush, George, 163, 167

Callard, Keith, 33

CENTO, 27, 63, 173, 243

China, 17, 22, 53, 58, 60-62, 90, 167, 168, 172, 176-181, 183, 195, 243-245, 246-256, 259, 264, 269, 277, 286, 293, 294, 298, 300, 308, 309, 322, 330, 338, 368, 369, 370-376, 383 393, 399, 405-407

    Aid to Pakistan, 61, 276

China Policy, 15, 52, 122, 147, 148, 154, 155, 165, 168, 174-177, 271-275, 287, 298, 315-323, 396, 401

Choudhury, G.W., 32, 34, 35, 39, 52, 91, 99, 373

Chou En-lai, 60

Church, Frank, 401

CIA, 91, 92, 113, 130, 257, 261, 269, 320, 345, 365

Cobb, Roger, 336, 337

Cognitive Theory, 304, 305, 324, 349, 357, 359, 361, 362, 363

Cold War, 26, 29, 39, 42, 47, 48, 54, 243, 396, 400

Committee on Foreign Affairs, 131

Committee on Foreign Raltions, 131

Congress, U.S., 13, 96, 97, 100, 110, 129-134, 137, 170, 293, 306, 378-382

Cozzolino, John, 346

Crisis Decision-Making, 3, 4, 24, 154-155, 182, 186, 187, 198, 209, 210, 238, 366

Cybernetic Paradigm, 196, 197, 226, 227-229, 235, 362

Defense Department, 13, 113, 124, 127, 147, 171, 319, 320, 368

Desirabilities, 19, 20, 21, 187, 241-243, 281, 308, 337, 338, 340, 351-356, 370, 371, 384, 389, 390

Deutsch, Karl, 215

Dougherty, James E., 219-220

Dulles, John Foster, 27, 42, 44, 50, 244

East Pakistan, 62, 78, 79, 80, 85, 87-93, 103, 141, 151, 153, 158, 160, 167, 195, 270, 295, 296, 368, 404

Easton, David, 215

Eisenhower Administration, 42, 121

Elder, Charles, 336, 337

Enterprise Episode, 258-264, 290

Farland, Joseph, 92, 93, 294, 295, 332, 374

Frelinghuysen, Peter, 131

Fulbright, William, 99

Gandhi, Indira, 156-160, 182, 291, 294-296, 299, 308, 309, 367

    Visit to Washington, 101-103, 151, 153, 155-160, 165, 295

George, Alexander, 284

Great Britain, 31, 39, 40, 45

Gupta, Shiv, 346

Gupta, Vinod, 285-289

Haas, Ernst, 67

Halperin, Morton, H., 307, 324, 326, 329, 331

Heins, Richard, 188

Helms, Richard, 91

Hermann, Charles and Margaret, 198, 199, 209-213

Hussain, Arif, 39, 41

Hilaly, Agha, 247

Incremental Model, 9, 13, 19, 20, 187, 188, 208, 218, 222, 224-226, 238, 239, 311-335, 391, 393

India

    American arms supply to, 30, 54

    American arms embargo of, 30

    Relations with Pakistan, 30-35, 47, 58, 60, 66-104, 150-184

Indo-Pakistani War of 1971, 1, 13, 16, 151-154, 159, 160, 165, 166, 170, 172, 176, 178, 183, 201, 202, 252, 255, 258, 275, 286, 302, 322, 386, 396

Indo-Pakistani War of 1965, 30, 60, 61, 276, 377, 379

Indo Soviet Friendship Treaty of August 9, 1971, 183, 266, 374

Integration Theory, 67-71

Islam, 37, 38, 39, 41

Jacob, Philip, 68

Jeffrey, R.C., 350, 355

Jervis, R., 284, 285

Jinnah, 32, 34

Johnson, Lyndon, 62-63, 399

Johnson, Richard Tanner, 125

Kahn, Liaquat Ali, 39

Kahn, Ayub, 41, 48, 50, 52, 54, 58, 61, 73-74

Kahn, Yahya, 15, 62, 73-87, 91, 95, 100, 101, 104, 151, 156, 158, 173, 180, 246, 247, 255, 287, 290-295, 299, 374, 376, 402

Kalb, Marvin and Bernard, 129

Kashmir, 35-36, 60, 270

Kaul, T.N., 157, 158, 407

Keating, Kenneth, 296, 332, 374

Kennedy, Edward, 96, 98-99, 100, 132-134, 378, 380, 401-402

Kennedy, John, 50, 52, 121, 291-292, 322

Kissinger, Henry, 19, 51, 90, 95, 101, 107, 112, 118, 119, 122-129, 136, 142-150, 159-184, 194-196, 199-203, 207, 242, 246, 247, 251-257, 261, 268, 269, 275-280, 293-300, 302, 309, 314, 318, 319, 323-330, 338, 370, 375, 377, 379, 381, 383, 393

Kusro, Amir, 48-49

Language Issue, 69-73

Legal Framework Order, 77-78

Lewis, Anthony, 135

Lindberg, Leon, 67

Lindblom, Charles, 224-225

Lippitt, Ronald, 202-203

Luce, R. Duncan, 192

Mao Tse-Tung, 290

McClelland, Charles, 216-217

Middle-Level Crisis, 1, 4, 14-19, 87, 96, 102, 104, 123, 136, 140-142, 181, 187, 207-214, 221, 237, 238, 278, 306, 307, 329, 333, 366, 385, 387, 388, 392-396, 403

Morganthau, Hans, 27-28, 67

Mountbatten Plan, 33

Mujib Sheik (Mujibar Rahman), 15, 81-86, 93, 100, 255, 368

Mukti Bahini, 89

Murphy Commission

Muslim League, 78

Mutual Defense Assistance Program, 44

National Security Council, 12, 106, 107, 113-125, 129, 136, 137, 142, 144, 145, 149-153, 162, 171, 287, 301, 314, 318, 326, 366, 394

    NSSMs, 123, 124

NATO, 44

Nayar, Baldev, Raj, 364

Nehru, 48, 287

Newhouse, John, 219, 237

New York Times, 135

Nixon, Richard, 19, 29, 95, 107, 111, 118, 120, 124, 134, 142-147, 158, 159, 160-168, 170-176, 183, 194, 196, 199-201, 207, 242, 245, 251, 254, 268, 269, 276, 280, 286-307, 315-327, 338, 370, 377, 383, 393, 395

Nixon Administration, 53, 67, 90, 91-94, 100-104, 107 119-123, 128, 136, 140, 144, 175-184, 247, 255, 259, 260, 265, 279, 292, 308, 316, 319, 322, 329-333, 364, 367, 369, 374, 381, 394, 395, 399, 400-405

Nixon Doctrine, 248, 267, 273, 277, 375

Nixon Report, 19, 159, 195, 242-256, 264-267, 271, 275-278, 280, 285, 315, 370, 371, 373

Noyes, James, 127, 370

One-Unit, 78, 79

Organizational Behavior, 196-207, 383

Organizational Model, 229, 230, 231

Outcomes, 192, 241, 243, 338, 347, 390

Packard, David, 178, 179, 320

Paige, Glenn, 219

Pakistan

    1970 Elections, 16, 17, 75-86, 94, 150, 368

    March 25 crackdown, 17, 66, 73, 86-89, 94, 95, 102, 151-153, 221, 253-254, 368, 402

    Foreign Policy of, 16, 28-30, 37-38, 40, 47, 53, 58, 60, 62, 65-104, 150-184, 246-249

    American arms embarge, 30, 61, 97

    Creation of 30, 31-35, 71

Pakistan People's Party, 80, 81, 83

Palmer, Norman, 56-57, 58

Pfaltzgraff, Robert, 219-220

Pfeffer, Irving, 189

Preference Ranking, 4-7, 12, 20, 21, 280, 332, 342, 348-358, 351, 354, 355, 385, 390

Priority Formulation, 3-8, 12, 14, 17, 19-22, 25, 139, 185, 187, 241-310, 327, 333, 337, 340, 360, 385, 387, 389, 390

Probabilities, 19-21, 187, 192, 241, 242, 337, 343, 344, 348, 351, 352, 353, 363, 384, 390

Psychological Model, 9, 13, 19, 187, 208, 218, 222, 225, 231-237, 238-241, 281-310, 338, 348, 390, 393

Ra'anan, Uri, 45

Raiffa, Howard, 192

Rann of Kutch Dispute, 61

Rational Man Model, 8, 9, 13, 18-19, 20, 187, 195, 206, 208, 218, 222-229, 238-280, 285, 340, 341, 348, 371, 383, 390, 392

Refugee Issue, 17, 35, 66, 88, 89, 96, 100, 102, 103, 132, 133, 150, 157, 160, 253, 255, 256, 378, 382

Risk, 185, 188-196, 238, 264, 343

Robinson, James, 198, 199

Rogers, William, 144, 145, 150, 161, 379, 381

Round Table Conference, 74

Rudolph, Lloyd and Susanne, 1-2, 24, 128, 138, 202-206, 372

Samaat-i-Islam, 78

Saunders, Harold, 124

Scheingold, Stuart, 67

SEATO, 27, 44, 47, 63, 243

Senior Review Group, 122, 129, 150, 151, 368

Shapiro, Michael, 283, 284

Seddiqui, Aslam, 29, 30

Simon, Herbert, 224, 226

Singh, Swaran, 380, 381

Sino-India Treaty of Peace, Friendship and Cooperation, 165-166

Sino-Indian War of 1962, 52-54, 59, 276

Sisco, Joseph, 127, 153-154, 158, 161, 164, 257, 270, 320, 375, 403

Six Points, 81-83

Smith, Donald, 36

Snyder, Richard, 232-233

SOPs (Standard Operating Procedures), 196, 229, 301, 311, 324, 325, 330

Spiro, Herbert, 215

State Department, 13, 88, 95, 107, 113, 124, 125, 127, 137, 142, 145-155, 159, 170-174, 201, 291, 315, 319-325, 330, 365-368, 380, 381, 382, 394

Steinbruner, John D., 1, 2, 8-13, 25, 188, 194, 197, 223, 227, 231, 283, 301, 302, 324, 348, 359

Stobaugh, Robert, 343

Strausz-Hupé, Robert, 27

Systems Theory, 214-222

Teune, Henry, 68

Truman Administration, 42

U-2 Incident, 49, 54

Uncertainty, 11, 12, 24, 185, 188-196, 238, 264, 307, 308, 343, 361, 363, 390

United Nations, 167, 255

United States

    Arms Supplies to Pakistan, 44, 46, 48, 63, 103, 133, 145, 288, 379, 380, 381

    Foreign Policy Structure, 4, 26, 27-30, 42, 43, 47, 53, 58, 90, 91-102, 105-139, 246-280, 309, 407, 408

    Presidential Power, 13, 19

    "Tilt" Policy, 16, 20, 128, 143, 161, 163-166, 168, 174, 175, 195, 199, 207, 254, 263, 290, 293, 294, 299, 308, 309, 315-324, 334, 377, 391, 395, 400, 401, 403

USSR, 43, 44, 49-53, 58, 90, 165, 180-183, 243-252, 264-270, 276, 279, 309, 317, 320, 322, 338, 367, 368, 371, 380, 400, 405, 408

Utility Theory, 5, 340, 341, 342

Value Formulation, 358-365

Van Hollen, Christopher, 133, 154, 161, 320

White, Ralph, 202-203, 284-285

Willett, Allan, 189, 190-191

Williams, Chester, 188

William, Maurice, 161, 320

Wint, Guy, 37

WSAG Meetings, 106, 107, 122, 129, 136, 137, 142, 151-154, 160-181, 195-200, 203, 207, 214, 253-257, 261, 270, 280, 296-298, 301, 309, 318, 319, 320, 328, 329, 331, 368, 377, 381, 394

Zeitlin, Arnold, 98